THE WORLD'S CLASSICS
FOUR COMEDIES

TITUS MACCIUS PLAUTUS (254 184 BC) was Rome's most successful playwright and perhaps the most influential comic author of all time. Like Shakespeare and Molière, he began his career as an actor in popular farces, which undoubtedly sharpened his unique sense of what made audiences laugh. Plautus' achievement is particularly remarkable since he is the earliest Roman author extant. His rise to fame coincided almost precisely with Rome's rise to world dominance. Plautus transformed the sedate, sentimental drama of Hellenistic Greece into boisterous musical farce, tailored to please the rough-hewn Romans of his day. In his comedies the strict, puritanical Roman social order is temporarily turned topsy-turvy—and the lowly slave reigns supreme.

Shakespeare's *Comedy of Errors* is an adaptation of *The Brothers Menaechmus* (in this volume). Molière rendered *The Pot of Gold* (also in this volume) when creating *The Miser*. Moreover, the huge success of *A Funny Thing Happened on the Way to the Forum* (a combination of several comedies) proves that Plautus is still very much alive on Broadway and in Hollywood.

ERICH SEGAL, formerly Professor of Classics at Yale, is a Fellow of Wolfson College, Oxford and author of the pioneering study *Roman Laughter: The Comedy of Plautus*.

He is also editor of The Oxford Readings in Greek Tragedy and The Oxford Readings in Aristophanes.

Erich Segal earlier published the first three plays in this volume without *The Pot of Gold*. On reading the first three translations, reviewers and lecturers commented:

'Enormously playable ... Scrupulously accurate to the meaning and spirit of the Latin, while, at the same time, dramatically effective as a medium for actors and audience.' (Dr Richard C. Beacham, Department of Theatre Studies, University of Warwick)

'It [*The Braggart Soldier*] is sayable and playable ... it recreates the original, losing only the nuances of diction, allusion, and rhythm that must be lost; it is superbly funny; and it is a poem.' (Dudley Fitts)

'Excellent translations.' (J. N. Hough, *Classical World*)

'I can see that these translations have been made with love, care, and enthusiasm, and I find them readable and amusing.' (Richmond Lattimore)

'Extremely successful in catching the sense and following the metre.' (Edmund Wilson)

THE WORLD'S CLASSICS

PLAUTUS

Four Comedies

The Braggart Soldier
The Brothers Menaechmus
The Haunted House
The Pot of Gold

Translated, with an Introduction and Notes, by
ERICH SEGAL

Oxford   New York
OXFORD UNIVERSITY PRESS

Oxford University Press, Great Clarendon Street, Oxford OX2 6DP

Oxford New York
Athens Auckland Bangkok Bogota Bombay
Buenos Aires Calcutta Cape Town Dar es Salaam
Delhi Florence Hong Kong Istanbul Karachi
Kuala Lumpur Madras Madrid Melbourne
Mexico City Nairobi Paris Singapore
Taipei Tokyo Toronto Warsaw

and associated companies in
Berlin Ibadan

Oxford is a trade mark of Oxford University Press

British Library Cataloguing in Publication Data
Data available

Library of Congress Cataloging in Publication Data
Plautus, Titus Maccius.
[Selections. English. 1996]
Four comedies / Plautus ; translated, with an introduction and
notes by Erich Segal.
(The World's classics)
Contents: The braggart soldier—The Brothers Menaechmus—The
haunted house—The pot of gold.
1. Plautus, Titus Maccius—Translations into English. 2. Latin
drama (Comedy)—Translations into English. I. Segal, Erich, 1937-
II. Title. III. Series.
PA6570.A3S4 1996 872'.01—dc20 95-44849
ISBN 0-19-283108-9 (pbk.)

3 5 7 9 10 8 6 4

Printed in Great Britain by
Caledonian International Book Manufacturing Ltd
Glasgow

For my daughters,

Francesca and *Miranda*

RIDETE QUIDQUID EST DOMI CACHINNORUM

PREFACE TO THE OXFORD EDITION

ONE magical summer evening in 1962, I saw an Italian translation of Plautus' *Casina* convulse a huge audience at the Stadio di Domiziano in Rome. Until that time, like so many academics, I had regarded Plautus as merely a name in literary history: a good man long ago, the best comic author in *ancient* Rome. That night I learned otherwise. Good old Plautus is still flourishing wherever great professional clowns do his comedy justice.

My first attempt at Plautine translation was *The Braggart Soldier*, which, to my amazement and delight, actually made people laugh when it was played at the Harvard Loeb Drama Center in 1963. Encouraged by requests from teachers and directors, I subsequently rendered two other comedies that I regarded to be among the playwright's best: *The Brothers Menaechmus* and *The Haunted House*.

When the first trio of plays was ready for publication, my then Yale colleagues Thomas Cole and Kenneth Cavander read and corrected the manuscript, while Hugh Lloyd-Jones of Oxford reassured me on what he termed 'justifiable conjectures'.

The occasion of the Oxford reprint enabled me to make further revisions and to add the fourth play, *The Pot of Gold*. I am grateful to T. J. Luce of Princeton, Walter Moskalew of Ball State University, and Carroll Moulton for their many suggestions. I have also benefited from seeing these plays produced, most recently by Richard Beacham at the University of Warwick.

These productions reassured me that Plautus is still alive and well and—I dare to hope—also living in the pages of this book.

E. S.

Wolfson College, Oxford
1995

PREFACE TO THE OXFORD EDITION

One magical summer evening in 1962, I saw an Italian translation of Plautus' *Casina* convulse a huge audience at the Stadio di Domiziano in Rome. Until that time, like so many academics, I had regarded Plautus as merely a name in literary history, a good man long ago, the best comic author in ancient Rome. That night I learned otherwise. Good old Plautus is still flourishing wherever great professional clowns do his comedy justice.

My first attempt at Plautine translation was *The Braggart Soldier*, which, to my amazement and delight, actually made people laugh when it was played at the Harvard Loeb Drama Center in 1963. Encouraged by requests from teachers and directors, I subsequently rendered two other comedies that I regarded to be among the playwright's best: *The Brothers Menaechmus* and *The Haunted House*.

When the first trio of plays was ready for publication, my then Yale colleagues Thomas Cole and Kenneth Cavander read and corrected the manuscript, while Hugh Lloyd-Jones of Oxford reassured me on what he termed 'justifiable conjectures'.

The occasion of the Oxford reprint enabled me to make further revisions and to add the fourth play, *The Pot of Gold*. I am grateful to T. J. Luce of Princeton, Walter Moskalew of Ball State University, and Carroll Moulton for their many suggestions. I have also benefited from seeing these plays produced, most recently by Richard Beacham at the University of Warwick.

These productions reassured me that Plautus is still alive and well and—I dare to hope—also living in the pages of this book.

E. S.

Wolfson College, Oxford
1995

CONTENTS

CONTENTS

INTRODUCTION

Seneca cannot be too heavy, nor Plautus too light.

WHEN Polonius trumpeted to Hamlet the arrival of 'the best players in the world', he paid them the ultimate compliment. For the heritage of modern tragedy goes back to Seneca (not Sophocles), and the fountainhead of modern comedy to Plautus (not Aristophanes). Each playwright was, in his way, a kind of enduring Roman bridge over which the classics crossed the Renaissance to our own day.

But let us return to the originals—in their original setting. Imagine it is the Harvest Festival in Rome, *c*.200 BC. The rustic Roman citizenry mills about, bored by the ceremonies through which it has been obliged to sit (or stand), 'drunk and disorderly' ('potus et exlex').[1] On a crude stage thrown together for the occasion, an actor appears. He shouts desperately for silence, hoping to turn the unruly mob into something resembling an audience. Then he speaks magic words:

'I bring you Plautus!'[2]

Suddenly, sweet silence. From the thousandth row, you can hear a pun drop.

The very name of Plautus means belly laughs, charm, wit, song—in a word, entertainment. Plautus knew what the public wanted and how they liked it. He gave them not only enough, but too much, which is the quintessence of all that evokes laughter.

The Comic Background

In 254 BC, the generally accepted date for Plautus' birth, Rome was still a relatively insignificant nation. But she was in the midst of the first of her three wars with Carthage, the powerful

---

[1] Cf. Horace, *Ars Poetica* 223 ff.: 'Only the attraction of novelty could keep the attention of the audience after the rites had been performed and they were inebriated and lawless.'

[2] *The Brothers Menaechmus* 3.

Phoenician colony in Africa. The prize was the Mediterranean world, and it did not take the Romans long to win it. By the time Plautus was in his teens, conquered Sicily had become the first Roman province. With Sicily's wealth and strategic position came an extra benefit: culture. From at least the sixth century BC, it had been a highly civilized island where all the arts had flourished, especially drama. In Sicily, for the very first time, the Romans saw theatres.

The First Punic War ended in 241 BC. In 240 BC, the first play was produced in Rome at the Harvest Festival (*ludi Romani*). It was a Latin adaptation of a Greek tragedy, done by a captured slave named Livius Andronicus.[3] The following year, Livius rendered both a comedy and a tragedy, and thus a tradition began: each year at this time the holidaying Romans would see stage plays rendered from Greek originals. Writing in this tradition, Plautus made his début at some unknown occasion after 215 BC. Since Livius Andronicus survives merely in fragments, Titus Maccius Plautus owns the distinction of being the earliest extant Latin author. We still have twenty of his comedies more or less complete (he may have composed as many as 130, and 'doctored' others).

What were the Greek models rendered by the Roman dramatists? As might be expected, their sources for tragedy were mainly Sophocles and Euripides. And yet the models for Latin comedy were not Aristophanic.

As we look back at Classical Greek literature, we can perceive two distinct types of comedy. First, there were the wild, loosely structured, bawdy, lyrical-satirical choral extravaganzas, whose most famous—but by no means only—practitioner was Aristophanes (*c*.448–380 BC). The *Birds*, in which a dispirited and dysfunctional old debtor rises (literally) to be crowned as the new Zeus in a city in the sky, is a paradigm of this type of play, referred to as Old Comedy. For various and complex reasons, however, the genre did not survive the fall of Athens in the Peloponnesian War (404 BC). The so-called New Comedy that even then was starting to evolve was radically different:

---

[3] The early history of the Roman theatre is sketched by Livy, 7. 2. For a convenient collection of this and other sources in translation, see Eric Csapo and William J. Slater (eds.), *The Context of Ancient Drama* (Ann Arbor, 1995), 207 ff.

typical (in plot and characterization), atopical, polite, and apolitical. It had neither chorus, nor songs, nor 'jokes' as such. In fact, 'Aristotle-on-Comedy' states that Old Comedy over-emphasized laughter, and New Comedy disregarded it.[4]

New Comedy presented stock characters in stock situations. Its locale was the city, its people the bourgeoisie, its plots romantic: boy meets/wants/has previously raped girl. The whole milieu was at once realistic (no Birds or Clouds on stage), and yet removed from reality. Reading these plays, we have no notion that during the time of their composition the Hellenistic world was torn constantly by war and strife. The tears shed are only those of the lover, sighing like a furnace. The story may begin with an outrage—to a maiden, long ago, in the dark—but all always ends well; Jack marries Jill. The final chord is always one of apology and conciliation. What a tame contrast with the Aristophanic finales, which usually conclude by celebrating the triumph of unrepentant outrage!

The only author of this genre who has left us anything but fragments is the legendary Menander (*c*.342–293 BC). He was made a legend by scores of ancient critics (none his contemporary) who celebrated him as the nonpareil of civilized comedy. To the Roman scholar Quintilian, for example, Menander was perfection itself, in speech, in character analysis, and in his portrait of life.[5] Plutarch regards him as the only reason for a civilized man to go to the theatre and enthusiastically lauds the playwright and his 'salt'.[6]

In the early part of the twentieth century the much-esteemed author existed only in fragments and quotable quotes. Yet since the late 1950s his *Dyskolos* (*The Grouch*) has been discovered entire, and *Samia* (*The Girl from Samos*) nearly so.[7] These papyrus finds confirmed the general impression that Menandrian comedy

---

[4] *Tractatus Coislinianus*, a document considered by some to epitomize Aristotle's (lost) views on comedy. See now Richard Janko, *Aristotle on Comedy: Towards a Reconstruction of Poetics II* (Berkeley, 1984).

[5] Quintilian, *Institutio Oratoria* 10. 1. 69.

[6] Plutarch, *Moralia* 854b–c. For good general overviews of Menandrian comedy, see the works by Goldberg, Moulton, Webster, and Zagagi listed in the Select Bibliography.

[7] See now the Penguin translation by Norma Miller, *Menander: Plays and Fragments* (London, 1987).

presented a series of polished, sedate character-studies of the Hellenistic leisured class. Perhaps some of his colleagues, such as Philemon or Diphilus,[8] were funnier, but it is unlikely that their plays remotely resembled the broad musical farce of the later fifth century BC. Suffice it to note here that when the Romans looked for Greek comedies to adapt, Aristophanes was completely out of the picture.

Enter Plautus

Although Plautus' plays are based on Greek originals, they have a character uniquely their own. The Roman playwright has refashioned the subdued dialogue of New Comedy into something rich and strange. What Elaine Fantham has aptly described as 'the kaleidoscopic brilliance of Plautine language'[9] is characterized by striking coinages, both verbal and imagistic.[10] Some are colourful metaphors like *lapides loqueris* (*The Pot of Gold* 151), 'you're babbling boulders'. Others are more surrealistic. For example, in *Captivi* 951, the slave, who typically exists in a violent atmosphere of menace and dire threats of punishment, is punningly referred to as *statua verberea*, 'a whipped-up statue'.[11]

Scholars have long debated the precise nature—and worth—of Plautus' changes to his Greek originals. It is fairly safe to state that he transformed what was simple metrical dialogue in the Greek to polymetrical songs (*cantica*) in the Latin; he added gags where there were none in the original; he poured on a plenitude of puns (there are virtually none in extant Menander). If he did not always change the plots, he would at least emphasize those aspects and figures that amused him most. His *Casina* illustrates this. Perhaps the strongest irony is the dramaturgical in-joke of the title itself. We know from internal evidence that this is one of the plays which has been renamed by Plautus. Thus he has deliberately called it after a person who does not appear, the

---

[8] See *The Haunted House* 1149 ff., and p. xxxi below.

[9] See *Comparative Studies in Republican Latin Imagery* (Toronto, 1972), 96.

[10] Ibid.

[11] Eduard Fraenkel, *Plautinisches im Plautus* (Berlin, 1922), revised by the author and translated into Italian by Franco Munari as *Elementi Plautini in Plauto* (Florence, 1960).

ultimate thumb in the nose to Greek New Comedy. The prologue explains the Roman playwright's intent. The lovely 'title character', the maiden Casina, will not arrive on stage during the play. Nor will the young man who is in love with her. The reason? *Plautus noluit*, 'Plautus didn't want to' (line 65). This is not merely an exercise of artistic volition, in order to bring the misadventures of a libidinous old codger to the fore. It is a deliberate subversion of the cardinal feature of Greek New Comedy. Youthful romance? *Plautus noluit.*

The second-century writer Aulus Gellius has preserved brief passages from *Plocium* (*The Necklace*) by Plautus' younger contemporary Caecilius, as well as the corresponding lines of the Menandrian original on which they were based.[12] Not only has the Roman playwright transformed the almost prosaic iambs of the Greek model into a Plautine 'song', he has changed the content as well, having larded the piece with what Gellius disapprovingly calls 'nescio quae mimica' ('some farcical rubbish'). This invaluable exercise in comparative literature was for centuries the touchstone for judging a Latin comic text in the light of its Greek model.[13]

Then came an unexpected windfall: in 1968, Eric Handley published a newly discovered papyrus containing a passage from Menander's *Dis Exapaton* (*The Double Deceiver*), the source of Plautus' *Bacchides*. After many centuries, we could once again make a very specific, detailed comparison between a Roman dramatist and his Greek original.[14]

In one sense, Handley's essay substantiated many of Eduard Fraenkel's brilliant conjectures about Plautine style.[15] But Handley concludes that with the new papyrus we can see 'on a very small scale but *by direct observation* how [Plautus] likes his colours strong, his staging more obvious, his comedy more comic'.[16] Subsequent interpreters have unanimously agreed on Plautus' preference for

---

[12] Gellius, *Noctes Atticae* 2. 23.

[13] See John Wright, *Dancing in Chains: The Stylistic Unity of the Comoedia Palliata* (Rome, 1974), still a valuable study of Roman comic style—he demonstrates that what we now accept as 'Plautine' was actually typical of the playwright's contemporaries as well.

[14] Handley's landmark contribution appeared as *Menander and Plautus: A Study in Comparison* (London, 1968).

[15] Ibid. 9 and n. 5.   [16] Ibid. 18.

the broader strokes of farce over such Greek New Comedy elements as realism, irony, pathos, and subtle characterization.

In addition, we can now understand the sly overtones of the Plautine slave Chrysalus' quip at line 649 of *Bacchides*: 'I have no time for ordinary servants like Parmeno and Syrus.' Handley's papyrus demonstrated that the slave in the Menandrian original was in fact called Syrus! Plautus changed both the appellation and the characterization of the bondsman for his own purposes.

The passage from *Bacchides* is typical of the playwright's metatheatrical practice—perhaps the ultimate dimension of his overall neglect of realism and divergence from the New Comedy originals. Niall Slater's provocative study of the 'phenomenon of theatrical self-consciousness'[17] in our poet is an eye-opening demonstration that a good deal of Plautus is about the process of writing Plautine comedy. His works abound in references to 'the play as play and the performers as players and playwrights'.[18] Indeed, perhaps the cleverest of clever slaves, Pseudolus, in the play which bears his name, compares his scheme to swindle his master to the creative act of dramaturgy:

> Just like a playwright when he's starting to compose,
> Seeking what is nowhere in the world—yet finds it,
> Transforming baseless lies into a semblance of the truth,
> Thus, I shall now become a playwright . . .
>
> (*Pseudolus* 401–4)

Both text and context glance at once forward and back. Even as they recall a famous fragment by the Greek playwright Antiphanes in which he describes the comic poet as having to 'invent things from thin air' (Fr. 191), they also prefigure the metatheatrical vision of Shakespeare of 'these our actors' in 'the great globe itself'.

Plautus is also the first professional dramatist in the modern sense. Neither Aristophanes nor Menander had to write for a living. For Plautus, however, the notions of his next play and his next meal were inextricably intertwined. Like Shakespeare and Molière (both of whom wrote in what may be described as 'the Plautine tradition'), the theatre was his career, his life, and his livelihood.

---

[17] Niall Slater, *Plautus in Performance* (Princeton, 1985), 9.   [18] Ibid. 14.

The Theatre and its Audience

What little we know of his biography does not help to explain how Titus Maccius Plautus rose from humble origins in Sarsina, northern Italy,[19] to become what a later Roman writer praised as 'the glory of the Latin tongue'.[20] And where did Plautus get the impulse for the melodies and broad slapstick which he added to his primly sober models? The most obvious answer is from his own genius. But there had always been at Rome a native type of subliterary comedy, known as the *fabulae Atellanae*, or Atellan farces, named after the Campanian village where the genre probably originated.[21] This crude entertainment presented little skits with stock low-life characters like Bucco, the babbling fool; Pappus, the foolish old codger; Dossenus, the hunchback buffoon; and Maccus, another type of simple fool. The spirit of these lusty, popular entertainments pervades Plautine comedy.

The playwright at one time may well have been an actor in one of the troupes performing these farces. Certainly his *nomen*, Maccius, bears a suspicious resemblance to one of the Atellan types, and his *cognomen* (Plautus) has been translated by some scholars as 'flatfoot', which may also suggest a previous career in baggy tunics. His ancient biography states enigmatically that Plautus made a fortune in some kind of show business: 'in operis artificum scaenicorum'.[22] It is a happy idea to imagine our author in a band of strolling players. The notion would certainly help to explain his unique instinct for pleasing the crowd.

There is little information and less evidence about theatre productions in the age of Plautus. To begin with, although there were three recorded attempts in the second century BC to build a permanent structure in Rome, the project was not realized until 55 BC, when the stone theatre of Pompey was finally constructed. The best that can be inferred is that the essential element of dramatic performance was what Plautus referred to as either a *scaena* or a *proscaenium*, a rather long, thin, wooden stage, assembled for the festival and then dismantled. From later

---

[19] See *The Haunted House* 770, and my note, p. 236.
[20] Aulus Gellius, *Noctes Atticae* 19. 8. 6: 'Plautus, linguae Latinae decus'.
[21] See the discussion of W. Beare in *The Roman Stage*[3] (London, 1964), 137–48.
[22] Plautus' biography is preserved by Aulus Gellius, *Noctes Atticae* 3. 3. 14.

theatrical designs we can assume there was some kind of simple backdrop and actors' quarters—which might have provided 'doorways' for the plot.

It is not known for certain whether the actors were masked, but since both New Comedy and the Atellan tradition included this convention, it is logical to assume that they were.[23] Some have speculated that the feminine roles were played by males (as in the Elizabethan theatre), although we know women did act in the coarse mimes. This may in part account for the limited variety of female roles in the comedies. There is no extant visual record, as there is for the Greek theatre, so we must rely upon the conjectures of scholars for many questions of scenic practice and stagecraft. Nor do we have any contemporary descriptions of the customs or histrionic style of the players. There seems, at any rate, to have been no three-actor rule as there was in Greek drama; therefore no doubling of roles by the actors was necessary.

Apparently, senators were privileged to have a special seating area, but we cannot tell if the others were all obliged to stand. What is certain is the heterogeneous character of the audience.[24] Although the entire Plautine *œuvre* mentions the word 'Roman' only once (*Poenulus* 1314)—a disputed passage at that—it is a single term which describes all the spectators, regardless of status or gender. Yet every disparate member of Plautus' audience was aware of the Roman value-system. They may not have been pious in their daily life, but they knew what *pietas* was: respect for parents, leaders, and divinities.

Plautus was, after all, an almost exact contemporary of Cato the Censor, who was an energetic campaigner for early Roman 'puritanical' mores. Roman society was governed by a series of restrictive, moralistic ordinances. Historian Crane Brinton describes the atmosphere:

---

[23] See Beare, *The Roman Stage*[3], 184 ff. and 303 ff. Slater, *Plautus in Performance*, 24, offers some imaginative 'evidence', interpreting the 'two voices' in a speech of the slave Epidicus (lines 81–101) as an address between the actor and his mask.

[24] Cf. A. S. Gratwick, *Cambridge History of Classical Literature*, ii. 81, citing the prologues to Plautus' *Poenulus* and Terence's *Hecyra*.

We here encounter clearly for the first time another persistent theme in the moral history of the West, and one that confronts the sociological historian with some difficult problems: sumptuary, prohibitory, 'blue law' legislation accompanied by official or semi-official educational propaganda toward a return to 'primitive' values.[25]

Throughout Plautine comedy these Roman values are alluded to only to be violated or overthrown—a deliberate comic subversion of Roman *gravitas*.

Plautine Comedy: Setting, Style, and Characters

Despite its Italian-Atellan touches, Plautus' comedy often explicitly alleges—indeed protests (too much, of course)—that it is Greek: see the absurd pronouncement by the prologue to *The Brothers Menaechmus*, lines 7 ff. Such places as Athens, Epidamnus, and Aetolia are only ostensible locales for the plays; in fact, as A. S. Gratwick has pointed out, the setting for Plautine comedy is a universalized *civitas graecoromana*, a cosmopolitan 'Plautinopolis' conterminous with the known civilized world.[26]

That said, however, the Roman playwright makes a good deal of comic hay out of his characters' ethnic protestations. When these figures are revelling, for example, they claim to be 'Greeking it up',[27] a notion which has special reverberations for his audience. The citizens of the early Roman republic were fundamentally a puritanical folk, prim, proper, abstemious, and reserved, who despised the Greeks for their dissolute ways. There is, then, an extra comic dividend when the Roman comedy hell-raisers are Hellenic. A famous example of Plautus' 'Greek irony' is the moment when the slave Stichus, in the process of arranging a little dinner-party, breaks the dramatic illusion to assure the spectators: 'We're allowed to do this sort of thing at Athens' (*Stichus* 448). But Plautus' Athens was no further from Rome

---

[25] Crane Brinton, *A History of Western Morals* (New York, 1959), 111.

[26] Gratwick, *Cambridge History of Classical Literature*, ii. 112–13.

[27] The verb *pergraecari* is used in *The Haunted House* 22, 64, 960—and in other Plautine comedies. Sometimes Plautus expresses it by *congraecare* (*Bacchides* 743), a similar verb which we may translate as 'Greek around'. Both these terms influenced the Elizabethan stereotype of a 'Merry Greeke'—one who acted frivolously and hedonistically.

than Beaumarchais's Seville was from Paris. Unlike Beaumarchais, or Montesquieu in the *Lettres persanes*, where Persian means Parisian, Plautus intends no satire. His only target is the funny-bone.[28]

The twin sources of Plautine style parallel the two strains which blended centuries later to become the special comedy of Molière. The critic Boileau rather snobbishly taxed his contemporary for combining the high and low comic styles, complaining that in *Les Fourberies de Scapin* Molière 'joined Terence and Tabarin', that is, he forced (Italian) *commedia dell'arte* to stand side by side with (Latin) classics. Without the depreciatory tone, we may paraphrase Boileau to suggest that Plautus 'joined Athens and Atella'. As in the case of Molière's combination, it was an inspired match.

I have already alluded to Plautus' songs. His was the first truly 'musical' comedy since the lyrics of Aristophanes had been replaced by the mundane iambics of New Comedy. But he was not the only Roman writer to add melody to a simpler text.[29] The operatic impulse seems to have been part of the Italian character from the very beginning. As he developed in the theatre, Plautus tended to add more and more songs to his plays. This is, in fact, one method employed by scholars to date his comedies. *The Braggart Soldier*, included in this volume, has no lyrics, and its simple metrical scheme suggests a date of composition early in his career.[30] *The Brothers Menaechmus* and *The Haunted House* each have five songs and the incomplete *Pot of Gold* has three; they were doubtless written later on, when Plautus had perfected his own style.

Nor, since Aristophanes, had an audience heard such vivacious

---

[28] See further Erich Segal, *Roman Laughter: The Comedy of Plautus*[2] (Oxford, 1987), 33–41.

[29] Fraenkel asserted that, among others, Ennius (239–169 BC), in adapting Roman tragedy from Greek models, changed Greek dialogue into Latin lyric, and vice versa: see *Elementi Plautini in Plauto*, 325 ff. The historian Livy, in discussing primitive Roman drama (7. 2), mentions a *satura* ('variety show') with assorted rhythmical music.

[30] In *The Braggart*, one brief interlude of anapaests ('Aristophanic' or 'Gilbertian' metre), lines 1011–93, interrupts the very simple iambics and trochees. The chief arguments tracing Plautus' development through his increasing use of lyrics are by W. B. Sedgwick: cf. 'The Dating of Plautus' Plays', *Classical Quarterly*, 24 (1930), 102 ff.

verbal abandon. What a language Plautus' characters speak!
Unlike the simple, forthright (good old Roman) style championed
by his conservative contemporary Cato, the dialogue is purple,
but not blue; it is racy, but not dirty.[31] Plautus is repetitive,
mock-elegant, mock-heroic, mock-everything. He invents all sorts
of delicious new words. As one of his slave characters—surely
speaking for his creator—expresses it: 'Nil moror vetera et volgata
verba' ('To hell with dated, dissipated diction!') (*Epidicus* 350).
Note the alliteration, by the way—a very Roman touch.

Plautus' verbal extravagance ranges from the super-superlative,
for example:

> Occisissumus sum omnium qui vivent!
>
> I'm the very dead-dead-deadest man alive!
>
> (*Casina* 694)

or Menaechmus' complaint that he is *exclusissimus*, the most
'kicked-out' man in the world (line 698), to the mini-diminutive,
such as his famous description of a lover's embrace:

> Papillarum horridularum oppressiunculae.
>
> Touchie-clutchie, itty-bitty-pretty-titty.
>
> (*Pseudolus* 68)

Plautus did not 'invent' any new comic figures, but he memor-
ably developed certain types with enormous zest and skill. The
most vivid are those characters who are in some way the enemies
of *la dolce vita*: greedy pimps (Plautus has an entire gallery, the
most infamous being Ballio in *Pseudolus*); bitchy wives (Plautus
has a veritable henhouse: Menaechmus' wife has plenty of company). Then there are the silly old codgers, credulous dupes like
Theopropides in *The Haunted House*, or senile Romeos like
Lysidamus in *Casina*. Clearly, the farcical figures are emphasized.
Menander sketched; Plautus painted with broad strokes.

But, without a doubt, his most brilliant—and favourite—
character is the clever slave. This type did not originate with

---

[31] Cato the Censor (234–149 BC), stern guardian of Roman morals, coined this
phrase as a formula for Roman speaking style: *Rem tene, verba sequentur* ('Just
stick to the subject, the words will follow'). Plautus, on the other hand, sticks to
the words—as many as possible.

Plautus (Xanthias in Aristophanes' *Frogs* is a much earlier example of a witty bondsman). But never before did the scheming servant take centre stage.[32]

As Gratwick observes, 'The slave is . . . at once a member of the audience and of the cast, the director of the action, and the intermediary between us and the more exotic characters. There is, as it were, no actor behind the mask of the slave.'[33] Pseudolus and Epidicus in the comedies that bear their names, Palaestrio in *The Braggart Soldier*, and Tranio in *The Haunted House* are all comic catalysts, the stars of their shows. If Greek New Comedy is essentially about love,[34] Plautine comedy is essentially about trickery, the *malitia* or 'shrewdness' that is celebrated in the brief epilogue to *Epidicus* (lines 732–3):[35]

Hic is homo est qui libertatem *malitia* invenit sua.
plaudite et valete. Lumbos porgite atque exsurgite.

Here's a lad who won his freedom, making good by being bad.
Now applaud, arise and stretch. Go home—we've nothing more to add.

The fact that the Roman slave who grovelled at the lowest rung of everyday society reigns supreme in Plautus epitomizes the topsy-turvy, Saturnalian quality of his comedy—just the right atmosphere for a Roman holiday.

A thousand handbooks and a million footnotes testify to the influence of Plautus throughout the ages. Masters of comedy have unceasingly filched from the storehouse of Plautine fun. In 1962, *A Funny Thing Happened on the Way to the Forum* had audiences rolling in the aisles in the same way Plautus had in ancient Rome—and with the very same jokes.

Yet, strangely enough, though Plautus' verve and gaiety brightened the stages of countless nations, it could not keep the

---

[32] See the chapter on this subject in Fraenkel, *Elementi Plautini*, 223 ff. and Segal, *Roman Laughter*[2], *passim*.

[33] Gratwick, *Cambridge History of Classical Literature*, ii. 107.

[34] See the interesting discussion on the love theme as treated by other New Comedy authors in William S. Anderson, *Barbarian Play: Plautus' Roman Comedy* (Toronto, 1993), 62 ff.

[35] *Malitia* is not unlike the Greek *poneria*, 'resourceful craftiness', which Cedric Whitman considered the distinguishing quality of the Aristophanic protagonist. Cf. his *Aristophanes and the Comic Hero* (Cambridge, Mass., 1964), 30 ff.

Roman theatre alive after his death. The epigram which marks Plautus' passing well describes the state of Roman comedy after 184 BC:

Postquam est mortem aptus Plautus, comoedia luget.
Scaena est deserta, dein risus ludus jocusque
Et numeri innumeri simul omnes conlacrimarunt.

When the playwright Plautus died,
Comedy broke down and cried.
Then the stage was empty, then all Laughter, Games and Fun
And all his boundless bouncy rhythms—wept as one.

(Baehrens, *Fragmenta Poetarum Romanorum*, p. 296)

The Braggart Soldier

Miles Gloriosus does not begin with a prologue. It opens instead with one of the touchstones of comic literature: the hero discussing himself (who else?) with a professional flatterer. This is a classic confrontation between *alazon* and *eiron*, the quintessential comic opposites originally described by Aristotle in the *Nicomachean Ethics*.[36] The *alazon* is the overstater, the bluffer, the great balloon of hot air. *Alazoneia*, braggadocio, has been aptly described as the comic counterpart of *hubris*, tragic pride. In contrast, the *eiron* is, as the word suggests, the *ironic* man, the understater, the needle of 'I know nothing' which takes the air out of the *alazon*'s 'I know everything'. In all of ancient literature, the greatest *eiron* is Plato's Socrates; the greatest *alazon* is Plautus' Pyrgopolynices.

In a scene of but seventy-nine lines, the Braggart Soldier's outrageous character is exposed to an audience who will wait anxiously through more than half the play to see him reappear. Pyrgopolynices ('terrific tower-taker') boasts of such mammoth achievements as having crushed exactly 7,000 men in a single day (line 45), and punching an elephant to smithereens (line 28). There may be a pun on the soldier's (Greek) name in line 1055:

---

[36] Aristotle, *Nicomachean Ethics* 4. 7. The effect is reinforced in the delayed prologue speech at line 86, where we learn that the title of the play's Greek original was none other than *Alazon*.

'noble king-killer, *sacker of cities*'. He is vain about his attractive-
ness to women. When his slave suggests that one of his female
admirers may be compared in beauty to himself, the soldier can
only remark: 'Oh, how gorgeous!' (line 968).

The *miles gloriosus* is by no means a Plautine invention, but
the boastful officer is one of his favourite characters and appears
in seven of the twenty extant plays—although never so promin-
ently as in this comedy. Certainly General Lamachus in Aristophanes' *Acharnians* is a blusterer of much the same ilk. However,
the type must have had a very special appeal for the Roman
spectators, many of whom were themselves soldiers. This audience had seen its commanders become world conquerors in real
life.

As the title character struts off pompously to the forum, the
tricky slave Palaestrio enters to deliver a long expository prologue.
He has a complicated story to convey. In 'good old Athens', the
Braggart Soldier abducted his master's girlfriend.[37] Loyal retainer
that he was, Palaestrio set out in pursuit (quite an independent
slave!) But, as fate would have it, he was captured by pirates and
given to none other than the Braggart himself, who had by this
time rented a mansion in Ephesus for himself and the kidnapped
girl. By chance, the soldier's house is *right next door* to that of
an old family friend of Palaestrio's Athenian master. Greek New
Comedy dealt constantly with the workings of chance. In this
prologue, Plautus mocks the convention.

The metatheatrical in-joking, however, soon takes a back seat
as the characterization of Palaestrio develops. In this early play,
he is the prototype of such tricky Plautine servants as Pseudolus
and Tranio (in *The Haunted House*). The imagery the playwright
lavishes on him must soon convince the audience that, if
Pyrgopolynices is the titular hero, Palaestrio is the real protagonist
(cf. lines 140–1). The plot revolves around his two 'mighty
machinations'. He is repeatedly an 'architect' (lines 901, 902,

---

[37] 'Girlfriend' is both anachronistic and inaccurate. 'Mistress' is rather Victorian
and does not suit a lively young woman like Philocomasium. *But she is not your
sister either*. Though not a pay-as-you-go courtesan like Acroteleutium, she can be
'owned', and is therefore some sort of slave. We have problems of vocabulary here,
not of sociology. I trust the reader will make the necessary adjustments of sensi-
bility. It is not impossible that in (one of) Plautus' Greek originals Philocomasium
was discovered to be free-born and could therefore marry Pleusicles.

915 ff., 1129), as well as a planner of strategy, an opponent of the enemy, an assailant from the ramparts, a company commander (lines 196 ff., 219–25, 266–7, 334, 813–15), and (climactically at line 1160), an *imperator*—in short, the real conquering hero of the piece. It is important to note that the spectator's pleasure in the portrayal of soldier and slave—*militia* hand in hand with *malitia*—is reciprocal. Both are profoundly playful impersonations, deriving their humour as much from the reversal of audience expectations as from their mutual, virtually symmetrical relationship.[38]

As if to embellish this structural feature, Palaestrio's 'campaigns' involve a substantial component of disguise, even by the standards of Plautine comedy.[39] When one of the soldier's slaves happens to spy the young lovers, Palaestrio must convince this thick-witted servant that he did not see Philocomasium, but her sister, who *just happened* (chance, again) to arrive in Ephesus the night before. To validate this claim, Palaestrio trains the girl to impersonate her own twin.

All this masquerading scares off the silly slave who had spied on the young couple, but does nothing towards getting Philocomasium ('lover of revelry', the pleasure principle personified) away from the soldier. And so Palaestrio needs a second stratagem.[40] With the help of an aged neighbour, he dresses up a courtesan to pretend that she is the old man's wife, desperately in love with the military marvel, and willing to go to any length—and expense—to win his amatory attentions. Pyrgopolynices will then hurriedly get rid of his current mistress. The scheme has a second purpose as well: to deflate the soldier's gargantuan ego and show the 'hero' to be a grovelling coward when confronted with the penalty for adultery—castration.

[38] John Arthur Hanson, 'The Glorious Military', 66, in T. A. Dorey and Donald R. Dudley (eds.), Roman Drama (New York, 1965), 66 points out that all but one of the Plautine comedies with a *miles gloriosus* also feature a *servus gloriosus*.

[39] There are, in fact, three masquerades in *The Braggart Soldier*: first Philocomasium as her own twin sister, then the courtesan as the amorous wife, then Pleusicles, the young lover, as a ship's captain. Needless to mention, Palaestrio wrote all three scripts.

[40] Much has been written about the fact that Plautus has combined two plots in this play, perhaps derived from two different Greek originals. This process is known as *contaminatio*, a term which has a pejorative connotation.

Palaestrio knows his military master, and brilliantly couches his proposition in terms that appeal to the soldier's greatest source of pride: not his valour, not even his beauty, but his wealth (1063 ff.). The slave feeds the soldier with ambiguous promises of 'profit' from this new affair, which he describes as *condicio nova et luculenta* (line 952), a phrase which could be understood either as a new love *or* business affair. He further stokes the fire of the soldier's *alazoneia* by presenting him with a ring which he calls *arrabonem amoris*, the 'first deposit on a love account' (line 957). The financial imagery had special, ironic resonance for the Roman audience, evoking the world of the forum and *negotium* (business).[41]

On every field of battle, the clever slave emerges victorious over the allegedly undefeated and unbeatable warrior. The farewell scene, when the girl, her many trunks of baggage, and Palaestrio himself are about to be given away by the departing soldier, is a masterpiece of irony. For those who suspect that Euripides in his late plays was really the godfather of New Comedy, there are some piquant similarities between this ironic leave-taking and the finale of the Greek playwright's *Helen* (Compare, for example, *Helen* 1419–20 with *The Braggart* 1321–5.) This may not prove any direct Euripidean influence, for Plautus himself has a predilection, as we have seen, for trickery by masquerade.

The Braggart Soldier has a long heritage on the comic stage. Even Terence's Thraso—in *The Eunuch*, his most successful play—owes quite a debt to Plautus. (Significantly, Terence is at pains to deny a contemporary charge of plagiarism at *The Eunuch* 23 ff.) We see the same characterization in the various captains of the *commedia dell'arte*, in Corneille's *L'Illusion comique*, in Nicholas Udall's *Ralph Roister Doister*, in Captain Bobadill of Ben Jonson's *Every Man in his Humour*, and, of course, in Falstaff, who is the greatest *alazon* of all time and perhaps also the best *eiron* as well.[42] If nothing else, the Braggart Soldier has commanded a legion of imitators.

---

[41] See the introduction to *The Brothers Menaechmus* (p. xxviii) and the fuller analysis in Segal, *Roman Laughter*[2], 53 ff.

[42] Cf. Falstaff's famous (and true) self-characterization: 'I am not only witty in myself, but the cause that wit is in other men' (*2 Henry IV*, I. ii. 10).

The Brothers Menaechmus

This is Plautus' only comedy of errors. His Hellenistic predecessors wrote so many that 'Miss Ignorance', a personification who speaks one of Menander's prologues (Agnoia in *She Who was Shorn*) has been called the presiding deity of New Comedy. Plautus usually preferred wit to ignorance, shrewd deceptions to naïve blunders. People in a comedy of errors are mere puppets; Plautus admired puppeteers, creative plotters like Palaestrio and Tranio. Since no one in *The Brothers Menaechmus* is clever, the laughter it arouses provides strong argument for that popular theory of the comic which sees the cue for guffaws as a feeling of audience superiority. Indeed, who would not feel superior to these fools who wander the streets of Epidamnus, where the presiding deity must surely be Miss Ignorance's dull-witted twin, 'Misunderstanding'?

Yet this is a fine, if untypical, Plautine comedy. It has enjoyed unceasing popularity over the ages, and not only in famous adaptations like Shakespeare's *Comedy of Errors* and Rodgers and Hart's *Boys from Syracuse*. It has always been the most-performed play of Plautus. Clearly, it has a very special appeal—in both its Plautine assets of song and snappy patter, and its atmosphere of holiday abandon, of carnival release from everyday rules. Moreover, it presents more simply than any comedy before or since the greatest of all wish-fulfilments: the surrogate self, the *alter ego* with no super-ego, the man who can get his pleasure free in every sense, because he is 'Jack in town and Ernest in the country'. Indeed, Plautus' twin-brother comedy might be aptly subtitled 'The Importance of Being Menaechmus'.[43]

The two houses on stage represent the conflicting forces in the comedy. They are not unlike the statues of Artemis and Aphrodite which frame the setting of Euripides' *Hippolytus*. In both dramas the action takes place in a magnetic field between poles of restraint and release. It is no coincidence that the house of Menaechmus I

---

[43] Plautus, *Menaechmi*, ed. Gratwick (Cambridge, 1993), 138. Gratwick points out that Plautus has very likely invented the name of the twins as a kind of comic commemoration of Menaechmus, the mathematician of Syracuse (mid-fourth century BC), 'famous for a solution of the problem of the duplication of the cube to the unmathematical, a sort of "twinning"'.

stands at the exit nearer the forum. For the local twin is bound by the business of everyday life, restrained by legal, financial, and social ties, especially by a wife who is constantly 'at work'. Across the stage, and nearer the harbour whence visitors come, dwells a lady of pleasure aptly named Erotium ('Passionella', if you will). Throughout the play, Plautus associates the word *industria* ('work') with Menaechmus' wife (e.g. line 123); to emphasize the contrast, he constantly refers to Erotium as *voluptas* ('pleasure').[44] It should be noted that Menaechmus' lawfully wedded spouse has no name at all; she is merely called 'wife'. Shakespeare, in his adaptation, reverses this, making the courtesan the lady with no name, and calling the twin's wife Adriana.

Plautus, of course, intends no allegory; he never intends anything but entertainment. And yet, without any conscious attempt on the part of the playwright, we see in the two on-stage houses in *The Brothers Menaechmus* a contrast between the atmosphere of everyday and that of holiday, or, as Freud would express it, the Reality Principle versus the Pleasure Principle. Needless to say, Pleasure emerges triumphant, for that is the essential theme of all comedy. But it is especially interesting to see why Menaechmus I needs a twin in order 'to win'.

The local, married brother is the hero of the play. Plautus gives him the larger and more lyrical role (Shakespeare, on the other hand, emphasizes the visiting twin). We first meet Menaechmus I in the midst of a domestic battle, describing himself as a hardened soldier in the war called marriage (lines 127, 129). He craves rest and recreation from this campaign; this is, in fact, what the play is about. He takes several steps in the direction of rest and recreation, that is, towards the other side of the stage, where passion lives incarnate. He orders a banquet, the bill of fare for which emphasizes various delicacies which were *forbidden to the Romans* (lines 209 ff.).[45] Plautus even concocts comic names for these illegal dishes, to emphasize how much Menaechmus is savouring the prospect of his breaking-of-the-rules banquet. And, of course, dessert will be Erotium, also rather unlawful. The

---

[44] *Eros*, of course, means passion, and *-ium* is an affectionate diminutive suffix; thus Erotium means 'Passion-ella'. Plautus loves to give his heroines such sensual names, e.g. Philocomasium in *The Braggart Soldier*, and Philematium in *The Haunted House*.

[45] Cf. Pliny, *Natural History* 8. 78 *passim*.

plans are elaborate, explicit, and titillating. Why, then, does Menaechmus leave the stage and head for—of all places—*the forum*, not to return till the party is over?

At the very moment when the local brother exits toward the business district, his long-lost twin enters from the harbour. This boy from Syracuse belongs to a great comic tradition: the lowly stranger who arrives in town, is mistaken for someone else of greater importance, and receives the cardinal comic joys: food, sex, and money. Xanthias in Aristophanes' *Frogs* is an earlier such type; a later one is Gogol's Klestakhov, the lowly government clerk who is mistaken for the Inspector-General. Like the Russian hero, Menaechmus II has come to town virtually penniless. As Messenio, his loyal slave, expresses it, 'We're travelling for summer—very, very light' (line 255). The sudden bounty seems too good to be true. Menaechmus II expresses his happy amazement as he emerges drunk and garlanded from the house of Erotium:

> By all the gods, what man in just a single day
> Received more pleasures, though expecting none at all:
> I've wined, I've dined, I've concubined, and robbed her blind!
> No one but me will own this dress after today.
>
> (473–7)

He also receives some of Erotium's jewellery, which, like the dress, has been stolen by Menaechmus I from his wife. Two comic fantasies are here fulfilled. Not only does someone else pick up the tab for the banquet, but the whore ends up paying the customer for sex! (We recall the Braggart Soldier, at the height of his *alazoneia*, drunk with joy at the prospect of being paid for his sexual attentions—lines 1059 ff.).

But what has kept our protagonist off-stage? He arrives, in fact, just in time to be too late, and though he sings elaborately of what has detained him, the cause may be summarized in a single word: business. While he was in the forum, a client stopped him and forced him to act as advocate in a complicated lawsuit.[46] Moreover, Menaechmus' punishment—for going to work on a

---

[46] Molière based his comedy *Les Fâcheux* (*The Annoying People*) on this same comic premiss: a man on his way to an amorous rendezvous, delayed by all sorts of blocking characters. Molière may have been inspired not only by Menaechmus I's plight, but by Horace's *Satire* 1. 9, where an annoying fan dogs the poet.

day set for play—is not yet complete. He is about to have an unpleasant encounter with his nameless wife, who will lock him out of his house, after which Erotium too will lock her door. He is then *exclusissimus* (line 698), the most 'kicked-out' man in the world. To add diagnosis to other injuries, he is then pronounced insane by a psychiatrist *gloriosus*, a hilarious quack whose professional questions are not unlike those posed by 'Socrates' in Aristophanes' *Clouds*. When one Menaechmus is at the acme of delight, the other is at the nadir of despair. The counterbalance is deliberate, and helps to explain the meaning of the entire comedy.

The hero of this play is a married man, a solid citizen of the town, who longs to go on a wild revel. In point of fact somebody named Menaechmus does enjoy all the forbidden delights of which the hero dreams. But it is *another Menaechmus*, who, although a mirror image (line 1062), is still different in three vital aspects: he is unmarried, unattached, and a non-citizen. In these three non-capacities, unmarried Menaechmus II can enjoy sex without 'sin', play without neglecting duty (he has no clients), and can even eat whatever he wants—foreigners are not subject to local dietary restrictions. In brief, Menaechmus II is *free*.

He is also non-existent. He is the creature of someone's imagination—specifically, Menaechmus I's. The fantasy fulfilled is that of a workaday Roman, caught up in the forum, dreaming of getting away—from everything and with everything. *The Brothers Menaechmus* is Roman comedy *par excellence*, and demonstrates once again that even when he departs slightly from his usual comic domain, Plautus never loses sight of his public's desires. Here he has given them exactly what they and Menaechmus I long for: a Roman holiday.

The Haunted House

The virtues of the 'little ghost story' cannot be overstated. Scintillating, polished, witty, and lyrical, *The Haunted House* is one of Plautus' masterpieces. Every single character is a credible characterization, and the theme—trickery—is Plautus' favourite. With typical bravado, the clever slave himself boasts that he has just concluded one of the greatest swindles of all time.[47] And with a saucy metatheatrical twist, Tranio cheekily advises his victim to relate his exploits to a famous comic playwright, in order to provide 'the perfect trickery plots'. This is yet another instance of Plautine slave-as-playwright, and in keeping with the subversive nature of the Latin author, he pretends that the bondsman is writing *Greek* New Comedy!

> Well, if you know Diphilus or Philemon,
> Go and tell them every way your slave's bamboozled you today.
> You'll provide the finest flim-flam plot for any comedy.

(1149–51)

The basic ingredients are all old hat, a familiar formula: the father has gone abroad (on business, of course) while the son stays home and lives it up. The revellers in the play take advantage of the absence of the Roman patriarch (for that is clearly what Theopropides is) to *pergraecari* 'act like Greeks' (lines 22, 64, 960).

Tranio has helped his master to purchase Philematium, a courtesan, whose name literally means 'my teeny-weeny kiss'. He frees her and they then join his friends in a non-stop carousal. The fact that the audience knows full well that the father's return is imminent only adds to the dramatic delectation.

The Haunted House presents a parade of richly drawn personalities. First, there is the puritanical (stolidly Roman) slave Grumio, whose boisterous bickering with Tranio begins the play and tosses out exposition in a far more lively manner than any prologue could.

Then there is Tranio's young master, who had previously been a paragon of Roman virtue. For once, a Plautine *adulescens* has a distinguishable personality, even if it be, as the lad himself sings, that of a dilapidated building (lines 84 ff.). Indeed, the house simile is consistently maintained throughout the play. The young man employs this imagery to substantiate Grumio's

---

[47] Cf. Slater, *Plautus in Performance*, 170: 'If Plautine drama represents any world, that world is the stage itself. Its characters are of players and playwrights, its plots the most theatrical of plots, its settings theatrical settings.'

accusation.[48] He has had a strict education to prepare him for a career in the forum (cf. lines 127 ff.) and he had once been an exemplary Roman, with all the significant qualities: *res*, *fides*,[49] *fama*, *virtus*, *decus*: property, trustworthiness, reputation, manliness, and decency.

Indeed, he was an example to others:

> I was a model of restraint and ruggedness to every boy.
> All the noblest people [*optumi*] looked to me for discipline.
>
> (154-5)

The play is so well crafted that the 'craven slave' (making a rare Plautine appearance) not only sustains the house metaphor, but even enters with a set speech that deliberately echoes and contrasts with the young man's song. Addressing his left hand, Phaniscus observes (870-1):

> If my hand is commanded, my roof will stay strong.
> Let it rain in on others, let others do wrong.

Unlike the dilapidation of the young man, this timorous bondsman is *probe tectum*, 'well roofed'.

The old father Theopropides, whose name ironically suggests omniscience (it is derived from the Greek verb 'to prophesy') is among the most colourful of Plautus' dupes—credulous, superstitious, and money-hungry. Coincidentally, these are not only qualities which make him an ideal victim but also quintessential Roman characteristics shared by the audiences of this period.

The moneylender Misargyrides is one of the great skinflints in Plautus' array of misers. Here is an obsessive caricature that Plautus enlarged in Euclio, the protagonist of *The Pot of Gold*. As usual, Tranio provides the aptest comment (lines 603-6):

MISARGYRIDES. My interest now, my interest, interest; pay me interest!
Will you please pay my interest to me right away?
I want my interest!

---

[48] Eleanor W. Leach uses Philolaches' comparison as the point of departure for her perceptive discussion of the play's imagery in '*De exemplo meo ipse aedificato*: An Organizing Idea in the *Mostellaria*', *Hermes*, 97 (1969), 318-32.
[49] See Explanatory Notes on *The Pot of Gold*, lines 583, 618.

TRANIO.   'Interest' here and 'interest' there.
The only interest this man has in life is 'interest'.

This fellow is so stingy he will not even 'expend' the energy to leave and return later for his promised payment. Hence he stays around—to confound matters further for Tranio.

Even a secondary figure like old Simo, the next-door neighbour, is a vivid characterization. Simo belongs to the same family of Plautine 'friendly old codgers' as Periplectomenus in *The Braggart Soldier*. Interestingly enough in this 'house play', while at one side of the stage the boys and girls are revelling and making love, Simo is fleeing his own home to avoid his unattractive wife's embraces (line 690 ff.) and sings a song which concludes: 'Better work in the forum than bed her at home' (lines 706–7). Thus, as in *The Braggart Soldier* and *The Brothers Menaechmus*, we find one house on stage standing for complete indulgence, the other for abstinence.[50]

The presence of a mercantile, parsimonious old man and a mercenary *flagitator* (debt-collector) on stage catalyses a cluster of financial images which help to unify the comedy on the level of language. When Theopropides unexpectedly returns from abroad, he greets the news that his son has bought a house with an ecstatic outburst (line 639):

His father's son he is, he is, he's going into business!

In fact, Philolaches has been neither filial nor frugal. His girlfriend's maid fears the lad will soon bankrupt himself for lack of *parsimonia* (line 235):

His cash will soon be gone, through dining, drinking day and night. He never saves a single thing. It's clear-cut gluttonizing.

The Roman audience, whose attention to balance sheets in real life is repeatedly emphasized by the ancient sources, would

---

[50] Cf. the introduction to *The Brothers Menaechmus*, p. xxvii. Elaine Fantham briefly discusses the figure of the married woman (*matrona*) in 'Sex, Status, and Survival in Hellenistic Athens: A Study of Women in New Comedy', *Phoenix*, 29 (1975), 72–3. Gratwick (*Cambridge History of Classical Literature*, ii. 110) bluntly remarks that apart from Alcumena in *Amphitryon*, 'the *matrona* in her housewifely setting is kept behind doors [in Plautus] as much as possible'.

not fail to appreciate the ironic echo in Tranio's exclamation when he learns of Theopropides' inopportune return (line 366): 'apsumpti sumus' ('We're bankrupt!') And yet the slave is not at a loss for trickery. To swindle his elder master, he concocts a fable about their house being haunted, thus making the old man too frightened even to enter it. The Romans had a particular predilection for ghost stories.[51]

However bright the play's other stars may glow, they are still only satellites to the shining Tranio. He may be the finest portrait of Plautus' favourite character: bouncy, brazen, bold, and brainy. His powers of improvisation are never on better display than in his haunted-house narrative, where at every cul-de-sac he reaches once again deeper into his bag of tricks. We can be no less extravagant in our praise of him than he is himself (lines 775–7):

> They say Kings Alexander and Agathocles
> Were two who did big things. Now would you say I'm third—
> Who solo does so many memorable things?

This exultant role is sung again and again by brilliant servants like Ben Jonson's Mosca, Molière's Scapin, and Beaumarchais's Figaro. In fact, Tranio voices a rather democratic notion which would later be celebrated as Figaro's philosophy (line 407): 'If a man has talent, it's no different if he's a slave or master!' He embodies the spirit of comedy. When his fellow slave Grumio warns him that his roguery may bring him punishment very soon, he retorts (line 71): 'I have my "now", let "very soon" come when it comes.' And even his 'now' is something very special. With Saturnalian audacity, he faces up to all that he has done, even boasting to his outraged master. (Note that he insolently draws attention to the financial profligacy which has bankrupted the old man's son—lines 200–1.) When surrounded by whippers, with but temporary refuge on a holy altar,[52] he is unregenerate, cheeky, and proud. The slave always remains

---

[51] Cf. Pliny, *Letters* 1. 7. 27 and the werewolf tale in Petronius' *Satyricon* 61 ff. There is a curious resemblance between Tranio's version of the 'spectre's' speech and the words of Hamlet's father (*Hamlet*, I. v. 77).

[52] The altar on to which Tranio leaps for sanctuary seems to have been part of the traditional Roman theatre set, perhaps used for a ceremony preceding the performance. The on-stage altar is also referred to in *The Pot of Gold* 606.

master of the situation, defying his antagonists and deifying himself.[53]

This is the supreme topsy-turvydom of Plautine comedy. On any ordinary occasion, a Roman Tranio would suffer a whipping —or even the gallows—for his malefactions. Today is different: tomorrow is another story, as Tranio himself admits (line 1178). For the moment, this creature of a single day, the figment of the 'now' imagination, is 'permitted the outrage, but spared the consequences'. The rules—and the audience—relax. Indeed, the latter testify to their complicity in Tranio's egregiously un-Roman rogueries just two lines later—with their applause.

The Pot of Gold

All of Plautus' most successful plays have a heritage. *The Braggart Soldier* anticipates Falstaff, *The Brothers Menaechmus* inspired *The Comedy of Errors*, and *The Pot of Gold* re-emerged as Molière's *Miser*. The text itself shows signs of reworking for subsequent performances, and was often emulated and adapted in late antiquity. For example, in 1497 it was staged in the original on the Quirinal in Rome and in 1564 presented (also in Latin) for Queen Elizabeth I.

The great appeal is, of course, old Euclio himself. While normally Plautus' characters are more sketches than portraits, the infamous skinflint is a noteworthy exception. He is at once funny and formidable and, for all his comic excesses, frighteningly real.

Euclio is a man obsessed, a true monomaniac whose every waking thought—and he does not sleep at all—is his hidden treasure. He lives in perpetual panic, ever suspicious that every passer-by on the street is equally mad and bent on robbing him.

He also has an unmistakable streak of cruelty. Unlike most Plautine masters, Euclio does not merely threaten his slaves with thrashings, but actually inflicts them. Moreover, in the case of his elderly maid Staphyla, he also terrifies her with gruesome threats like eye-gouging, stabbing, and cutting her tongue out.

---

[53] Cf. line 1104. On 'the divinity of the clever slave', see Segal, *Roman Laughter*[2], ch. 4, esp. 131 ff.

And his violence is not restricted to servants. He even beats a rooster to death.

Of all Plautus' *dramatis personae*, only Euclio may be described as having a psychology—albeit an abnormal one. He is driven by unseen forces to behave in a compulsive, antisocial manner. How can the old man live a normal life when he is continually breaking off conversations to run inside and check on his gold?

As dramaturgy, the play itself is hardly a masterpiece. It is little more than a series of hostile confrontations—and attempted blows—between Euclio and everyone else. The text also shows signs of awkward revision. Indeed, at first glance, Megadorus' tirade against dowried women—a familiar Roman satirical subject—seems strangely out of place and out of character. Probably composed by a later hand and encrusted on to the manuscript, its only apparent relation to the original drama is a slightly heartless attitude.

With his typical slapdash construction, Plautus uses the familiar New Comedy motif of the-girl-raped-at-the-festival-by-a-stranger (and her resultant pregnancy) as his threadbare plot[54] (one thinks of Euripides' *Ion*[55].) The story does not bear much scrutiny, as the prologue never explains why young Lyconides waits the full nine months to approach Euclio and ask for her hand; or, indeed, why no one seems to notice that the girl is gaining weight. By contrast, Terence would have made the love-affair the focal point of his drama.

An expository prologue begins the play. It is spoken by the Household God who has been watching over the hidden gold for generations. He has only recently decided to reward the *pietas* of Euclio's daughter Phaedria by revealing the secret treasure to her father.

Curiously, for all its wealth of information, the prologue gives us no idea of Euclio's extraordinary personality. It could, for example, have taken some of the humorous material from Strobilus' descriptive conversation with Congrio (lines 298 ff.), mentioning just one of the old man's innumerable quirks, like

[54] Cf. Fantham, 'Sex, Status and Survival in Hellenistic Athens', 53.

[55] Bernard Knox, 'Euripidean Comedy', in Alan Cheuse and Richard Koffler (eds.), *The Rarer Action: Essays in Honor of Francis Fergusson* (New Brunswick, NJ, 1970).

hoarding his nail shavings or sleeping with a bag on his face to
save his breath.

Still, the first scene accomplishes this dramatically. When the
miser bursts out of his door, hurling blows and abuse at his
maidservant, the poor woman reveals to the audience the extent
of her master's psychosis (lines 70–2 ff.):

> Why, every single day he kicks me out ten times.
> I don't know what affliction's taken hold of him.
> He stays up all the night ...

After this she discloses a piquant detail which the Household
God has forgotten to mention, namely that Phaedria is on the
verge of giving birth. In short, this scene is an excellent introduction to the leading character. It has been argued that Euclio
is a deliberate Roman caricature: Roman frugality brought to its
comic extreme. The historian Polybius emphasizes what sticklers
the Romans were when it came to financial matters, although
he says that this is a praiseworthy quality. Indeed, he states
approvingly that in Rome, 'absolutely no one gives you *anything*
he possesses of his own free will.'

After this explosive scene, a middle-aged—and middle-class—
couple appears: Megadorus, the wealthy neighbour and his
bourgeois sister, Eunomia. Though the setting of *The Pot of
Gold* is ostensibly Athens, they are as Roman as can be.

By force of platitudinous prolixity, the matron persuades her
brother to take a wife. He in turn launches into a lengthy diatribe
against the bad habits of rich women and vows to wed none
other than Euclio's undowried daughter. Indeed, at the outset,
this scene would appear extraneous. On the other hand, the
underlying theme of the entire play is 'dowry', both material and
metaphorical. Megadorus—whose name means 'great gift'—is
open and generous in relinquishing all claims on a financial
settlement from Euclio's daughter (he thinks her virtues are
enough). At the end of the play, Euclio is converted to generosity,
creating a kind of 'eunomia' (harmony, good integration) among
the citizenry. It is, as in all the best comedies, the ultimate
reintegration of society.[56]

[56] Cf. Northrop Frye, 'The Argument of Comedy', *English Institute Essays* (New
York, 1949), 61.

Eunomia (whose son happens, by coincidence, to be the one who compromised the girl) agrees with appropriate deference. Never one to do things by halves, the inveterate bachelor resolves to marry that very day and immediately approaches his quirky neighbour who, of course, suspects that Megadorus' real passion is for his hidden treasure (lines 184-5 ff.):

A trick—I sense a trick when rich men speak so lavishly to poor.
That fellow knows that I have gold, why else would he be so polite?

Temporarily overcoming his suspicions, Euclio agrees to the match and both men go their separate ways to prepare for the ceremony.

To concoct a feast Megadorus hires some professional caterers —familiar figures on the Greek New Comedy stage. Following the usual stereotype these cooks are depicted as boastful and rivalrous, better known for their kleptomania than their cuisine. Meanwhile, the old man proves to be psychologically incapable of expending the tiniest sum (lines 371-7):

I tried to screw my courage up today
To have some fun—enjoy my daughter's wedding.
I went to shop for fish—but it was overpriced.
The lamb was overpriced, the beef was overpriced
The veal was overpriced, the pork and tuna too.
And they were all the more expensive since I had no money.
I stormed away, unable to buy anything!

Note how the old man specifies that he had *tried* to let go, but was unable to bring himself to do so.

After raving endlessly about his fears, Euclio suddenly sees them realized: his pot is stolen. This occasions two famous scenes, both of which made a lasting impression on Molière. In a stirring monologue (lines 713 ff.) Euclio addresses the audience, alternately accusing them and imploring them for help. The French playwright adds the ultimate touch—having the protagonist seize his own hand in a Dr Strangelovian fashion, accuse himself of the deed, and demand that *he* be tortured.

The other classic moment is what the French call a quiproquo (lines 731 ff.). Here young Lyconides 'confesses' to his misdeeds. His references to Phaedria's predicament are mistaken by

Euclio for allusions to his pot of gold and the confusion is rich
in humour. Yet this also demonstrates the miser's ultimate
dehumanization by greed. He confuses his precious daughter
with his inanimate possessions.

At a maddening moment in the narrative, the text breaks off,
leaving scholars to debate forevermore the author's dramatic
intentions. We are left to seek out the resolution from the two
arguments—versified epitomes appended to the manuscripts of
the play. Both indicate that when Euclio recovers his pot, he
bestows it upon the newly-weds.

This is a lovely irony. The skinflint displays surprising generosity,
giving his son-in-law the dowry which—throughout the entire
play—he protested he did not have.

The Pot of Gold attracted attention once again in the mid-
1950s when the new Menander papyri were discovered, especially
Dyskolos (*The Grouch*), the only complete play of his we possess.
Many critics noted the similarity of setting in both the Greek
and Roman plays, the affinities in characterization and detail
between the two central figures. Moreover, since Menander's
title-character Knemon is misanthropic, too stingy to spend money
on a proper sacrifice, and has a daughter with whom a local
bourgeois youth falls in love, some have even declared the play
a direct model for *The Pot of Gold*. But that is going too far.

There seems to be a gallery of misers in Greek New Comedy[57]
(showing some similarity to the famous study of *Characters* by
Menander's philosophical contemporary, Theophrastus). For
example, Smikrines in *The Arbitration*, who 'feared that the
smoke from his fire would escape with something' directly
anticipates lines 300–1 of the Latin play.

Whatever its source, *The Pot of Gold* seems to have been
written towards the end of Plautus' career. There are several
complex 'lyric' passages and, according to scholars, an allusion
(475 ff.) to the *Lex Oppia*. This legislation to curb female
extravagance was passed in 215 BC and, despite Cato the Elder's
vigorous objection, repealed in 195 BC.[58] (Cf. Livy's account in
34. 1 ff. which echoes some key words such as *vehicula*, *pallas*,

[57] Stockert, *Plautus Aulularia* (Stuttgart, 1983), 14 ff., surveys the many possible
Menandrian models for the play.
[58] See Explanatory Note on line 504.

and *purpuram*.) There is also a probable reference (line 408) to the Senate's landmark decree in 186 BC outlawing the secret cult of Bacchus.

The Pot of Gold is a good example of the 'Plautinification' of Greek New Comedy. The original Hellenistic play was similar in theme but far different in tone. Plautus has remoulded it on his Roman potter's wheel and turned a sentimental drama into a farce.

Perhaps the most important aspect of *The Pot of Gold* is that it gave Molière the inspiration to create one of his most brilliant comedies. Harpagon is an even more radical characterization than Euclio; for whereas the Roman miser has a few natural traits—like the ability to give away his daughter and, we assume, ultimately his treasure—Molière's monomaniac is the quintessence of unyielding avarice as well as a heartless father, hated by everyone. Indeed, his obsession is so severe that at times Molière's play—as Goethe long ago observed—achieves tragic dimensions. Plautus would have been astonished at what a greater artist had done with his raw material.

The manuscript of *The Pot of Gold* itself is incomplete not only in its structure, but in a great many of its verses. Some of the jokes are obscure—a constant source of frustration for the translator and, no doubt, the reader. Yet we must be thankful for what we have. *The Pot of Gold*, if not a great play, is none the less great theatre.

NOTE ON THE TRANSLATIONS
AND THE TEXT

WHEREVER possible, the renderings are line for line: the Latin text is indicated in the introduction to each play. As far as English allows, I have tried to approximate the metre of Plautus. This was a relatively easy task for *The Braggart Soldier*: I merely wrote English lines in iambs and trochees (and in one place anapaests), to correspond to the Latin. I did likewise for the iambic and trochaic lines of the other three comedies, but the metre of their songs only remotely resembles the polymetric lyrics of the Plautine original. In other words, I took a few rhythmic and verbal liberties—else the task of translation would have been impossibly complicated.

There is no rhyme in the original Latin (except, perhaps, such uncommon instances as *The Brothers Menaechmus* 595 ff.), but I have added it where it might be called for in the analogous situation on the English-speaking stage. The prologues are an obvious example. Also, to emphasize Plautus' ternary crescendos such as:

> Sine ultro veniat; quaeri*tet*, deside*ret*, expec*tet*

I have rhymed as follows:

> Do let her come unbidden, sir: to yearn, to burn, to wait her turn.

On rare occasions, a metaphor has been altered, but always in the service of Plautus' joke. I have zealously tried to avoid anachronisms, and where the dialogue sounds very snappy and modern, I have added explanatory notes to assure the reader he is getting the real Roman stuff.

I have *not* divided the plays into acts and scenes, for there is no evidence that Plautus himself did so. The divisions we see in some modern editions were made only in 1500 by J. B. Pius. Since these translations are also intended to be acted, I have suggested where logical intermissions might be placed. Interestingly enough, the first three plays in this volume have a very natural break just about half-way through; perhaps this requires further scholarly investigation. There are no stage directions in the ancient manuscripts. Those included here are one translator's intuitive guesses.

With the few exceptions that are signalled below, the translations in this volume were based on the Latin editions listed in the following paragraph.

Unfortunately, I obtained A. S. Gratwick's excellent *Menaechmi* edition (Cambridge, 1993), at too late a stage in the publication of this book, but found the commentaries of N. Moseley and M. Hammond (Cambridge, Mass., rev. edn., 1968) to be similarly helpful, as was the *Mostellaria*² edition of E. Sonnenschein (Oxford, 1907, repr. 1966). For *Aulularia*, E. J. Thomas's school text, *T. Macci Plauti Aulularia* (Oxford, 1913), was useful, as was W. Stockert's Teubner edition, *Plautus Aulularia* (Stuttgart, 1983). The texts were clarified at many points by Alfred Ernout's Belles Lettres edition (Paris, 1932). Textual remarks on *Aulularia* are included among the Explanatory Notes to that play.

Miles

Lines 215–28: with Fraenkel, giving the lines to Palaestrio.

Line 584: favouring Tyrrell's suggestion of *capitulo* for *populo impio*.

Line 658: with Lindsay *et al.*, reading O *lepidum semisenem*.

Line 894: with Ernout, preferring *mala mulier mers*.

Line 997: *Bitant* for *bitat*.

Line 1000: Redistributing the lines as in Ernout.

Line 1337: with Lindsay *et al.*, reading Palaestrio's line as *Fio miser*.

Line 1365: with Ernout, Tyrrell, giving line to Pyrgopolynices.

Menaechmi

Lines 152–3: *Pulchre habeamus* for *sepulcrum habeamus*.

Line 333: redivided.

Line 613: line 614 after line 619, following Kiessling, whom Ernout accepts.

Line 914: line 914 bracketed by Lindsay.

Mostellaria

Lines 286, 290–1 bracketed. See Ernout ad loc.
Lines 306–7 omitted. See Sonnenschein ad loc.
Lines 537–8: lacuna in lines 537–8 conjectured.
Lines 622 ff. redistributed as in Leo, Ernout, Sonnenschein.
Line 645: as in Sonnenschein.
Lines 864–6 omitted (fragmentary).
Lines 1055–60 are fragmentary.

SELECT BIBLIOGRAPHY

Anderson, William S., *Barbarian Play: Plautus' Roman Comedy* (Toronto, 1993).

Arnott, W. Geoffrey, *Menander*, i (Cambridge, Mass., 1979).

—— 'The Greek Original of Plautus' *Aulularia*', *Wiener Studien*, 101 (1988), 181–91.

—— *Menander, Plautus, and Terence, Greece and Rome*, New Surveys in the Classics, 9 (Oxford, 1975).

Barsby, J. A. (ed.), *Plautus, Bacchides* (Warminster, 1986).

Beacham, Richard C., *The Roman Theatre and its Audience* (London, 1991).

Beare, W., *The Roman Stage*³ (London, 1968).

Chalmers, Walter R., 'Plautus and his Audience', in T. A. Dorey and Donald R. Dudley (eds.), *Roman Drama* (New York, 1965), 21–50.

Csapo, Eric, and Slater, William J. (eds.), *The Context of Ancient Drama* (Ann Arbor, 1995).

Dorey, T. A., and Dudley, D. R. (eds.), *Roman Drama* (New York, 1965).

Duckworth, George E., *The Nature of Roman Comedy* (Princeton, 1952). Revised by Richard Hunter (London, 1994).

Fantham, Elaine, *Comparative Studies in Republican Latin Imagery* (Toronto, 1972).

—— 'Sex, Status and Survival in Hellenistic Athens: A Study of Women in New Comedy', *Phoenix*, 29 (1975), 44–74.

Garton, Charles, *Personal Aspects of the Roman Theater* (Toronto, 1975).

Gentili, Bruno, *Theatrical Performances in the Ancient World* (Amsterdam, 1979).

Goldberg, Sander, *The Making of Menander's Comedy* (London, 1980).

—— *Understanding Terence* (Princeton, 1986).

Gratwick, A. S., 'Drama', in *Cambridge History of Classical Literature* (Cambridge, 1982), ii. 77–127.

—— (ed.), *Plautus Menaechmi* (Cambridge, 1993).

Green, J. R., *Theatre in Ancient Greek Society* (London, 1994).

Hammond, Mason, Mack, Arthur M., and Moskalew, Walter (eds.), *Plautus, Miles Gloriosus* (Cambridge, Mass., 1961).

Handley, E. W., *Menander and Plautus: A Study in Comparison* (London, 1968).

Hanson, John Arthur, 'Scholarship on Plautus since 1950', Parts I and II, *Classical World*, 59 (1965–6), 101 ff., 141 ff.

—— 'The Glorious Military', in T. A. Dorey and Donald R. Dudley (eds.), *Roman Drama* (New York, 1965), 51–85.

Hunter, R. L., *The New Comedy of Greece and Rome* (Cambridge, 1985).

Janko, Richard, *Aristotle on Comedy: Towards a Reconstruction of Poetics II* (Berkeley, 1984).

Konstan, David, *Roman Comedy* (Ithaca, NY, 1983).

Lawall, Gilbert, and Quinn, Betty Nye (eds.), *The Menaechmi* (Oak Park and Bristol, 1981).

Lodge, Gonzalez, *Lexicon Plautinum*, 2 vols. (Leipzig, 1924–33).

Mairhofer, H., *Der direkte Einfluss Plautus auf die englische Komödie*, Diss. (Vienna, 1952).

Moseley, Nicholas, and Hammond, Mason (eds.), *Plautus, Menaechmi* (Cambridge, Mass., 1961).

Moulton, Carroll, 'Aristophanes', in T. J. Luce (ed.), *Ancient Writers: Greece and Rome* (New York, 1982), i. 291–312.

—— 'Menander', in *Ancient Writers: Greece and Rome* (New York, 1982), i. 435–47.

Muecke, Frances, 'Plautus and the Theater of Disguise', *Classical Antiquity*, 5 (1986), 216–29.

Sandbach, F. H., *The Comic Theatre of Greece and Rome* (London, 1977).

—— 'Terence', in T. J. Luce (ed.), *Ancient Writers: Greece and Rome* (New York, 1982), i. 541–54.

Schaaf, L., *Der Miles Gloriosus des Plautus und sein griechisches Original* (Munich, 1977).

Segal, Erich, 'Scholarship on Plautus 1965–1976', *Classical World*, 74 (1981), 353–433.

—— *Roman Laughter: The Comedy of Plautus* 2nd edn. rev. (Oxford, 1987).

—— 'The Comic Catastrophe: An Essay on Euripidean Comedy', in A. Griffith (ed.), *Stage Directions: Essays in Ancient Drama in Honour of E. W. Handley* (London, 1995), 1–10.

Slater, Niall, *Plautus in Performance* (Princeton, 1985).

—— 'The Dates of Plautus' *Curculio* and *Trinummus Reconsidered*', *American Journal of Philology*, 108 (1987), 264–9.

Stark, Ekkehard, *Die Menaechmi des Plautus und kein griechisches Original* (Tübingen, 1989).

Webster, T. B. L., *An Introduction to Menander* (Manchester, 1974).

Wiles, David, 'Taking Farce Seriously: Recent Critical Approaches to Plautus', in J. Redmond (ed.), *Themes in Drama*, x. *Farce* (Cambridge, 1988), 261–71.

Wiles, David, *The Masks of Menander: Sign and Meaning in Greek and Roman Performance* (Cambridge, 1991).

Wright, John, *Dancing in Chains: The Stylistic Unity of the Comoedia Palliata* (Rome, 1974).

—— 'Plautus', in T. J. Luce (ed.), *Ancient Writers: Greece and Rome* (New York, 1982), i. 501–23.

Zagagi, Netta, *Tradition and Originality in Plautus: Studies in the Amatory Motifs in Plautine Comedy* (Göttingen, 1980).

—— *The Comedy of Menander: Convention, Variation and Originality* (Bloomington, Ind., 1995).

THE BRAGGART SOLDIER

(*Miles Gloriosus*)

DRAMATIS PERSONAE

PYRGOPOLYNICES, *a soldier*
ARTOTROGUS, *his parasite*
PALAESTRIO, *slave to the soldier (formerly to Pleusicles)*
PERIPLECTOMENUS, *an old man of Ephesus*
SCELEDRUS, *slave to the soldier*
PLEUSICLES, *a young man from Athens*
LURCIO, *slave to the soldier*
PHILOCOMASIUM, *a girl abducted by the soldier*
ACROTELEUTIUM, *a courtesan*
MILPHIDIPPA, *her maid*
A SLAVE BOY
CARIO, *Periplectomenus' cook*

The entire action takes place on a street in Ephesus, before the adjoining houses of PYRGOPOLYNICES *and* PERIPLECTOMENUS.

THE BRAGGART SOLDIER

Enter PYRGOPOLYNICES, *followed by his parasite**
ARTOTROGUS *and several minions who carry
his monstrous shield*

PYRGOPOLYNICES [*posing pompously, declaiming in heroic
    fashion*]. Look lively—shine a shimmer on that shield of
    mine
Surpassing sunbeams—when there are no clouds, of course.
Thus, when it's needed, with the battle joined, its gleam
Shall strike opposing eyeballs in the bloodshed—bloodshot!
Ah me, I must give comfort to this blade of mine
Lest he lament and yield himself to dark despair.
Too long ere now has he been sick of his vacation.
Poor lad! He's dying to make mincemeat of the foe.
    [*Dropping the bombastic tone*] Say, where the devil is
    Artotrogus?
ARTOTROGUS.   He's here—
By Destiny's dashing, dauntless, debonair darling,   10
A man so warlike, Mars himself would hardly dare
To claim his powers were the equal of your own.
PYRGOPOLYNICES [*preening*]. Tell me—who was that chap I
    saved at Field-of-Roaches,
Where the supreme commander was Crash-Bang-Razzle-
    Dazzle
Son of Mighty-Mercenary-Messup, you know, Neptune's
    nephew?
ARTOTROGUS. Ah yes, the man with golden armour, I recall.
You puffed away his legions with a single breath
Like wind blows autumn leaves, or straw from thatch-
    roofed huts.
PYRGOPOLYNICES. A snap—a nothing, really.
ARTOTROGUS.   Nothing, indeed—that is
Compared to other feats I could recount—[*aside*] as false
    as this.   20

[*To the audience, as he hides behind the soldier's shield*]

If any of you knows a man more full of bull
Or empty boastings, you can have me—free of tax.
But I'll say this: I'm crazy for his olive salad!

PYRGOPOLYNICES. Hey, where are you?

ARTOTROGUS [*popping up*]. Here! And then that elephant in
India—
The way your fist just broke his arm to smithereens.

PYRGOPOLYNICES. What's that—his *arm*?

ARTOTROGUS.   I meant his leg, of course.

PYRGOPOLYNICES. I gave him just an easy jab.

ARTOTROGUS.   A jab, of course!
If you had really tried, you would have smashed his arm
Right through his elephantine skin and guts and bone!   30

PYRGOPOLYNICES. No more of this.

ARTOTROGUS.   Of course. Why bother to narrate
Your many daring deeds to me—who knows them all.
[*Aside, to the audience*] It's only for my stomach that I
stomach him.
While ears are suffering, at least my teeth are suppering.
And so I yes and yes again to all his lies.

PYRGOPOLYNICES. What was I saying?

ARTOTROGUS.   Oh, I know precisely what.
It's done, by Hercules.

PYRGOPOLYNICES.   What's done?

ARTOTROGUS.   Well, something is.

PYRGOPOLYNICES. Have you—

ARTOTROGUS.   Your tablets? Yes, of course, a stylus too.

PYRGOPOLYNICES. How expertly you suit your mind to know
my own.

ARTOTROGUS. I ought to know your habits well-rehearsedly   40
And see to it I sniff your wishes in advance.

PYRGOPOLYNICES. How good's your memory?

ARTOTROGUS.   It's perfect, sir. In Cilicia,
A hundred fifty. In darkest I-robya, hundreds more.
Add thirty Sardians, those Macedonians, and there's
The total men you've slaughtered in a single day.

PYRGOPOLYNICES. 'The total men', your final sum is—

ARTOTROGUS.   Seven thousand.

PYRGOPOLYNICES. I believe you're right. You're good at your
accounts.*

ARTOTROGUS. I didn't even write it down; it's all by heart.

PYRGOPOLYNICES. My god, you've got a memory!

ARTOTROGUS. Food feeds it.

PYRGOPOLYNICES. Well, if you keep behaving as you have,
you'll eat 50
Eternally. I'll always have a place for you at dinner.

ARTOTROGUS [*inspired by this*]. And then in Cappadocia, you
would have slain
Five hundred with one blow—except your blade was dull.

PYRGOPOLYNICES. Just shabby little soldiers, so I let them
live.

ARTOTROGUS. Why bother to repeat what every mortal
knows—
There's no one more invincible in all the earth
In duties or in beauties than—Pyrgopolynices!
Why, all the women love you—who can blame them,
either—
Since you're so ... so attractive? Why, just yesterday
Some women grabbed me by the tunic—

PYRGOPOLYNICES. Yes, what said they?

ARTOTROGUS. They badgered me with asking—'Isn't that
Achilles?' 60
'No,' said I, 'it's just his brother.' 'Ah,' said one,
'That's why he looks so beautiful and so genteel!
Just look at him—that handsome head of hair he has!
Oh, blessèd are the women that can sleep with him!'

PYRGOPOLYNICES. They really said all that?

ARTOTROGUS. And then both begged me
To parade you by today so they could see you.

PYRGOPOLYNICES. How wretched to be such a handsome
man.

ARTOTROGUS. How true.
They are a bother, screeching and beseeching me 70
For just one little look at you. And sending for me!
That's why I can't give all my time to serving you.

[*Suddenly, duty calls*

PYRGOPOLYNICES. Now is the hour, fall in! On to the forum
To seek the mercenaries I conscripted yesterday.
I must distribute salaries to all enlisted.
King Seleucus has urgently appealed to me*

To gather fighting men for him and sign them up.
I have decreed this day devoted to the king's demands.
ARTOTROGUS. Then off we go!
PYRGOPOLYNICES.   Faithful fellows—follow!*

> [PYRGOPOLYNICES *leads his minions off*
> *Enter* PALAESTRIO

PALAESTRIO [*to the audience*]. Now, folks, if you'll be kind
    enough to hear me out,   80
Then I'll be kind and tell you what our play's about.
Whoever doesn't want to listen, let him beat it
And give a seat to one of those in back who need it.
    I'll tell you why we've gathered in this festive spot,
What comedy we will enact, its name and plot.
This play is called the *Alazon* in Greek,
A name translated 'braggart' in the tongue we speak.
This town is Ephesus; that soldier is my master
Who's just gone to the forum. What a shameless crass
    bombaster!
He's so full of crap and lechery, no lies are vaster.*   90
He brags that all the women seek him out *en masse*.
The truth is, everywhere he goes they think he's just an ass.
The local wenches claim they've tired out their lips,
But not from kissing him—from making nasty quips.
    Not very long have I been slaving as his slave,
I want you all to know how I became his knave,
And whom I slaved for prior to this slavish lot.
So listen very closely, folks, here comes the plot!
    My master back in Athens was a fine young man.
In good old Athens, he was crazy for a courtesan.*   100
She loved him too. Yes, that's the kind of love that's best.
Then he was sent to Naupactus—a governmental quest
Of great importance. While my master served the state,
The soldier came to Athens—by some trick of Fate.
He made advances to my master's little friend.
He played up to her mother and began to send
Cosmetics, costly catered cookery and wine—
The soldier and the bawd were getting on just fine.
Right when the soldier saw his chance for something shady

He bamboozled the old bawd—the mother of the lady   110
(That's the girl my master loved). He took her daughter
In secret on a ship, and made for open water.
To Ephesus—against her will—is where he brought her.
    Now when *I* learn he's kidnapped Master's concubine,
As fast as possible, I get a ship of mine.
I head for Naupactus to tell him of the fact,
But just when we get out to sea we are attacked—
And pirates take the ship. Fate's will be done,   120
And I was finished, though I scarcely had begun.
    The pirate made the soldier here a gift of me
And when the soldier took me home—what do I see?
The girl from Athens—my old master's concubine—
Who, when she saw me, winked and gave a sign
Not to address her. Later, when the coast was clear,
She wept and told me how unhappy she was here.
She longed to flee to Athens—in a phrase:
She loved my master from the good old days
And hated no one as she did this military guy.   130
On learning of the woman's inner feelings, I
Compose a letter, sign and seal it secretly
And get a merchant to deliver it for me
To my old master—he who still adored
This girl here. And my note to come was not ignored!
He came! He's staying with a neighbour right next door—
A wonderful old man his family knew before,
Who's been a blessing to my amorous young man,
Promoting our affair in every way he can.
    Now here within I've started mighty machinations   140
To make it easy for the lovers' . . . visitations.
The soldier gave the girl a bedroom of her own.
No one but she can enter it, it's hers alone.
So in this bedroom I have tunnelled through the wall,
Right to the other house in secret she can crawl.
Our neighbour knows of this—in fact, he planned it all!
    So good for nothing is this fellow slave of mine—
The one the soldier picked to guard the concubine—
That with our artful artifice and wily ways
We'll coat this fellow's eyeballs with so thick a glaze,

We'll make him sure he doesn't see what's really there!
Don't *you* be fooled: one girl today will play a *pair*.   150
And so the girl that comes from either house will share
A single face, the same one claiming to be twins.
We'll fool that guard of hers until his head just spins!
But wait—I hear the creaking of our neighbour's door.
Here comes that nice old fellow I described before.

Old PERIPLECTOMENUS *comes out of his house,*
still shouting back angrily at the slaves within

PERIPLECTOMENUS. After this, by Hercules, if you don't beat
   the daylights out of
Anyone who's on our roof, I'll make your raw sides into
   rawhides!
[*In exasperation, to the audience*] Now my neighbours see
   the show of all that happens in my house—
Looking right down through my skylight!* [*Back to his
   slaves*] Listen, I command you all:
Anyone you see on our roof, coming from the soldier's
   house—
That's excepting for Palaestrio—throw 'em down into the
   street!   160
Should they claim to be pursuing monkeys, pigeons or the
   like,
You'll be finished if you don't just pound and pummel 'em
   to pulp!
Make it so they won't be able to infringe upon our gambling
   laws.
See to it they won't even have bones enough for rolling
   dice!*

PALAESTRIO. Someone from our house has done a naughty
   thing, from what I hear—
The old man's commanded that my fellow slaves be beaten
   up.
Well, he said except for me—who gives a hoot about the
   rest?
I'll go see him.

PALAESTRIO *steps into view*

PERIPLECTOMENUS. Isn't this Palaestrio now coming toward
   me?
PALAESTRIO. How are you, Periplectomenus?
PERIPLECTOMENUS.   There aren't many men I'd
   Rather meet right now than you, Palaestrio.
PALAESTRIO.   What's going on? 170
   Why are you in such an uproar with our household?
PERIPLECTOMENUS.   We're all finished!
PALAESTRIO. What's the matter?
PERIPLECTOMENUS.   It's discovered!
PALAESTRIO.   What's discovered?
PERIPLECTOMENUS.   On my roof—
   Someone from your household has been spying on us,
      through the skylight,
   Where he saw Philocomasium in my house, with my guest—
   Kissing.
PALAESTRIO. Who saw this?
PERIPLECTOMENUS.   A fellow slave of yours.
PALAESTRIO.   But which, I wonder.
PERIPLECTOMENUS. I don't know, the fellow got away too
   fast.
PALAESTRIO.   Oh, I suspect—that
   I'm a dead man.
PERIPLECTOMENUS. As he fled, I cried, 'Why are you on my
   roof?'
   He replied, still on the run, 'I had to chase our little monkey.'
PALAESTRIO. Pity me—I'll have to die—all for a worthless
   animal!   180
   But the girl—is she still in your house?
PERIPLECTOMENUS.   She was when I came out here.
PALAESTRIO. Quick—have her cross back to our house, so
   the slaves can see her there.
   Make her hurry—that's unless she'd rather see her faithful
      slaves
   Just for her affair become fraternal brothers—on the cross!*
PERIPLECTOMENUS. She'll be told. [Going off] If that is all . . .
PALAESTRIO.   It isn't. Also tell the girl to
   See to it she doesn't lose her woman's ingenuity.
   Have her practice up her tricks and female shrewdness.

PERIPLECTOMENUS. What's this for?

PALAESTRIO. She must force the fellow who found her into
full forgetfulness.

Even if he saw her here a hundred times, have her deny it.

She has cheek, a lot of lip, loquacity, audacity,

Also perspicacity, tenacity, mendacity.

If someone accuses her, she'll just outswear the man with
oaths.   190

She knows every phoney phrase, the phoney ways, the
phoney plays.

Wiles she has, guiles she has, very soothing smiles she has.

'Seasoned' women never have to get their spices at the
grocer's—*

Their own garden grows the pepper for their sharp and
saucy schemes.

PERIPLECTOMENUS. I'll convey this all to her, if she's still
there. [Stops, amazed] What's going on?

What are you debating there inside yourself?

PALAESTRIO. Some silence, please,

While I call my wits to order to consider what to do

In retaliation: to outfox my foxy fellow slave, who

Saw her kissing in your house. We've got to make the
seen . . . unseen.

PERIPLECTOMENUS [starts to head for his house]. Cogitate—
while I withdraw and go in here. [Turns] Well, look at
him!   200

Standing pensive, pondering profundities with wrinkled
brow.

Now he knocks upon his head—he wants his brains to
answer him.

Look—he turns. Now he supports himself with left hand
on his left thigh.

Now he's adding something with the fingers of his right
hand. Now he

Slaps his right thigh—what a slap! What to-do for what to
do!

Now he snaps his fingers, struggles, changes posture every
second.

Look—he shakes his head. No, no, what he's invented
doesn't please him.

He'll cook up a plan that's well done—not half baked—I'm
    sure of that.

Look—he's going in for building—with his chin he crowns
    a column.

Cut it out! That type of building doesn't please me—not at
    all.   210

For I hear a foreign poet also has his face so columned*—

But he has two guards to keep him columned like that all
    the time.

Bravo! *Molto bello*, standing slavewise and theatrically*

He won't rest at all today until he finds the plan he's
    seeking.

Now I think he has it.

PALAESTRIO.   Hey—get busy, man, don't slip to sleep.*

That's unless you'd rather be on guard right here and [*points
    to his own back*] scarred right here.

Hey, have you been drinking? Hey, Palaestrio, I'm talking
    to you.

Rouse yourself! Wake up, I say; it's dawn, I say—

[*as if answering himself*]   I hear you, sir—

[*exhorting himself again*] Don't you see the enemy is
    threatening your rear? Come on and think!

Get us aid and reinforcements. No more napping; let's get
    scrapping!   220

Ready an offensive for the foe; prepare defences too!

Cut the enemy's supply line, then we'll fortify our own.

So our rations and equipment get to you and to our legions

Safely: do it quickly. What we need is instant action!

Come, concoct a cunning clever new campaign, and quickly
    too.

Make the visible invisible, undo every deed that's done.

PERIPLECTOMENUS. What fantastic feats he's fixing, fortified
    with fortitude!

PALAESTRIO. Tell me that you'll take command yourself and
    then I'll rest secure,

Knowing we can crush the foe.

PERIPLECTOMENUS [*magnanimously*]. I do accept the office
    and do   230

Take command!

PALAESTRIO. I think you'll win the prize you seek.

PERIPLECTOMENUS [*paternally and gratefully*]. May Jupiter
    Shower blessings on you. Won't you share your plans?

PALAESTRIO.   Be silent, sir,
    While I show you through the landscape of my 'plot', so
       you'll be sharing
    Equally in all the plans.

PERIPLECTOMENUS.   I'll guard them as I would my own.

PALAESTRIO. Master hasn't normal skin—it's thicker than an
    elephant's.
    He's about as clever as a stone.*

PERIPLECTOMENUS.   That much I know myself.

PALAESTRIO. Here's the whole idea, here's the notion that I'll
    set in motion:
    I will say Philocomasium has got a real twin sister
    Who has just arrived from Athens with a young man she's
       in love with.
    These two 'sisters' are alike as drops of milk. We'll say the
       lovers   240
    Stay at your house, as your guests.

PERIPLECTOMENUS.   Bravo—it's a brilliant plan!

PALAESTRIO. Should this fellow slave of mine make accusations
    to the soldier,
    Claiming that he saw the girl there kissing someone else,
       why then
    I'll accuse my fellow slave of having spied on you and seen
       the
    Sister with her lover, kissing and embracing.

PERIPLECTOMENUS.   Oh, that's fine!
    If the soldier questions me, I'll back you up.

PALAESTRIO.   Remember that the
    Sisters are identically alike. Remind the girl as well, so
    When the soldier asks her, she won't foul it up.

PERIPLECTOMENUS.   A perfect ploy!
    [*Suddenly*] Wait—what happens if the soldier wants to see
    'em both *together*?
    What do we do then?

PALAESTRIO.   It's easy; there are thousands of excuses: 250
    'She's not home, she took a walk, she's sleeping, dressing,
       washing,
    Dining, drinking, busy, indisposed, it's just impossible.'

If we start this on the right foot, we can put him off for
  ever.
Soon he'll get to thinking all the lies we tell him are the
  truth.
PERIPLECTOMENUS. This is just terrific.
PALAESTRIO.   Go in—if the girl is there, then have her
  Hurry home. And train her, make things plainer and explain
  her all.
She must fully comprehend our plan, the web we're weaving
  with her
New twin sister.
PERIPLECTOMENUS. You shall quickly have a girl who's very
  quick.
What else?
PALAESTRIO. Be off.
PERIPLECTOMENUS. I'm off.

> [*The old man rushes off into his house,
> leaving* PALAESTRIO *to ponder his next move*

PALAESTRIO.   Now I myself must go back home
And by secret subterfugitive investigation find out   260
Who of my fellow servants chased that monkey on the roof
  today.
Surely he'll have shared the secret with the other household
  slaves,
Whispering of Master's mistress, telling people how he saw
  her
Here—within our neighbour's house—embracing some
  unknown young man.
'I can't keep it secret, I'm the only one who knows,' he'll
  say.
When I find the man who saw her, my equipment will be
  ready.*
All is ready; I'm resolved to storm and take the enemy.
If I can't discover him, I'll sniff just like a hunting dog
Till I can pursue the little fox by following his footprints.
Wait—our door is creaking—I had better quiet down for
  now.   270
Look—here comes my fellow slave, the one they picked to
  guard the girl.

Enter SCELEDRUS, *one of the soldier's household
slaves. Normally a nervous nail-biter,
he is now completely bewildered*

SCELEDRUS. If I wasn't walking in my sleep today up on that
  roof, I
  Know for sure, by Pollux, that I saw Philocomasium,
  Master's mistress, right here in our neighbour's house—in
  search of trouble.

PALAESTRIO [*aside*]. There's the man who saw her kissing. I
  can tell from what he said.

SCELEDRUS. Who is that?

PALAESTRIO.   Your fellow slave. How goes it, Sceledrus?

SCELEDRUS.   Palaestrio!
  I'm so glad to see you.

PALAESTRIO.   Why? What's up? What's wrong?
                                      Please let me know.

SCELEDRUS. I'm afraid—

PALAESTRIO.   Of what?

SCELEDRUS.   Today I fear we slaves are really *leaping* into
  Trouble and titanic tortures!

PALAESTRIO.   So leap solo, you yourself—
  I don't care the slightest bit for any leaping—up or down. 280

SCELEDRUS. Maybe you don't know the crime committed in
  our house today.

PALAESTRIO. Crime? What sort of crime?

SCELEDRUS.   A dirty one!

PALAESTRIO.   Then keep it to yourself.
  I don't want to know it.

SCELEDRUS.   Well, I won't allow you *not* to know it!
  Listen: as I chased our monkey over neighbour's roof
  today—

PALAESTRIO. Sceledrus, I'd say one worthless animal pursued
  another.

SCELEDRUS. Go to hell!

PALAESTRIO.   *You* ought to go—on with your little
  tale, I mean.

                      [SCELEDRUS *glares at* PALAESTRIO,
                      then goes on with his story

SCELEDRUS. On the roof, I chanced by chance to peek down
  through our neighbour's skylight—

And what do I see? Philocomasium! She's smooching with
  some
Utterly unknown young man!

PALAESTRIO [*horrified*].   What scandal, Sceledrus, is this?

SCELEDRUS. There's no doubt of it, I saw her.

PALAESTRIO.   Really?

SCELEDRUS.   With my own two eyes. 290

PALAESTRIO. Come on, this is all illusion, you saw nothing.

SCELEDRUS.   Look at me!
Do my eyes look bad to you?

PALAESTRIO.   Ask a doctor; don't ask me!
                [*He now becomes the friendly adviser*
By the gods, don't propagate this tale of yours so indis-
  creetly.
Now you're seeking trouble head-on, soon it may seek
  you—*head off!*
And unless you can suppress this absolutely brainless banter,
Double death awaits you!

SCELEDRUS.   What's this 'double' death?

PALAESTRIO.   Well, I'll explain it:
First, if you've accused our master's mistress falsely, you
  must die.
Next, if what you say *is* true, you've failed as guard—you
  die again.

SCELEDRUS. I don't know my future, but I know I'm sure of
  what I saw.

PALAESTRIO. Still persisting, wretch?

SCELEDRUS. Look, I can only tell you what I saw. Why— 300
  She's inside our neighbour's house right now.

PALAESTRIO [*with mock surprise*].   What's that, she's not
  at home?

SCELEDRUS. You don't have to take my word. Go right inside
  and look yourself.

PALAESTRIO. Yes, indeed I will!
       [*He strides with severity into the soldier's house*

SCELEDRUS.   And I'll wait here and ambush her, the
  Minute our young filly trots from pasture to her storehouse
  stall.*
             [*He reflects a moment, then groans*
What am I to do? The soldier chose me as her guardian.

If I let this out—I die. Yet, if I'm silent, still I die,
Should this be discovered. Oh, what could be wickeder
    than women?
While I was on the roof there, she just left her room and
    went outside!
Bold and brazen badness, by the gods! If master learns of
    this,
Our whole household will be on the cross, by Hercules. Me
    too!   310
[*Resolves himself*] Come what may, I'll shut my mouth.
    Better stilled than killed, I say.
[*Exasperated, to the audience*] I can't guard a girl like this
    who's always out to sell herself!

PALAESTRIO *marches out of the soldier's house,*
a very stern look on his face

PALAESTRIO. Sceledrus! Is there a man more insolent in all
    the earth, or
Born beneath more angry or unfriendly stars—
SCELEDRUS.   What's wrong? What's wrong?
PALAESTRIO. You should have your eyes dug out for seeing
    what was never there.
SCELEDRUS. Never where?
PALAESTRIO.   I wouldn't give a rotten nut for
                                              your whole life!
SCELEDRUS. Tell me why—
PALAESTRIO.   You even dare to ask me?
SCELEDRUS.   Well, why can't I ask?
PALAESTRIO. You should really have that tattletaling tongue
    of yours cut off.
SCELEDRUS. Should I—why?
PALAESTRIO.   My friend, the girl's *at home*—
    the one you said you saw
In our neighbour's house with some young man, hugging
    and kissing him.   320
SCELEDRUS. It's amazing you don't eat your carrots. Why,
    they're cheap enough.*
PALAESTRIO. Carrots, why?
SCELEDRUS.   To aid your eyesight.

PALAESTRIO.   Gallows bird! It's you who needs 'em.
  You're the blind man, my sight's perfect—and I'm sure the
  girl's at home.
SCELEDRUS. She's at home?
PALAESTRIO.   At home she is.
SCELEDRUS.   Oh, cut it out; you're fooling with me.
PALAESTRIO. Then my hands are very dirty.
SCELEDRUS.   Why?
PALAESTRIO.   Because I fool with filth.
SCELEDRUS. Damn your hide!
PALAESTRIO. No, Sceledrus, it's *your* hide that is now at stake.
  That's unless you make some changes in your visions and
  derisions.
  Wait—our door is creaking.
SCELEDRUS [*at the old man's door*]. I shall stay right here
  and block *this* door,
For it's sure she can't cross over if she doesn't use the door!
PALAESTRIO. What's caused all this scurvy scoundrelism,
  Sceledrus? She's *home*.   330
        [SCELEDRUS *keeps blocking the old man's door,*
        looking straight ahead, trying to reassure himself
SCELEDRUS. I can see . . . I know myself . . . I trust myself
  implicitly.
  No one bullies me to make me think she isn't in this house.
          [He spreads his arms across the doorway
Here—I'll block the door. She won't sneak back and catch
  me unawares.
PALAESTRIO [*to the audience*]. There, he's where I want him.
  Now I'll push him off the ramparts.
  [*To* SCELEDRUS] Do you want me to convince you of your
  stupi-vision?*
SCELEDRUS.   Try it!
PALAESTRIO. And to prove that you don't know what eyes or
  brains are for?
SCELEDRUS.   Well, prove it!
PALAESTRIO. Now . . . you claim the concubine's in there.
SCELEDRUS.   Why, I *insist* she is,
  And I saw her kissing some young man as well—a perfect
  stranger.

PALAESTRIO. There's no passage from this house to our house,
    you know that—

SCELEDRUS [*impatiently*]. I know it.

PALAESTRIO. There's no balcony or garden, just the skylight—

SCELEDRUS.   I know *that* too! 340

PALAESTRIO. Well . . . if she's in *our* house and I bring her
    out so you can see her,
  Would you say you're worthy of a whipping?

SCELEDRUS [*nods*].   Worthy.

PALAESTRIO.   Guard the door—
  See she doesn't sneak out on the sly and slip across to our
  house.

SCELEDRUS. That's my plan.

PALAESTRIO.   I'll have her standing in the
    street here right away.

            [PALAESTRIO *dashes into the soldier's house*

SCELEDRUS [*muttering to himself*]. Go ahead and do it! I'll
    soon know if I saw what I saw.
  Or if—as he says he will—he'll prove the girl is still at
  home.
  [*Tries to reassure himself*] After all, I have my eyes. I never
  borrow someone else's. . . .
  [*Having second thoughts*] Yet he's always playing up to
  her—and he's her favourite:
  First man called to dinner, always first to fill his face with
  food.
  And he's only been with us about three years—not even
  that.*   350
  Still, I tell you, no one's slavery could be more savoury.
  Never mind, I'd better do what must be done, that's guard
  this door.
  Here I'll stand, by Pollux. Never will they make a fool of
  me!

            [SCELEDRUS *stands with his arms spread across
            the doorway to the old man's house*

        PALAESTRIO *enters from the soldier's house,
            leading the girl* PHILOCOMASIUM

PALAESTRIO. Remember your instructions.

PHILOCOMASIUM.   I'm astonished I'm admonished so.

PALAESTRIO. I'm worried you're not slippery enough.

PHILOCOMASIUM.   What? I could make
A dozen decent damsels devils with my surplus shrewdness!

PALAESTRIO. Now concentrate on trickery. I'll slip away from
    you.

> [PALAESTRIO *strides jauntily up to* SCELEDRUS,
> *who is still blocking the old man's door with
> all possible concentration*

How are you, Sceledrus?

SCELEDRUS [*staring straight ahead*]. I'm on the job. Speak—
    I have ears.

> [PALAESTRIO *looks at* SCELEDRUS' *pose, amused*

PALAESTRIO. You know, I think you'll travel soon in that
    same pose—beyond the gates
With arms outstretched—to bear your cross.

SCELEDRUS.   Oh yes? What for? 360

PALAESTRIO. Look to your left. Who is that woman?

SCELEDRUS.   Oh—by all the gods—
That girl—she's the master's concubine!

PALAESTRIO.   You know, I think so too.
Well, hurry, now's your time—

SCELEDRUS.   What should I do?

PALAESTRIO.   Don't dally—*die!*

PHILOCOMASIUM. Where is this 'loyal' slave who falsely brands
    an honest woman
With unchastity?

PALAESTRIO [*points to* SCELEDRUS]. Right here! He told me
    all the things I told you.

PHILOCOMASIUM. You say you saw me—rascal—kissing in
    our neighbour's house?

PALAESTRIO. And with an unknown man, he said.

SCELEDRUS.   By Hercules, I did.

PHILOCOMASIUM. You saw me?

SCELEDRUS.   With these eyes, by Hercules.

PHILOCOMASIUM.   You'll lose them soon—
They see more than they see.

SCELEDRUS.   By Hercules, I won't be frightened
Out of seeing what I really saw!

PHILOCOMASIUM.   I waste my breath   370
  Conversing with a lunatic. I'll have his head, by Pollux!
SCELEDRUS. Oh, stop your threats! I know the cross will be
  my tomb.
  My ancestors *all* ended there—exactly like my forefathers—
  and five-fathers.*
  And so these threats of yours can't tear my eyes from me!
  [*Meekly motioning* PALAESTRIO *to one side*] But—could I
  have a word with you, Palaestrio? . . . Please tell me:
  Where *did* she come from?
PALAESTRIO.   Home, where else?
SCELEDRUS.   From home?
PALAESTRIO. [*checking* SCELEDRUS' *eyes*]. You see me?
SCELEDRUS.   Sure.
  But it's amazing how she crossed from one house to the
  other!
  For certainly we haven't *got* a balcony, no garden,
  Every window's grated. [*To* PHILOCOMASIUM] Yet I'm sure
  I saw you here inside.
PALAESTRIO. What—criminal—you're still accusing her?
PHILOCOMASIUM.   By Castor, now 380
  I think it must have been the truth—that dream I dreamed
  last night.
PALAESTRIO. What did you dream?
PHILOCOMASIUM.   I'll tell you both, but
  please pay close attention:
  Last night it seemed as if my dear *twin sister* had arrived
  In Ephesus from Athens—with a certain man she loved.
  It seemed as if they both were staying here next door as
  guests.
PALAESTRIO [*aside*]. Palaestrio dreamed all this up. [*To* PHILO-
  COMASIUM] Go on—continue, please.
PHILOCOMASIUM. It seemed—though I was glad my sister
  came—because of her,
  There seemed to be a terrible suspicion cast upon me.
  Because it seemed that, in my dream, one of our slaves
  accused me,
  [*To* SCELEDRUS] Just as you're doing now, of having kissed
  a strange young man,   390

When really it was my *twin sister* kissing her beloved.
And so I dreamt that I was falsely and unjustly blamed.
PALAESTRIO. What seemed like dreams now happen to you
    wide awake!
By Hercules—a real live dream! [*To* PHILOCOMASIUM] Go
    right inside and pray!
[*Casually*] I think you should relate this to the soldier. . . .
PHILOCOMASIUM.   Why, of course!
I won't be falsely called unchaste—without revenge!
                    [*She storms into the soldier's house.*
                    PALAESTRIO *turns to* SCELEDRUS
SCELEDRUS. I'm scared. What have I done? I feel my whole
    back itching.
PALAESTRIO. You know you're finished, eh?
SCELEDRUS.   Well, now at least I'm sure she's home.
And now I'll guard our door—wherever she may be!
                    [SCELEDRUS *plants himself astride the soldier's
                    door in the same position he used to block
                    the old man's doorway*
PALAESTRIO [*sweetly*].   Sceledrus—
That dream she dreamt was pretty similar to what went
    on—   400
Even the part where you suspected that you saw her kissing!
SCELEDRUS. I don't know what I should believe myself. I
    thought I saw
A thing . . . I think . . . perhaps . . . I didn't see.
PALAESTRIO.   You're waking up—
Too late. When Master hears of this, you'll die a dandy
    death.
SCELEDRUS. I see the truth at last. My eyes were clouded by
    some fog.
PALAESTRIO. I knew it all along. She's always been inside the
    house.
SCELEDRUS. I can't say anything for sure. I saw her, yet I
    didn't . . .
PALAESTRIO. By Jupiter, your folly almost finished us for good!
In trying to be true to Master, *you* just missed disaster!
But wait—our neighbour's door is creaking. I'll be quiet
    now.   410

Enter PHILOCOMASIUM *again,*
this time from the old man's house

PHILOCOMASIUM [*in a disguised voice*]. Put fire on the altar;
  let me joyfully give thanks
To Diana of Ephesus. I'll burn Arabian incense.*
She saved me in the turbulent Neptunian territory,
When I was buffeted about, beset by savage seas.

SCELEDRUS. Palaestrio, Palaestrio!

PALAESTRIO [*mimicking him*].   O Sceledrus! What now?

SCELEDRUS. That girl that just came out—is that our master's
  concubine,
Philocomasium? Well—yes or no?

PALAESTRIO.   It seems like her,
Yet it's amazing how she crossed from one house to the
  other.
If it is she . . .

SCELEDRUS.   You mean you have your doubts?

PALAESTRIO.   It seems like her.

SCELEDRUS. Well, let's accost her. Hey, what's going on,
  Philocomasium?   420
What were you doing in that house? Just what's been going
  on?
Well, answer when I talk to you!

PALAESTRIO.   You're talking to yourself—
She doesn't answer.

SCELEDRUS.   You! I'm speaking to you, wicked woman!
So naughty with the neighbours—

PHILOCOMASIUM [*coldly*].   Sir, with whom are
  you conversing?

SCELEDRUS. Who else but you?

PHILOCOMASIUM.   Who are you, sir? What do
  you want with me?

SCELEDRUS. Asking me who am I?*

PHILOCOMASIUM.   Why not?—I don't know you, so I ask.

PALAESTRIO. I suppose you also don't know who *I* am.

PHILOCOMASIUM.   Well, you *and* he—
Are both a nuisance.

SCELEDRUS.   You don't know us?

PHILOCOMASIUM.   Neither one.

SCELEDRUS.   I'm scared, I'm scared.
PALAESTRIO. Scared of what?
SCELEDRUS.   I think we've lost our own
    identities somewhere—
Since she says she doesn't know us!
PALAESTRIO [*very seriously*]. Let's investigate this further.   430
    Sceledrus—are we ourselves—or are we other people now?
    Maybe, unbeknownst to us, one of our neighbours has
    transformed us!
                    [SCELEDRUS *ponders this for a split second*
SCELEDRUS. I'm myself for sure.
PALAESTRIO. Me too. Hey, girl—you're going after trouble.
                    [PHILOCOMASIUM *ignores him completely*
PALAESTRIO. Hey, Philocomasium!
PHILOCOMASIUM [*coolly*]. What madness motivates you, sir,
    to
Carelessly concoct this incoherent name to call me?
PALAESTRIO [*sarcastically*].   Well now,
    Tell me—what's your real name, then?
PHILOCOMASIUM.   My name is Dicea.
SCELEDRUS.   No, you're wrong, the
Name you're forging for yourself is phoney, Philocomasium.
    You're not *decent*, you're *in*decent—and you're cheating
    on my master!*
PHILOCOMASIUM. I?
SCELEDRUS.   Yes, you.
PHILOCOMASIUM.   But I only arrived from Athens
    yesterday,
With my faithful lover, an Athenian young man.
SCELEDRUS.   Then tell me—   440
What's your business here in Ephesus?
PHILOCOMASIUM.   Looking for my dear twin sister.
Someone said she might be here.
SCELEDRUS [*sarcastically*].   Oh, you're a clever girl!
PHILOCOMASIUM. No, I'm foolish, by the gods, to stand here
    chattering with you two.
    I'll be going. . . .
SCELEDRUS.   No, you won't be—
                                    [*He grabs her*

PHILOCOMASIUM.   Let me go!

SCELEDRUS.   You're caught red-handed!
I won't let you—

PHILOCOMASIUM.   Then beware the noise—when my hand
     meets your cheek.
Let me go!

SCELEDRUS [to PALAESTRIO]. You idiot, don't stand there;
     grab her other arm!

PALAESTRIO. I don't want to get my back involved in this.
     Who knows—*
Maybe she's our girl . . . or maybe someone else who *looks*
     like her.

PHILOCOMASIUM. Will you let me go or not?

SCELEDRUS.   You're coming home, no matter what!
If you don't, I'll drag you home.

PHILOCOMASIUM.   My home and master are in Athens— 450
Athens back in Attica. I'm only staying as a guest here.
[*Pointing to the soldier's house*] I don't know and I don't
     care about that house—or who you are!

SCELEDRUS. Go and sue me! I won't ever let you go unless
     you swear that*
If I do you'll come inside.

PHILOCOMASIUM.   Whoever you are, you're forcing me.
All right, if you let me go, I give my word to go inside.

SCELEDRUS. Go then.

                                            [*Releases her*
PHILOCOMASIUM.   Go I shall . . . goodbye!

                              [*She dashes into the old man's house*

SCELEDRUS.   That's typical: a woman's word.

PALAESTRIO. Sceledrus, you let the prize slip through your
     fingers. No mistaking—
She's our master's mistress. *Now*—you want to be a man
     of action?

SCELEDRUS [*timidly*]. Tell me how.

PALAESTRIO [*boldly*].   Bring forth a sword for me!

SCELEDRUS [*frightened*].   What will you do with it?

PALAESTRIO [*imitating his master's bombastic manner*]. I'll
     burst boldly through these portals and the man I see
     inside   460

Kissing Master's mistress, I shall slash to slivers on the
spot!

SCELEDRUS [*meekly*]. So you think it's she?

PALAESTRIO.   There's no two ways about it.

SCELEDRUS.   What an actress—
So convincing . . .

PALAESTRIO [*shouts*]. Bring me forth my sword!

SCELEDRUS.   I'll do it right away.

> [SCELEDRUS *dashes headlong into the sol-*
> *dier's house.* PALAESTRIO, *convulsed with*
> *laughter, addresses the audience*

PALAESTRIO. All the king's horses and all the king's men could
never act with such great daring,

Never be so calm, so cool, *in anything*, as one small *woman*!

Deftly she delivered up a different accent for each part!

How the faithful guard, my foxy fellow slave, was fully
flim-flammed!

What a source of joy for all—this passage passing through
the wall!

> PALAESTRIO *laughs gleefully as* SCELEDRUS *peeks*
> *out of the soldier's house, then sheepishly*
> *approaches*

SCELEDRUS. Say, Palaestrio . . . forget about the sword.

PALAESTRIO.   What's that? Why so?

SCELEDRUS. She's at home . . . our master's mistress.

PALAESTRIO.   Home?

SCELEDRUS.   She's lying on her couch. 470

PALAESTRIO [*building up to a frightening crescendo*]. Now it
seems you've found the trouble you've been looking for,
by Pollux!

SCELEDRUS. Why?

PALAESTRIO.   Because you dared disturb a lady who's
our neighbour's guest.

SCELEDRUS. Hercules! How horrible!

PALAESTRIO.   Why, there's no question, she must be the
Real twin sister of our girl—and *she's* the one that you saw
kissing!

SCELEDRUS. Yes, you're right. It's clearly she, just as you say.
Did I come close to

Getting killed! If I'd said a word to Master—
PALAESTRIO.   Now, be smart:
Keep this all a secret. Slaves should always know more
    than they tell.
I'll be going. I don't want to get mixed up in all your
    mischief.
I'll be at our neighbour's here. I don't quite care for your
    confusions.
If when Master comes he needs me, he can send for me in
    here.   480

> [PALAESTRIO *strides into the old man's house*

SCELEDRUS. At last he's gone. He cares no more for Master's
    matters
Than if he weren't slaving here in slavery!
Well, *now* our girl's inside the house, I'm sure of that;
I personally saw her lying on her couch.
So now's the time to pay attention to my guarding.

> [SCELEDRUS *paces before the soldier's*
> *door, concentrating on his guarding*

> PERIPLECTOMENUS *rushes out angrily from*
> *his own house*

PERIPLECTOMENUS. By Hercules, those men must take me for
    a sissy—
My military neighbour's slaves insult me so!
Did they not lay their hands upon my lady guest—
Who yesterday arrived from Athens with my friend?
[*Indignantly to the audience*] A free and freeborn girl—
    manhandled and insulted!   490
SCELEDRUS. Oh, Hercules, I'm through. He's heading to
    behead me.
I'm scared this thing has got me into awful trouble—
At least that's what I gather from the old man's words.
PERIPLECTOMENUS [*aside*]. Now I'll confront him. [*To*
    SCELEDRUS] Scurvy scoundrel Sceledrus!
Did you insult my guest right by my house just now?
SCELEDRUS [*near panic*]. Dear neighbour, listen please—
PERIPLECTOMENUS.   *I* listen? *You're* the slave!
SCELEDRUS. I want to clear myself—
PERIPLECTOMENUS.   How can you clear yourself,

When you've just done such monstrous and disgraceful
    things?
Perhaps because you're used to plundering the foe
You think you're free to act here as you please, scoundrel? 500
SCELEDRUS. Oh, please, sir—
PERIPLECTOMENUS.   May the gods and goddesses
    not love me
If I don't arrange a whipping for you—yes,
A good long-lasting lengthy one, from dawn to dusk.
For one, because you broke my roof tiles and my gutters,
While you chased another monkey—like yourself.
And then for spying on my guest in my own house,
While he was kissing and embracing his own sweetheart.
And *then* you had the gall to slander that dear girl
Your master keeps—and to accuse me of atrocious things!
And *now* you maul my lady guest—right on my doorstep! 510
Why, if I don't have knotted lashes put to you,
I'll see to it your master's hit by more disgrace
Than oceans are by waves during a mighty storm!
                    [SCELEDRUS *trembles with fright*
SCELEDRUS. I'm so upset, Periplectomenus, I just don't know
Whether I'd better argue this thing out with you,
Or else—if one is not the other—she's not *she*—
Well then, I guess I should apologize to you.
I mean—well, now I don't know *what* I saw at all!
Your girl looks so much like the one we have—that is,
If they are not the same—
PERIPLECTOMENUS [*sweetly*]. Look in my house; you'll see. 520
SCELEDRUS. Oh, could I?
PERIPLECTOMENUS. I insist. Inspect—and take your time.
SCELEDRUS. Yes, that's the thing to do.
                    [*He dashes into the old man's house*
PERIPLECTOMENUS [*calling at the soldier's house*]. Philoco-
    masium, be quick!
Run over to my house—go at a sprint—it's vital.
As soon as Sceledrus goes out, then double quick—
Run right back to your own house at a sprint!
[*Getting a bit excited himself*] Oh, my goodness, now I'm
    scared she'll bungle it.
What if he doesn't see her? Wait—I hear the door.

SCELEDRUS *re-enters, wide-eyed and confused*

SCELEDRUS. O ye immortal gods, there never were two girls
  more similar,
  More similar—and yet I know they're not the same.   530
  I didn't think the gods could do it!
PERIPLECTOMENUS.   Well?
SCELEDRUS.   I'm whipped.
PERIPLECTOMENUS. Is she your girl?
SCELEDRUS.   It is and yet it isn't her.
PERIPLECTOMENUS. You saw . . . ?
SCELEDRUS.   I saw a girl together with your guest,
  Embracing him and kissing.
PERIPLECTOMENUS.   Was it yours?
SCELEDRUS.   Who knows?
PERIPLECTOMENUS. You want to know for sure?
SCELEDRUS.   Yes!
PERIPLECTOMENUS.   Hurry to your house
  And see if your girl's there within. Be quick—
SCELEDRUS.   I will.
  That's good advice. Wait—I'll be back here right away.

                [SCELEDRUS *rushes into the soldier's house*

PERIPLECTOMENUS. By Pollux, never was a man bamboozled
  better,
  More wittily, in wilder or more wondrous ways.
  But here he comes. . . .

      SCELEDRUS *re-enters, on the brink of tears,*
      and throws himself at PERIPLECTOMENUS' *feet*

SCELEDRUS.   Periplectomenus, I beg of you,   540
  By all the gods and men—by my stupidity—
  And by your knees.
PERIPLECTOMENUS.   What do you beg of me?
SCELEDRUS.   Forgive
  My foolishness and my stupidity. At last
  I know that I've been thoughtless—idiotic—blind!
  [*Sheepishly*] Philocomasium . . . is right inside.
PERIPLECTOMENUS.   Well, gallows bird—
  You've seen them both?
SCELEDRUS.   I've seen.

PERIPLECTOMENUS.   Would you please call your master?

SCELEDRUS [*beseeching*]. I do confess I'm worthy of a whop-
    ping whipping,

And I do admit that I abused your lady guest.

But I mistook her for my master's concubine—

The soldier has appointed me her guardian.   550

Two drops of water from a single well could not be drawn

Much more alike than our girl's like your lady guest.

[*Quietly*] I also peeked down into your house through the
    skylight,

I do confess.

PERIPLECTOMENUS. Why not confess? I saw you do it!

And there you saw my guests—a man and lady—kissing—
    Correct?

SCELEDRUS.   Yes, yes. Should I deny the things I saw?

But, sir, I thought I saw Philocomasium.

PERIPLECTOMENUS. Did you consider me a man so vile and
    base

To be a party to such things in my own house,

And let my neighbour suffer such outrageous harm?   560

SCELEDRUS. At last I see how idiotically I've acted.

I know the facts now. But it wasn't done on purpose.

I'm blameless—

PERIPLECTOMENUS. But not shameless. Why, a slave should
    have

His eyes downcast, his hands and tongue in strict control—

His speech as well.

SCELEDRUS.   If I so much as mumble, sir,

From this day on—and even mumble what I'm sure of—

Have me tortured. I'll just give myself to you.

But now I beg forgiveness.

PERIPLECTOMENUS [*magnanimously*]. I'll suppress my wrath

And think you really didn't do it all on purpose.

So—you're forgiven.

SCELEDRUS.   May the gods all bless you, sir!   570

PERIPLECTOMENUS. Now, after this, by Hercules, you guard
    your tongue

And even if you know a thing, *don't* know a thing—

And *don't* see even what you see.

SCELEDRUS.   That's good advice.
  I'll do it. Have I begged enough?
PERIPLECTOMENUS.   Just go away!
SCELEDRUS. Do you want something else?*
PERIPLECTOMENUS.   Yes—*not* to know you!

> [PERIPLECTOMENUS *turns away from*
> SCELEDRUS *in disgust and walks aside*

SCELEDRUS [*suspiciously*]. He's fooling me. How easily he
    just excused me.
  He wasn't even angry. But I know what's up:
  The minute that the soldier comes home from the forum,
  They'll grab me in the house. He and Palaestrio,
  They have me up for sale—I've sensed it for a while now. 580
  By Hercules, I won't snap at their bait today.
  I'll run off somewhere, hide myself a day or two,
  Till this commotion quiets and the shouting stops.
  I've earned myself much more than one man's share of
    troubles.

> [SCELEDRUS *runs off*

PERIPLECTOMENUS. Well, he's retreated. Now, by Pollux, I'm
    quite sure
  A headless pig has far more brains than Sceledrus.
  He's been so gulled he doesn't see the things he saw.
  His eyes, his ears, his every sense has now deserted him
  To join our cause. Well, up to now, so far so good.   590
  That girl of ours came up with quite a fine performance.
  Now to our little senate, for Palaestrio*
  Is there inside my house and Sceledrus is gone.
  We now can have a meeting with the whole committee.
  I'd better go inside before they vote without me!

> [He goes into his own house
>   The stage is empty for a moment, then
> PALAESTRIO *tiptoes out of the old man's house*

PALAESTRIO [*motioning to the others who are still inside*].
  Pleusicles, have everybody wait inside a little longer.
  Let me reconnoitre first to see if there are spies around to
  Stop the meeting we're about to have. We need a place
    that's safe,

Some place where no enemy can plunder any plans we've
    made.
What you plan out will not pan out, if your enemy can use
    it.   600
Useful things for enemies become abuseful things for you.
Clearly, if the enemy should somehow learn about your
    plans, they'll
Turn the tables on you, shut your mouth and tie your
    hands. And so
Whatever you had planned to do to them, they'll do to you
    instead!
Now I'll peek around, look right and left, to see there's no
    one here, no
Hunter using ears for nets so he can 'catch' our secret
    plans.
[*Looks to either side*] Good—the coast is clear all up and
    down the street. I'll call them out.
Hey, Periplectomenus and Pleusicles, produce yourselves!* 610

They come out eagerly

PERIPLECTOMENUS. Here—at your command.
PALAESTRIO. Commanding's easy when your troops are good.
    How about it now—that plan we figured out inside—shall
    we now
    Carry on with it?
PERIPLECTOMENUS. We couldn't do it better.
PALAESTRIO.   What do you think,
    Pleusicles?
PLEUSICLES [*mindlessly devoted*]. What could be fine with
    you and not be fine with me?
No one's more my friend than you are.
PALAESTRIO.   Nicely and precisely put.
PERIPLECTOMENUS. That's the way he should be talking.
PLEUSICLES.   Yet it makes me miserable; it
    Troubles and torments me too—
PERIPLECTOMENUS. What troubles you? Speak up, my boy!
PLEUSICLES. That I burden someone who's as old as you with
    childish trifles.
These concerns are so unworthy of your noble qualities—

Asking you for so much help in what is really my concern: 620
Bringing reinforcements to a lover, doing different duties,
Duties which most men of your age would prefer to dodge—
    not do!
I'm ashamed to bring annoyance to you in your twilight
    years.

PALAESTRIO. You're a novel lover if you blush at doing any-
    thing!
You're no lover—just the palest shadow of what lovers
    should be.

PLEUSICLES. Troubling a man of his age with a youthful love
    affair?

PERIPLECTOMENUS. What's that? Do I seem so six-feet-under
    to you—is that so?
Do I seem to be so senile, such a coffin candidate?
After all, I'm barely fifty-four years old—not even that.
I've got perfect vision still, my hands are quick, my legs are
    nimble.   630

PALAESTRIO. Maybe he's white-haired on top, but not inside
    his head—that's sure.
All the qualities that he was born with haven't aged a bit.

PLEUSICLES. I know that, by Pollux, what you say is true,
    Palaestrio.
He's been absolutely youthful in his hospitality.

PERIPLECTOMENUS. Try me in a crisis, boy. The more I'm
    pressed the more you'll note how
I'll support your love affair—

PLEUSICLES.   No need to note—I know it well.

PERIPLECTOMENUS [*casually boasting*]. Experience, experience
    . . . the only way of finding out.
Only he who's loved himself can see inside a lover's soul.
Even I still have a little lively loving left in me.   640
All my taste for joy and pleasure hasn't dried up in me yet.
I'm the perfect party guest—I'm quick with very clever
    quips.
And I never interrupt another person when he's talking.
I refrain from rudeness, I'm restrained with guests and never
    rowdy.
I remember to contribute just my share of conversation.

And I also know to shut my mouth when someone else is
   talking.
I'm no spitter, I'm no cougher and I'm not forever sneezing.
I was born in Ephesus, I'm not an Animulian.*
PALAESTRIO. Mezzo-middle-aged at most, with all the talents
   he describes!
Certainly a Muse has shown this man how to be so amusing. 650
PERIPLECTOMENUS. I can show you that I'm even more
   amusing than you say:
Never at a party do I screw around with someone's girl,
Never do I filch the food or take the goblet out of turn.
Never do I let the wine bring out an argument in me.
Someone gets too nasty? I go home and cut the conversation.
Give me love and loveliness and lots of laughter at a party.
PALAESTRIO. All your talents seem to tend toward charm and
   graciousness, by Pollux.
Show me three men with such talents and I'll pay their
   weight in gold!
PLEUSICLES. Never—you won't find another man as old as he
   who is so
Thoroughly delightful and so good a friend to anyone.   660
           [PERIPLECTOMENUS *is enjoying the compliments,*
           but he doesn't like being called an old man
PERIPLECTOMENUS. I'll make you admit I'm really just a
   youngster in my way.
Wait until you see the countless splendid services I'll render:
Do you need a lawyer—one that's fierce and angry? Here
   I am.
Do you need a mild one? I'll be smoother than the silent sea.
I'll be oh so softer than the southern breeze in early spring.
I can also be the most lighthearted of your dinner guests,
Or the perfect parasite, or else supply a super supper.
As for dancing—even fruity fairies haven't got *my* grace.*
           [*Acting very impressed*, PALAESTRIO
           turns to PLEUSICLES
PALAESTRIO [*to* PLEUSICLES]. What else could you wish for if
   you'd even wish for something else?
PLEUSICLES. Just the talent to express my gratitude for every-
   thing.   670

Thanks to you [*to* PERIPLECTOMENUS] and thanks to you,
  for taking such good care of me.
I must be a burdensome expense to you—
PERIPLECTOMENUS.   You silly boy!
  What you spend for enemies or for a nasty wife's expense,
  What you lay out for a guest, a real true friend of yours,
    is *profit!**
  Thank the gods I can afford to entertain you as I'd like to.
  Eat! Drink up! Indulge yourself, let laughter overflow the
    brim!
  Mine's the house of freedom—I am free—I live my life for
    me.
  Thank the gods, I'm rich enough. I could've married very
    well,
  Could've led a wealthy wife of high position to the altar. 680
  But I wouldn't want to lead a barking dog into my house!*
PALAESTRIO. Yet remember—children can be pleasant—and
  it's fun to breed 'em.
PERIPLECTOMENUS. You can breed 'em, give me freedom!
  That, by Hercules, is fun!
PALAESTRIO. You're a good adviser—for yourself as well as
  other people.
PERIPLECTOMENUS. Sure it's sweet to wed a *good* wife—if
  there's such a thing on earth.
  I'd be glad to marry someone who would turn to me and
    ask me,
  'Dearest husband, buy some wool, so I can make some
    clothing for you,
  First a tunic, soft and warm, and then a cloak for winter
    weather,
  So you won't be cold.' You'd never hear a wife say things
    like that!
  Why, before the cock would crow, she'd shake me from
    my sleep and say,   690
  'Husband! Give me money for a New Year's gift to give
    my mother!
  It's Minerva's festival, so give to give the fortune-teller,
  Dream interpreter, diviner, sorceress and soothsayer!
  She tells fortunes from your eyebrows—it's a crime to leave
    her out!

How about the laundry girl? She couldn't do without a gift.
Look how long it's been since we have tipped the grocer's
    wife—she's angry with us.
And the midwife has complained—we didn't send her quite
    enough!
What! Will we send nothing to the one who's nursed our
    household slaves?'
These and other ruinations that a woman brings have kept
    me
Single, so I'm not subjected to this sort of sordid speeches. 700
PALAESTRIO. All the gods have blessed you, for, by Hercules,
    if you let go of
Freedom just one second, it's no easy thing to get it back.
PLEUSICLES. Don't you think it's noble for a man of wealth
    and high estate to
Bring up children as a sort of monument to his good name?*
PERIPLECTOMENUS. I have relatives aplenty, so what need have
    I of children?
I live happily and well, I suit myself, do what I please.
When I die, my relatives can split the money that I leave
    'em.
Now they're up at dawn to come and ask me if I've slept
    all right. 709
When they sacrifice, they give me bigger portions than their
    own.
And they take me out to banquets, have me home for
    lunch, for dinner.
They're so sad if they can send me only something small
    and simple.
They compete in giving, as I secretly repeat inside:
'Let them chase my money; they're all eagerly supporting
    me!'
PALAESTRIO. Ah, you really know the way to live; you know
    what life is for.
If you're having fun, it's just as good as having twins or
    triplets.

> [PERIPLECTOMENUS *seems anxious to talk*
> *on any topic, so he now pursues this one*

PERIPLECTOMENUS. If I really had 'em, I'd be miserable because
    of them—

Worrying about their health. Why, if my son had fever, I
would   720

Think he's dying. If he drank too much or tumbled off his
horse,

I would always be afraid he broke his neck or broke a leg.

PALAESTRIO. Here's a man who rightfully has riches. He
should live for ever.

He keeps wealthy, ever healthy—and he's out to help his
friends.

PLEUSICLES. What a charming chap! By all the gods and
goddesses above,

Gods should all decide how long we live by a consistent
system.

Just as the inspector fixes selling prices in the market,

Merchandise of quality is priced according to its merits,

Merchandise that's rotten gets a price that makes its owner
poorer,

That's the way a person's life should be determined by the
gods.   730

Men with charm and lots of talent should have long and
lengthy lives;

Rotten men and rogues should be deprived of life without
delay.

We'd be minus many scoundrels if the gods would use this
system,

And the dirty deeds committed would be fewer. Further-
more,

Men would be of quality—and life would be a better
bargain.

[PERIPLECTOMENUS *is flattered, but he*
playfully chides the young man

PERIPLECTOMENUS. Only silly fools find fault with what the
gods above decree.

Only fools would scold the gods. Let's stop this stupid stuff
for now.

[*He starts to go off*

Now I'll buy the groceries to entertain my guest with
something

Worthy of us both, a welcome of good wishes *and* good
dishes!

PLEUSICLES. Please—I've been a terrible expense to you
  already. Surely
  No guest can accept such friendly treatment as you've
    offered me and   740
  Not become an inconvenience after three days in a row.
  After *ten* days, he becomes an *Iliad* of inconvenience!
  Even if his host is willing, still the servants start to mutter.
PERIPLECTOMENUS. I've instructed servants in this house to
  stick to serving me,
  Not to give me orders or to have myself depend on them.
    Why, if
  What I want displeases them—too bad! I'm captain of the
    ship.
  Willy-nilly, they'll do what they're ordered—or be beaten
    up.
  Now I'd better get on with the groceries . . .
                               [*He starts to amble off*
PLEUSICLES.   Well, if you must—
  Please don't buy extravagantly—anything is fine for me. 750
        [PERIPLECTOMENUS *now stops to discuss this topic*
PERIPLECTOMENUS. Stop that kind of talk, that stale cliché is
  older than the hills.
  Really, now you're talking like *hoi polloi*—you know the
    kind, who
  When they're at the table and the dinner's set before 'em
    say,
  'Did you go to all this trouble just for *me*—you shouldn't
    have.
  Hercules, it's madness. Why, there's food enough for ten at
    least!'
  Much too much for them! But while they're frowning, they
    are downing it!
PALAESTRIO. That's the way it is exactly. [*To* PLEUSICLES] He
  speaks soundly and profoundly.
PERIPLECTOMENUS. Never will you hear these people, when a
  feast is set before 'em,
  Say, 'Remove this . . . take this plate away . . . take off the
    ham . . . I simply couldn't.
  Take this bit of pork away . . . this eel would be much
    better cold.'   760

'Take' . . . 'remove' . . . 'be off' are words you'll never hear
from one of them.

No, they leap to reach the food, with half their bodies on
the table.

PALAESTRIO. Bad behaviour well described.

PERIPLECTOMENUS.   I haven't told the hundredth part of

What I could expound upon if only we had time to talk—
          [PALAESTRIO *seizes this opportunity to cut*
              PERIPLECTOMENUS' *monologue short*

PALAESTRIO. Right! But we had better turn our thoughts to
what we're doing now.

Listen closely, both of you. [*To* PERIPLECTOMENUS] I'll need
your services in this,

Periplectomenus. I've figured out a lovely scheme to help us

Take our curly-headed soldier to the barber's for a trimming.*

And we'll give our lover here the chance to get his sweetheart
back, and

Take her off from here for good!

PERIPLECTOMENUS.   Now there's a plan I'd like to hear! 770

PALAESTRIO. First, I'd like to ask you for that ring of yours.

PERIPLECTOMENUS [*suspiciously*].   How will you use it?

PALAESTRIO. When I have the ring you'll have the reason—
and my whole invention.

PERIPLECTOMENUS. Here's the ring.

PALAESTRIO.   And here's your reason

in turn, the little scheme that

I've been setting up.

PLEUSICLES.   We're listening to you with well-washed ears.

PALAESTRIO. Master is the wildest wenching wanton man who
ever was—

Or who ever will be for that matter.

PERIPLECTOMENUS.   I believe it too.

PALAESTRIO. He supposes he surpasses Paris in his handsomeness.

He thinks all the women here just cannot help pursuing
him.

PERIPLECTOMENUS. I know several husbands here who wish
that statement were the truth!*

But proceed, I know too well he's what you say, Palaestrio. 780
Get on to the point, be brief, don't beat around the bush,
   my boy.

PALAESTRIO. Could you find a woman for me—someone
   beautiful and charming,
Someone full of cleverness and trickery from tip to toe?

PERIPLECTOMENUS. Freed or free-born girl?

PALAESTRIO.   It doesn't matter, just be sure and get me
One who's money-loving, and who earns her keep by being
   kept.
One who's got a mind—she doesn't need a heart—no
   woman has one.

PERIPLECTOMENUS. Do you want a . . . green one . . . or a ripe
   one?

PALAESTRIO. Just be sure she's juicy.
Get the freshest, most appealing girl you possibly can find.

PERIPLECTOMENUS. Say—I have a client—a luscious, youngish
   little courtesan!
But—why do you need her?

PALAESTRIO.   Bring her home to your house, right away. 790
Have her in disguise, so she'll look like a married woman—
Hair combed high, with ribbons and the rest. She must
   pretend that*
She's your wedded wife. Now train the girl!

PERIPLECTOMENUS.   I'm lost. What's all this for?

PALAESTRIO. You'll soon see. Now, does she have a maid?

PERIPLECTOMENUS.   A very clever one.

PALAESTRIO. We'll have need of her as well. Now tell the
   woman and her maid the
Mistress must pretend that she's your wife—who's dying
   for the soldier boy.
We'll pretend she gave her little maid this ring—to give to
   me.
I'll give it to him, pretending I'm the go-between.

PERIPLECTOMENUS.   I hear you—
Don't assume I'm deaf. I know my ears are both in fine
   condition.*

PALAESTRIO. I'll pretend it's been presented as a present from
   your wife so 800

She could . . . get together with him. I know him—he'll be
  in flames!
Nothing gets that lecher more excited than adultery!
PERIPLECTOMENUS. If you asked the Sun himself to find the
  girls you've asked me for,
He could never find a pair more perfect for the job. Relax!
PALAESTRIO. Fine, hop to it then. We need 'em right away.

> [*Periplectomenus exits*

Now, Pleusicles—
PLEUSICLES. At your service.
PALAESTRIO.   When the soldier gets back
  home, remember *not* to
Call your girl Philocomasium.
PLEUSICLES.   What should I call her then?
PALAESTRIO. Dicea.
PLEUSICLES. Yes, of course, the name we just agreed upon.
PALAESTRIO.   Now go.

> [PLEUSICLES *remains stationary for*
> *a moment, 'memorizing' the name*

PLEUSICLES. I'll remember. [*To* PALAESTRIO] But I'd like to
  ask you *why* I should remember.
PALAESTRIO. When you have to know, I'll tell you. For the
  moment, just keep still,   810
While the old man does his part—and very soon you'll play
  your role.
PLEUSICLES. Then I guess I'll go inside.

> [*He starts to walk off*

PALAESTRIO [*calling after him*]. And follow orders carefully!

> [PLEUSICLES *walks slowly into the*
> *house, rehearsing to himself*

PALAESTRIO [*to the audience, with a broad smile*]. What
  storms I'm stirring up—what mighty machinations!
Today I'll snatch that concubine back from the soldier—
That is, if all my troops remain well disciplined.*   815
Now I'll call him. Hey, Sceledrus! If you've got time
Come out in front. Palaestrio is calling you.

> *A pause. Not* SCELEDRUS, *but another slave,*
> LURCIO *by name, appears at the door,*
> *extremely drunk*

LURCIO. He's busy now.*

PALAESTRIO. At what?

LURCIO. He's pouring . . . as he sleeps.

PALAESTRIO. Did you say 'pouring'?

LURCIO. 'Snoring' 's what I meant to say.
But snoring, pouring—isn't it about the same?   820
[LURCIO starts to reel off-stage.
PALAESTRIO stops him

PALAESTRIO. Hey—Sceledrus inside asleep?

LURCIO. Except his nose.
That's making quite a noise. [Confidentially] He took some
    secret snorts
'Cause he's the steward and was spicing up the wine.
[LURCIO again turns to go;
PALAESTRIO again stops him

PALAESTRIO. But wait, you scoundrel, you're the guy's
    substeward—wait!

LURCIO. Your point?

PALAESTRIO [indignantly]. How could he let himself just go
    to sleep?

LURCIO. He closed his eyes, I think.

PALAESTRIO. I didn't ask you that!
Come here! You're dead if I don't know the truth at
    once!
Did you serve him the wine?

LURCIO. I didn't.

PALAESTRIO. You deny it?

LURCIO. I do, by Hercules. He told me to deny it.   830
I also didn't pour four pints into a pitcher.
He also didn't drink 'em all warmed up at dinner.

PALAESTRIO. You also didn't drink?

LURCIO. Gods blast me if I did.
I wish I'd drunk.

PALAESTRIO. How come?

LURCIO. Because I guzzled it instead.
The wine was overheated and it burned my throat.

PALAESTRIO. Some slaves get drunk, while others get weak
    vinegar!
Our pantry has some loyal steward and substeward!

LURCIO. You'd do the same, by Hercules, if you had charge.

You're acting jealous now 'cause you can't copy us.   840
[*He turns to go once again*

PALAESTRIO. Wait, wait, you scoundrel! Has he drunk like
this before?
And just to help your thinking let me tell you this:
If, Lurcio, you lie, you'll suffer horribly.

LURCIO. Oh, really now? Then you can tattle what I've told
To get me kicked out from my storeroom stuffing job,
And pick a new substeward when *you're* put in charge.

PALAESTRIO. By Pollux, no, I won't. Come on, be brave and
speak.

LURCIO. He never poured a drop, by Pollux. That's the truth.
He'd order me to do it—and I'd pour for him.

PALAESTRIO. That's why the jars were always standing on
their heads!   850

LURCIO. By Hercules, that isn't why the jars were jarred.
Inside the storeroom was this very slippery spot.
A two-pint pot was leaning on the casks nearby;
It often would get all filled up—ten times or so.
I saw it filled and emptied. Mostly it got filled.
And then the pot danced wildly and the jars were jarred.*

PALAESTRIO. Get in! You held that storeroom bacchanal
yourselves.
By Hercules, I'll go bring master from the forum.
[PALAESTRIO *takes a few steps toward the forum,*
then stops to listen to LURCIO'*s lament*

LURCIO. I'm dead. Master will crucify me when he comes
And finds out what's been done because I didn't tell him.   860
I'll run off somewhere so I can postpone the pains.
[*To the audience*] Folks, please don't tell Palaestrio, I beg
of you.
[*He starts to tiptoe off.* PALAESTRIO
scares him with a shout

PALAESTRIO. Hey—where're you going?

LURCIO [*nervously*].   I'll be back. I'm on an errand.

PALAESTRIO. For whom?

LURCIO.   Philocomasium.

PALAESTRIO.   Go—rush right back!

LURCIO. Do me a favour, will you? If while I'm away

There's punishment distributed ... please take my share.

[LURCIO scampers off

PALAESTRIO [*to the audience*]. Ah, now I understand our
young girl's strategy.
With Sceledrus asleep, she sends his underling
Off on some business while she sneaks across.
[*Looks off-stage to his left*] But here's our neighbour with
the girl I requisitioned—   870
And, oh, is she good-looking! All the gods are with us.
She's dressed so finely—most unprostitutishly.
This whole affair now seems most charmingly in hand!

PERIPLECTOMENUS *enters with a girl on either arm.*
One is the courtesan ACROTELEUTIUM,
a reasonably young old pro, and the other
is her maid MILPHIDIPPA

PERIPLECTOMENUS [*to the girls*]. Now I've explained this
whole thing to you both from start to finish,
Acroteleutium and Milphidippa. If you haven't grasped
This artful artifice as yet, I'll drill you once again.
But if you understand it all, then we can change the subject.

ACROTELEUTIUM. Now don't you think I'd be a stupid idiot
to undertake
An unfamiliar project or to promise you results,
If I were unacquainted with the whole technique—the art
of being wicked?   880

PERIPLECTOMENUS. Forewarned's forearmed, I say.

ACROTELEUTIUM.   Not to a real professional—
A layman's words are little use. Why, didn't I myself,
The minute that I drank the smallest drop of your proposal,
Didn't *I* tell *you* the way the soldier could be swindled?

PERIPLECTOMENUS. But no one ever knows enough. How
many have I seen
Avoid the region of good sense—before they even found it.

ACROTELEUTIUM. But when it's wickedness or wiles that's
wanted of the woman,
Why, then she's got a monumentally immortal memory.
It's only when it comes to something fine or faithful
That suddenly she's scatterbrained—and can't remember.   890

PERIPLECTOMENUS. Well, that's what I'm afraid of. Here your
    job is double-edged:
  For when you do the soldier harm, you're doing *me* a
    favour.
ACROTELEUTIUM. Relax, you're safe as long as we don't know
    we're doing good.
PERIPLECTOMENUS. What mangy merchandise a woman is.
ACROTELEUTIUM.   Just like her customers.
PERIPLECTOMENUS. That's typical. Come on.
PALAESTRIO.   I ought to go ahead and meet them.
  It's good to see you, sir, so charmingly accompanied.
PERIPLECTOMENUS. Well met, Palaestrio. Look—here they
    are—the girls
  You ordered me to bring—and in their costumes.
PALAESTRIO [*pats him on the back*].   You're my man!
  Palaestrio salutes Acroteleutium.
ACROTELEUTIUM.   Who's this   900
  Who speaks to me as if he knew me?
PERIPLECTOMENUS.   He's our . . . architect.
ACROTELEUTIUM. My greetings to the architect.
PALAESTRIO.   The same to you. Has he
  Indoctrinated you?
PERIPLECTOMENUS. The girls I bring are well rehearsed.
PALAESTRIO. I want to hear how well. The fear of failure
    frightens me.
PERIPLECTOMENUS. I didn't add a thing to those instructions
    that you gave me.
              [ACROTELEUTIUM *approaches* PALAESTRIO
                and speaks to him in a very blasé manner
ACROTELEUTIUM. Now look, you want the soldier to be
    swindled, right?
PALAESTRIO.   That's right!
ACROTELEUTIUM. Neatly, sweetly, and completely—everything's
    arranged.
PALAESTRIO. I want you to pretend to be his wife—
ACROTELEUTIUM.   I *am* his wife.
PALAESTRIO. Pretend that you're enamoured of the soldier—
ACROTELEUTIUM.   So I will be.
PALAESTRIO. Pretend that I'm the go-between for this—with
    Milphidippa.

ACROTELEUTIUM. You should have been a prophet—all you   910
say will soon come true.

PALAESTRIO. Pretend this ring was given by your little maid
to me

To offer to the soldier with your compliments.

ACROTELEUTIUM.   That's true!

PERIPLECTOMENUS. Why bother to remind the girls of things
they know?

ACROTELEUTIUM.   It's good.

Remember if you're dealing with a first-rate architect,

And if this man designs a ship with well-drawn plans,

You'll build the ship with ease if everything's laid out and
set.

Now we've a keel that's accurately laid and nicely set,

Our architect has helpers who are not exactly . . . amateurs,

So if our raw material is not delayed *en route*,   920

I know our capabilities—we'll have that ship in no time.

PALAESTRIO [*to* ACROTELEUTIUM]. I guess you know my
military master—

ACROTELEUTIUM.   What a question!!

How could I *not* know such a public menace, such a big-
mouth,

Fancy-hairdoed, perfumed lecher?!

PALAESTRIO.   Hmm—does he know you?

ACROTELEUTIUM. He never saw me, so how could he?

PALAESTRIO.   Ah, that's lovely talk.

I'm sure the action will be lovelier.

ACROTELEUTIUM.   Now just relax—

Leave him to me. If I don't make a fancy fool of him,

Then put the blame on me completely.

PALAESTRIO.   Fine, now go inside

And concentrate completely on this project.

ACROTELEUTIUM [*going*].   Just relax.

PALAESTRIO. Periplectomenus, take them inside. I'm for the
forum.   930

I'll find my man, I'll offer him this ring and I'll insist

That it was given to me by 'your wife', who's dying for
him.

[*Pointing to* MILPHIDIPPA] As soon as we get back here
from the forum, send her out,

Pretending she was sent to him in secret.

PERIPLECTOMENUS.   Fine—relax.

PALAESTRIO. Just keep on the alert. I'll bring him here already
stuffed.

[PALAESTRIO *rushes out toward the forum*

PERIPLECTOMENUS. Now walk and talk successfully! Oh, if
we work this out,

And if my guest gets back the soldier's concubine today,

I'll send you such a gift—

ACROTELEUTIUM [*casually*].   Say—is the girl co-operating? 940

PERIPLECTOMENUS. Absolutissimo, bellissimo.

ACROTELEUTIUM [*facetiously*].   Swellissimo.

When all our roguery is pooled together, I'm convinced,

We'll never meet defeat by any trickier deceit.

PERIPLECTOMENUS. Let's go inside and then rehearse our parts
with care.

We all must follow our instructions nicely and precisely,

So when the soldier comes, there'll be no blunders.

ACROTELEUTIUM.   You're the slow one.

[PERIPLECTOMENUS *leads the two
women into his house*

*The stage is empty for a brief moment [musical
interlude?], then enter* PYRGOPOLYNICES, *smiling
with pleasure at his accomplishments this
morning.* PALAESTRIO *follows at his heels, trying
to get his master's attention*

PYRGOPOLYNICES [*smiling smugly*]. What a pleasure when
affairs go well—exactly as you planned them.

I've already sent a parasite of mine to King Seleucus,

Leading mercenaries I conscripted for His Majesty.

While they guard his kingdom, I shall have a little relaxation. 950

PALAESTRIO. Come now, think of your affairs, not King
Seleucus'. Why, look, a

Promising new venture's been proposed to me as go-
between.*

PYRGOPOLYNICES [*condescendingly*]. Well, I'll put the other
things aside and give you my attention.

Speak—I now surrender both my ears to you and to this
venture.

PALAESTRIO [*suspiciously*]. Reconnoitre first—is there a snare
  to catch our conversation?
I'm commanded to pursue this business with all secrecy.

> [PYRGOPOLYNICES '*scouts*' *the area,*
> *then whispers to* PALAESTRIO

PYRGOPOLYNICES. No one.

PALAESTRIO [*giving the ring*].
> Take this—it's the first deposit on a love account.

PYRGOPOLYNICES. What's this? Where'd you get it?

PALAESTRIO.   From a lovely and lively lady
Who adores you and who longs to have your handsome
  handsomeness.
She has had her maid give me this ring to forward on to
  you.   960

PYRGOPOLYNICES. But who is she—is she free-born or some
  manumitted slave?

PALAESTRIO. Feh! How could I dare negotiate for you with
  freedwomen—
You're already swamped with offers from the well-born
  girls who want you!

> [PYRGOPOLYNICES *smiles and*
> *continues his questions*

PYRGOPOLYNICES. Wife or widow?

PALAESTRIO.   Wife *and* widow.

PYRGOPOLYNICES.   Tell me how a woman can be
  Both a wife and widow?

PALAESTRIO.   Easy: she is young, her husband's old!

PYRGOPOLYNICES. Goody!

PALAESTRIO.   She's delectable and dignified.

PYRGOPOLYNICES.   Tell me no lies—

PALAESTRIO. She alone could be compared to *you* in beauty.

PYRGOPOLYNICES.   Oh, how gorgeous!
  Who is she?

PALAESTRIO.   The wife of old Periplectomenus, next door.
How she's dying for you, longing to escape—she hates the
  old boy.   970
I've been asked to beg you—to beseech you—let her have
  a chance to
Give herself completely.

PYRGOPOLYNICES.   Hercules, why not? If she is willing—

PALAESTRIO. Willing? *Thrilling!*

PYRGOPOLYNICES [*suddenly remembering*]. Say—what shall we do about the girl at home?

PALAESTRIO. Let her go—wherever she would like to. *And it just so happens*
  Her twin sister and her mother have arrived to fetch the girl.

PYRGOPOLYNICES. What—her mother's come to Ephesus?

PALAESTRIO.   Those who saw so say so.

PYRGOPOLYNICES. Hercules—the perfect chance for me to kick the woman out!

PALAESTRIO. Yes, but you should do it in the 'perfect' way.

PYRGOPOLYNICES.   All right, what's your advice?

PALAESTRIO. Don't you want to have her hurry from your house with no hard feelings?

PYRGOPOLYNICES. Yes yes yes.

PALAESTRIO.   Here's what to do: you're rich enough, so let the girl have   980
  All the gold and all the jewels and all the things you dressed her up with.
  Better not upset her; let her take the stuff where she would like.

PYRGOPOLYNICES. That sounds good. But watch out when I let her go this other woman
  Doesn't change her mind!

PALAESTRIO.   Oh, feh! Don't be absurd—the girl adores you!

PYRGOPOLYNICES [*preening*]. Venus loves me!

PALAESTRIO. Quiet now—the door is open—hide yourself.

      MILPHIDIPPA *enters from the old man's house*

  That one coming out is madam's clipper ship, the go-between who
  Brought the ring that I just gave to you.

PYRGOPOLYNICES.   By Pollux, she's not bad, not Bad at all!

PALAESTRIO. A chimpanzee—a harpy set beside her mistress!
  Look at her there—hunting with her eyes and using ears as traps.   990

MILPHIDIPPA [*to the audience*]. There's the circus where I
must perform my little act right now.

I'll pretend that I don't see them—I won't even know they're
there.

PYRGOPOLYNICES [*whispering to* PALAESTRIO]. Shh . . . let's
listen in to see if there's a mention made of *me*.

MILPHIDIPPA. Are there men about who care for others'
business, not their own,

Idlers who don't earn their supper, who might spy on what
I'm doing?

I'm afraid of men like these, lest they obstruct me or delay
me—

If they come while mistress crosses over—burning for *his*
body.

How she loves that man—too beautiful, too too magnificent,
the

Soldier Pyrgopolynices.

PYRGOPOLYNICES [*aside*]. This one's mad about me too!
She just praised my looks.

PALAESTRIO.   By Pollux, her speech needs no
further rubbing.   1000

PYRGOPOLYNICES. How is that?

PALAESTRIO.   Because her words are bright
enough—already polished.

And why not? She speaks of you—she has a shining subject,
too!

PYRGOPOLYNICES. Say, her mistress surely is a gorgeously
attractive woman.

Hercules, I'm getting sort of warm for her already, boy.

PALAESTRIO. Even when you haven't seen her yet?

PYRGOPOLYNICES [*ogling* MILPHIDIPPA]. I take your word for
it.

Meanwhile, 'clipper ship' here whets my appetite for love.

PALAESTRIO.   No, you don't, by Hercules!

Don't you fall in love with her—that girl's engaged to *me*.
If you should

Wed the mistress, *she* becomes my bride at once.*

PYRGOPOLYNICES [*impatiently*].   Then speak to her.

PALAESTRIO. All right, follow me.

PYRGOPOLYNICES.   I'll be your follower.

    [They approach MILPHIDIPPA, *who still pretends
not to see them. She gets even more melodramatic.*

MILPHIDIPPA.   Would I could find him—
  Find the man I've left the house to meet. Oh, heaven grant
  me this!*   1010

PALAESTRIO. All you dreamed will appear, you can be of
  good cheer—there is certainly no cause for fearing,
  For the person that's speaking knows just who you're
  seeking—

MILPHIDIPPA.   My goodness—who is this I'm hearing?

PALAESTRIO. Of your council a sharer—and also a bearer of
  counsel, should you be confiding it.

MILPHIDIPPA. Oh no, heaven forbid, what I'm hiding's not hid!

PALAESTRIO.   Well, you may or may not still be hiding it.

MILPHIDIPPA. Tell me how that can be?

PALAESTRIO.   It's not hidden from
       me—but I'm trusty, a tacit and mum one.

MILPHIDIPPA. Can you give me a sign that you know our
  design?

PALAESTRIO. Let us say that a woman loves someone.

MILPHIDIPPA. There are hundreds who do—

PALAESTRIO.   Ah, but ever so
  few send a gift given straight from their finger.

MILPHIDIPPA. Ah, now I understand, I've the lay of the land
  now—and no more uncertainties linger.
  Are there spies hereabouts?

PALAESTRIO [*pointing to the soldier*]. We're both with and
  without.

        [MILPHIDIPPA *motions* PALAESTRIO *to one side*

MILPHIDIPPA.   I must see you alone, so I beckoned.

PALAESTRIO. Well, for many or few words?

MILPHIDIPPA.   I only want two words.

PALAESTRIO [*to the soldier*]. I'll be back with you in a second.   1020

PYRGOPOLYNICES. What of me—hey, explain—must I stand
  here in vain, looking fiery, fierce . . . fascinating?

PALAESTRIO. Yes, sir, stand there in view—I'm just working
  for you.

PYRGOPOLYNICES [*in great heat*]. But I'm wasting away with
  this waiting!

PALAESTRIO. But it's best to go slow, for I'm sure you well
    know of the kind of low mind that her stock has.

PYRGOPOLYNICES. Yes yes yes—on with your quest—do what
    you think is best.

PALAESTRIO [aside to MILPHIDIPPA]. This man has no more
    brains than a rock has!
  Now I'm back here with you—ask me.

MILPHIDIPPA.   What shall I do?
  What's your method for storming our Troy here?*
  Can you give me a plan?

PALAESTRIO.   Just pretend if you can, that you're
    dying with love—

MILPHIDIPPA [nodding].   For our boy here!

PALAESTRIO. Don't forget when you speak, praise his face
    and physique—and his courage in every endeavour.

MILPHIDIPPA. Now you don't have to harp, I've got everything
    sharp. As I showed you before, I'm quite clever.

PALAESTRIO. In respect to the rest, you resolve what is best—
    hunt a hint in whatever I'm saying.

PYRGOPOLYNICES [chafing at the bit]. Well, I wish we would
    start and you'd tell me my part in all this—come back
    here—you're delaying!   1030

      [PALAESTRIO scampers back to the soldier's side

PALAESTRIO. Here I am, don't be nervous, I'm back at your
    service—

PYRGOPOLYNICES. Tell me what she has said—

PALAESTRIO.   It's her mistress—
  Why, the poor dear's been sighing and crying—near dying—
    in short, she's in terrible distress.
  For she's crazy about you and can't live without you, so
    she sent out her maid on this mission.

PYRGOPOLYNICES. Let her come—

PALAESTRIO.   Why so pliant? Do act
    more defiant, disdainful of this proposition.
  Shout—why did I annoy you, debase, hoi-polloi you?—
    pretend that this whole affair piques you.

PYRGOPOLYNICES. Say, there is something to that, I'll certainly
    do that.

PALAESTRIO [aloud]. Shall I call this woman who seeks you?

PYRGOPOLYNICES. Let her come if she wants something.

PALAESTRIO.   Come if you want something, woman.

MILPHIDIPPA [*hurling herself at the soldier's feet*]. O beauty
    so beaming!

PYRGOPOLYNICES. What a clever young dame—she remembers
    my name.

    [*To* MILPHIDIPPA] May the gods grant whatever you're
    dreaming—

MILPHIDIPPA. Why, to live out this life as your own wedded
    wife.

PYRGOPOLYNICES. That's too much!

MILPHIDIPPA.   Oh, it's not *my* desire—
    It's for mistress I woo—she's just dying for you.

PYRGOPOLYNICES. My dear girl, there are thousands on fire. 1040
    And there just isn't time—

MILPHIDIPPA.   Oh, by Castor, sir, I'm quite
    aware that you've so high a rating.

    You're a man so attractive, in action so active—and 'fiery,
    fierce . . . fascinating'.

    [*Aloud to* PALAESTRIO] And there never could be one more
    godlike than he—

PALAESTRIO.   He's *not* human—you're right, no debating.

    [*Aside*] Why, it couldn't be plainer—a vulture's humaner
    than he is.

PYRGOPOLYNICES [*not hearing this*]. I'll act more imposing.
    I must put on a show since she's praising me so—

PALAESTRIO [*aside to* MILPHIDIPPA]. What an ass—will you
    look at him posing!

    [*Aloud, to the soldier*] Will you deign a reply to her
    mistress's cry? You remember, I spoke a while back of
    it.

PYRGOPOLYNICES. I don't quite understand—from *which one*?
    The demand is so great that I cannot keep track of it.

MILPHIDIPPA. Well, she took from her hand something grand,
    something handsome, to hand you in elegant fashion.

    Look—you're wearing the ring I was bidden to bring—
    from a woman who's burning with passion.

PYRGOPOLYNICES. All right, what's her request—speak out,
    woman, I'm pressed.

MILPHIDIPPA.   How she wants you—oh, please
    don't reject her!   1050

She lives only for you—who knows what she may do—
she's near death—but *you* could resurrect her!

PYRGOPOLYNICES. What's her wish now?

MILPHIDIPPA.   To touch you,
to clasp you, to clutch you—she cries for complete
consummation.

And unless you relieve her, I truly believe her to be very
near desperation.

O Achilles so fair, won't you answer my prayer—save this
pretty one all the world pities.

Oh, produce something kind from your merciful mind—
noble king-killer, sacker of cities!

PYRGOPOLYNICES. Ah, these girls who adore me do nothing
but bore me.

[*To* PALAESTRIO] You shouldn't be letting me near all this.
Do you think it's your job—giving me to the mob?

PALAESTRIO [*to* MILPHIDIPPA]. Hey there, woman, I hope that
you hear all this!

Look, I've told you before—must I tell you once more?
This great stud always must be rewarded.

He can't give out his seed to just any old breed—it's too
valuable not to be hoarded!   1060

MILPHIDIPPA. Let him make his demand; we have cash here
on hand.

PALAESTRIO. Well . . . one talent—not silver, but golden.
And he never takes less—

MILPHIDIPPA.   By the gods, I confess that he's
cheap at that price; we're beholden!

PYRGOPOLYNICES. Oh, I'm not one for greed, I've got all that
I need. To be frank, I've got wealth beyond measure:

Golden coins by the score—by the thousands and more—

PALAESTRIO.   Not to mention a storehouse of treasure!
Silver too, not in pounds, no, not even in mounds, but in
mountains, like Aetna—or higher.

MILPHIDIPPA [*aside*]. Oh, ye gods, how he's lying!

PALAESTRIO [*aside to her*]. And how I'm supplying him fuel—

MILPHIDIPPA.   And I'm stoking the fire!

But do hurry, I pray, send me back right away.

PALAESTRIO [*aloud*]. Will you deign, sir, to give her an
answer?

Say you do or you don't, say you will or you won't—
MILPHIDIPPA.   Save a suffering wretch while you can, sir!
Why torment her so long? She has done you no wrong.
PYRGOPOLYNICES [*magnanimously*]. Have her come here to
me for a viewing.
You may say that I'm willing; I'll soon be fulfilling her
dreams—
MILPHIDIPPA [*excitedly*]. Just as you should be doing!   1070
Being very astute you will do what is mutual—
PALAESTRIO [*waving her off*]. Experts need no further cuing.
MILPHIDIPPA. You're so kind to be heeding my passionate
pleading and letting me speak to your soul myself!
[*Aside to* PALAESTRIO] Well, speak up—how's my act?
PALAESTRIO [*aside to* MILPHIDIPPA]. As a matter of fact, I
have all I can do to control myself!
MILPHIDIPPA. That's why I turned aside. I was trying to hide—
[*She breaks into giggles*]
PYRGOPOLYNICES [*completely involved in self-praise*]. Do you
know this occasion is stellar?
Do you know the great honour I lavish upon her?
MILPHIDIPPA.   I know, and I'll certainly tell her.
PALAESTRIO. The demand is so great I could ask for his weight
in pure gold—
MILPHIDIPPA.   By the gods, you'd receive it!
PALAESTRIO. And the women he lies with he fecundifies with
real heroes—and would you believe it—
The children he rears live for eight hundred years—
MILPHIDIPPA [*aside*]. Oh, please stop it, you joker—I'm crying!
PYRGOPOLYNICES. My dear boy, there are many who live a
millennium—from age to age without dying!
PALAESTRIO. Oh, I knew it but hid it—and I underdid it so
she wouldn't think I was lying.
MILPHIDIPPA. Oh, I'm simply aghast—why, how long will *he*
last—if his sons are of such great duration?   1080
PYRGOPOLYNICES. Jove was born of the Earth just preceding
my birth—I was born one day after Creation.*
PALAESTRIO. And what is more—had he been born before, *he*
would be in the heavens now, reigning!
MILPHIDIPPA [*aside to* PALAESTRIO]. Please—one more and

I'll crack! By the gods, send me back—let me go with
some breath still remaining.

PALAESTRIO [*aloud*]. Don't stand lazily by—go—you've got
your reply.

MILPHIDIPPA.   Yes—I'll go and I'll bring back madam now.
How her spirits will soar! [*To* PYRGOPOLYNICES] Do you
want something more?

PYRGOPOLYNICES.   To be no handsomer than I am now.
It is so aggravating to be devastatingly handsome . . .

PALAESTRIO.   Go on, girl!

MILPHIDIPPA.   I'm going.

PALAESTRIO. Now remember, be smart—use your head
and your heart. Have *her* heart fairly dance, have her
glowing!

[*Aside to* MILPHIDIPPA] And if our girl's in there, have her
cross and prepare—say the soldier's returned to his
station.

MILPHIDIPPA. She's with mistress inside; they found a place
to hide where they took in our whole conversation.   1090

PALAESTRIO. That was smart—what they're hearing will help
them in steering their own course with good navigation.

MILPHIDIPPA. Come—you're holding me back—

PALAESTRIO.   I'm not holding you actually, nor am I—
[*gives a knowing glance*] no further mention now.

                                                 [MILPHIDIPPA *exits*

PYRGOPOLYNICES. Have your mistress make haste, I have
no time to waste. I shall give this my foremost attention
now.

                    [PYRGOPOLYNICES *paces back and forth, deep*
                         in thought, then turns to PALAESTRIO
Palaestrio, you're my adviser, what about
My concubine? For clearly it's impossible.
To ask the new one in before the other's out!

PALAESTRIO. Why ask me for advice on what to do? I've told
you
How to do it gently—with the most compassion:
Let her keep the jewels and fancy clothes you gave her.
Tell her to prepare 'em, wear 'em, bear 'em off.   1100
Say the time is ripe for her to go back home—

Her mother's here with her twin sister—say that too.
It's fitting she go home accompanied by them.

PYRGOPOLYNICES [*worried*]. How do you *know* they're here?

PALAESTRIO.   Why, with these very eyes
I saw our lady's twin.

PYRGOPOLYNICES.   And have the sisters met?

PALAESTRIO. Yes.

PYRGOPOLYNICES [*lecherously*]. How's the twin—good-
looking?

PALAESTRIO.   Sir! You want
To grab at everything!

PYRGOPOLYNICES [*more lechery*]. Where did she say the
mother is?

PALAESTRIO. Aboard the ship, in bed with swollen and infected
eyes.
The skipper told me—that's the man who brought 'em
here.
He happens to be staying as our neighbour's guest.   1110

PYRGOPOLYNICES. How's *he*—is he good-looking?

PALAESTRIO.   Cut it out! Indeed—
You really have been quite the model stud—
Pursuing both the sexes—male and female!*
Enough of this!

PYRGOPOLYNICES [*a bit cowed, changing the subject*]. Now
this advice you've given me—
I would prefer your speaking to her of the matter.
You seem to get on well with her in conversation.

PALAESTRIO. What better than to go yourself; it's your affair.
Just say that it's imperative you take a wife.
Say your relations tell you and your friends compel you.

PYRGOPOLYNICES. You think so?

PALAESTRIO.   Would I tell you what I didn't think? 1120

PYRGOPOLYNICES. I'll go inside. Meanwhile, you stay before
the house
And guard. As soon as *she* appears, you call me out.

PALAESTRIO [*confidently*]. Just do your own part well.

PYRGOPOLYNICES.   Consider it as done!
If she's unwilling, then I'll kick her out by force!

PALAESTRIO. Oh, do be careful. It's much better that she
leave

With no hard feelings. So just give her what I told you—
The gold, the jewels and all the stuff you dressed her up
with.

PYRGOPOLYNICES. Ye gods, I hope she'll go!

PALAESTRIO.   I think that you'll succeed.
But go inside—don't wait.

PYRGOPOLYNICES   I'll follow your advice.

[PYRGOPOLYNICES *dashes into his house.*
PALAESTRIO *smiles broadly as he watches
his master, then turns to the audience*

PALAESTRIO. Well, folks, did I exaggerate a while ago   1130
In what I said about this concupiscent captain?
Now I need Acroteleutium, or else
That little maid of hers, or Pleusicles. By Jupiter!
My luck is coming through for me at every turn!
For just the ones I wanted most of all to see,
I see—coming together from the house next door!

Enter ACROTELEUTIUM *from the old man's house,
leading* MILPHIDIPPA *and* PLEUSICLES

ACROTELEUTIUM [*to the others*]. Follow me and look around
to see there's no one spying on us.

MILPHIDIPPA. I see no one here—except the man we want to
see.

PALAESTRIO. Well met!

MILPHIDIPPA. How're you doing, architect?

PALAESTRIO.   Feh, I'm no architect.

MILPHIDIPPA.   What's that?

PALAESTRIO. Why, compared to you, my talent couldn't bang
two boards together.   1140

MILPHIDIPPA. Come now, don't exaggerate—

PALAESTRIO [*smiling*].   Why, you're a filly full of felony!
And you polished off the soldier charmingly.

MILPHIDIPPA.   We haven't finished.

PALAESTRIO. Smile a little; this affair is well in hand—at least
for now.
Simply keep on giving helpful help as you have done so far.
Soldier boy is there inside, beseeching her to go away:
'Please go back to Athens with your mother and your sister!'

PLEUSICLES.   Great!

PALAESTRIO. And he gave her all the gold, the jewels, the
    stuff he dressed her up with

As a gift—to go away. He's following the plan I gave him!

PLEUSICLES. It looks easy: he is all insistence—she gives no
    resistance.

PALAESTRIO. Don't you know that when you're climbing
    upward in a well that's deep,

You're in greatest danger of a fall when nearest to the top. 1150

We have almost drawn this from the well, but if he gets
    suspicious,

We'll get nothing out of him—so now's the time to be our
    sharpest.

We have raw materials aplenty for the job, that's clear.

Three girls, [to PLEUSICLES] you're a fourth, and I'm a
    fifth—the old man is a sixth.

We six have a large reserve of rogueries to draw upon.

Name a city—we could storm and conquer it with all our
    tricks.*

Pay attention now—

ACROTELEUTIUM.   That's why we've come—to find out
    what you want.

PALAESTRIO. Nice of you to say. Now I'll command you in
    your line of duty.

ACROTELEUTIUM. You'll command commendably. I'll do my
    best for your request.   1160

PALAESTRIO. Lightly . . . brightly . . . and in spritely fashion—
    fool the soldier boy.

  I command it.

ACROTELEUTIUM. Your command's a pleasure.

PALAESTRIO.   You've got the way?

ACROTELEUTIUM. I pretend I'm torn apart for love of . . . him,
    that I've divorced my present husband,

Since I'm burning so to marry . . . him.

PALAESTRIO [smiling].   It's all in order now.

One more thing—this house is *yours*—since it was in your
    dowry. Say the*

Old man has gone off already, since the separation's final.

We don't want our man afraid to enter someone else's
    house.

ACROTELEUTIUM. Well advised.

PALAESTRIO.   When he comes out, be
   hesitant—don't come too close.

   Act as if you're too ashamed to place your beauty near his
      own.   1170

   Be in awe of all his riches; lavish praise upon his looks, his

   Splendid face and figure, charm, his personality, et cetera.

   Have you been rehearsed enough?

ACROTELEUTIUM.   Of course. Won't it be quite enough to

   Render you a polished piece of work? I know you'll find
      it flawless.

PALAESTRIO. Fine. [*To* PLEUSICLES] It's your turn now to be
   commanded in your line of duty.

   When what we've discussed is done, and she goes in—you
      come at once.

   Get yourself disguised the way the skipper of a ship would
      dress:

   Have a wide-brimmed hat—rust-brown—and on your eye
      a woollen patch.

   Also have a rust-brown cloak—since that's the colour sailors
      wear.

   Fasten it to your left shoulder, tie it round with one arm
      bare.   1180

   One way or another, you must seem the master of a ship.

   All these clothes are there inside—the old man owns some
      fishing boats.

                                   [PLEUSICLES *nods, having taken*
                                      great pains to memorize all this

PLEUSICLES. Well, when I am here . . . all dressed up like you
   just described . . . what then?

PALAESTRIO. Come here—and pretend you're fetching Philocomasium for her mother.

   Say that if she's going to Athens she must hurry to the
      harbour.

   Also have them carry all the things she wants to take on
      board.

   [*Affecting an old-salt accent*] If she doesn't come, you'll
      cast off anyway—the wind is fair.

PLEUSICLES. Pretty picture—please proceed.

PALAESTRIO.   Then right away he'll urge the girl to
  Hasten, hurry—don't keep Mother waiting.
PLEUSICLES [*admiringly to the others*]. He's poly-perceptive! 1190
PALAESTRIO. I'll have her request my aid in taking luggage to
  the harbour.
  He'll command me to escort her. When I'm there, be sure
    of this—
  Straightaway I'll be away, straight . . . back to Athens.
PLEUSICLES.   When you're there,
  You won't be a slave for three days longer. I'll release you.
PALAESTRIO. Quickly now, and dress yourself.
PLEUSICLES.   There's nothing else?
PALAESTRIO.   Just don't forget.
PLEUSICLES. I'll be going . . .

                               [*He goes*

PALAESTRIO [*to the women*]. You two hurry in as well, since
  any minute
  He'll be coming out again, I know.
ACROTELEUTIUM [*taking leave*]. Your wish is our command.
PALAESTRIO. Everybody go—retreat! [*Turns*] And just in time
  —our door is open!
  [*To the audience*] Here he comes—so chipper—he's 'suc-
  ceeded'! Fool—he gapes at nothing!

    PYRGOPOLYNICES *bursts out, overjoyed with himself*

PYRGOPOLYNICES. I've succeeded! I got what I wanted as I
  wanted it—   1200
  Sweetly and completely she agreed.
PALAESTRIO.   What took so long in there?
PYRGOPOLYNICES. Never was I loved as madly as that little
  woman loves me.
PALAESTRIO. Oh?
PYRGOPOLYNICES. I needed countless words; she was the
  toughest nut to crack.
  Finally, I triumphed. Did I give her gifts! I gave her
  Everything that she demanded. [*Sheepishly*] I even had to
  give her . . . you.
PALAESTRIO [*mock shock*]. Even me! How could I live away
  from you?

PYRGOPOLYNICES.   Stiff upper lip.
   I would like to have you back, and yet there was no other
     way. I
   Couldn't get the girl to go without you—I tried everything,
     she
   Overwhelmed me.
PALAESTRIO [*dramatically*]. Well, I trust the gods—and you,
   of course. I know that
   After this, though 'twill be bitter, parted from the best of
     masters,   1210
   This at least will comfort me: that your surpassing beauty
     will have—
   Through my humble efforts—won that lady. I will now
     arrange it.
PYRGOPOLYNICES. Ah, what need of words. If you succeed,
   you'll be a free man—
   And a rich man.
PALAESTRIO.   I'll succeed.
PYRGOPOLYNICES [*impatiently*]. I'm bursting—hurry!
PALAESTRIO.   Self-control!
   Take it easy, don't be so ... hot-blooded. Wait—she's
   coming out.

        PALAESTRIO *pulls the soldier aside,*
      as MILPHIDIPPA *leads* ACROTELEUTIUM
         from the old man's house

MILPHIDIPPA [*aside to* ACROTELEUTIUM]. Oh, mistress, there's
   the soldier.
ACROTELEUTIUM. Where?
MILPHIDIPPA.   Right to your left.
ACROTELEUTIUM.   I see.
MILPHIDIPPA. Take just a hasty glance so he won't know
   we're looking at him.
ACROTELEUTIUM. All right, by Pollux, now's the time for bad
   girls to be worse girls.*
MILPHIDIPPA. You take the lead.
ACROTELEUTIUM [*melodramatically*]. Please tell me—did you
   see the man in person?
   [*Aside*] Don't speak too softly—let 'im hear.

MILPHIDIPPA [*proudly*].   I spoke to him myself, 1220
Quite calmly, easily—and just as long as I desired.

PYRGOPOLYNICES. You hear?

PALAESTRIO.   I hear. She's overjoyed just to
have talked to you.

ACROTELEUTIUM. Oh, what a lucky woman!

PYRGOPOLYNICES.   How they love me.

PALAESTRIO.   You deserve it.

ACROTELEUTIUM. What a miracle—you got to him and begged
him to submission.

I heard one needed letters, or a page—like for a king.

MILPHIDIPPA. Indeed, it took a bit of effort getting through
to him.

PALAESTRIO. You're a legend with the women.

PYRGOPOLYNICES.   I accept the will of Venus.

ACROTELEUTIUM [*picking up a cue*]. I give my thanks to Venus
and I beg her and beseech
That I may be successful with the one I love and long for.
May he be kind to me and not deny me my desire.   1230

MILPHIDIPPA. I hope so too. And yet so many women long
for him.
He spurns them all, despises them—except for you alone.

ACROTELEUTIUM. I'm terribly tormented, since he's so discri-
minating,
That, seeing me, his eyes will make him change his mind.
Why, his own splendidness will spurn with speed my plain
appearance.

MILPHIDIPPA. He won't. Be of good cheer.

PYRGOPOLYNICES [*taken—and taken in*]. How she disparages
herself.

ACROTELEUTIUM. I'm frightened you exaggerated my good
looks to him.

MILPHIDIPPA. Oh, I was careful—you'll be prettier than I
described.

ACROTELEUTIUM. If he won't take me for his wife, then I'll
embrace his knees
And I'll implore him. Otherwise, if I can't win him over, 1240
I am resolved to die. I know I cannot live without him.

[PYRGOPOLYNICES *starts toward*
her with open arms

PYRGOPOLYNICES. I must prevent that woman's death. I'll
go—

PALAESTRIO [restraining him]. Oh, not at all!

You're cheapening yourself to give yourself so liberally.

Do let her come unbidden, sir: to yearn, to burn, to wait
her turn.

Now, do you want to lose your reputation? Don't do that!

No man was ever loved by woman thus—except for two:

Yourself and Phaon, Sappho's lover on the Isle of Lesbos.*

ACROTELEUTIUM. Dear Milphidippa, call him out—or I'll go
in myself!

MILPHIDIPPA. Let's wait at least till someone else comes out.

ACROTELEUTIUM.   But I can't wait—
I'm going in!

MILPHIDIPPA.   The doors are locked.

ACROTELEUTIUM.   I'll break 'em.

MILPHIDIPPA [rushing to the soldier's door]. You're insane! 1250

ACROTELEUTIUM. But if he's ever loved, or if his wisdom
match his beauty,

Then he'll forgive whatever I may do because of love.

PALAESTRIO [to the soldier]. The poor girl's burning up for
love of you.

PYRGOPOLYNICES [trembling]. It's mutual!

PALAESTRIO [hushing him]. Don't let her hear!

MILPHIDIPPA.   You're standing stupefied—why don't you knock?

ACROTELEUTIUM. The man I love is not inside.

MILPHIDIPPA.   How do you know?

ACROTELEUTIUM.   I smell.

My nose would sense it if he were inside.

PALAESTRIO.   A prophetess!

PYRGOPOLYNICES. She loves me, therefore Venus gave her
powers of prophecy.

ACROTELEUTIUM. He's near—somewhere—the man I long to
see. I smell him!

PYRGOPOLYNICES. She sees more with her nose than with her
eyes.

PALAESTRIO. She's blind with love.

          [ACROTELEUTIUM begins an elaborate fainting act

ACROTELEUTIUM. Oh, hold me!

MILPHIDIPPA.   Why?

ACROTELEUTIUM.   I'm falling!

MILPHIDIPPA.   Why?

ACROTELEUTIUM.   Because I can't stand up! 1260
My soul's retreating through my eyes—

MILPHIDIPPA.   By Pollux, then you've seen
The soldier!

ACROTELEUTIUM. Yes!

MILPHIDIPPA.   I don't see—where?

ACROTELEUTIUM.   You'd see him if you loved him!

MILPHIDIPPA. What's that? Why, if you'd let me, I would
love him more than you do!

PALAESTRIO. It's obvious that every woman loves you at first
sight.

PYRGOPOLYNICES [in a confidential tone]. I don't know if I
told you, but my grandmother was . . . Venus.*

ACROTELEUTIUM. Dear Milphidippa, please go up to him.

PYRGOPOLYNICES [preening].   How she reveres me!

PALAESTRIO. Well, here she comes.

MILPHIDIPPA.   I want you—

PYRGOPOLYNICES [aside].   I want you!

MILPHIDIPPA.   As you commanded,
I've brought my mistress out.

PYRGOPOLYNICES. I see.

MILPHIDIPPA.   Well, tell her to approach.

PYRGOPOLYNICES. Your pleas have forced me not to hate her
as I do the others.

          [PYRGOPOLYNICES starts toward ACROTELEUTIUM,
          but MILPHIDIPPA suddenly blocks his way

MILPHIDIPPA. If she approaches nearer you—she couldn't
speak a word.   1270
For when she simply looks at you, her eyes cut off her
tongue.

PYRGOPOLYNICES. I'll cure milady's malady.

MILPHIDIPPA.   Oh, how she shaked and quaked
When she beheld you.

PYRGOPOLYNICES.   Mighty men in armour do the same—
I do not wonder that a woman does. What does she want?

MILPHIDIPPA. She wants to live a lifetime with you, so—
come to her house.

PYRGOPOLYNICES [*hesitantly*]. I—to her house? She's married
   —why—her husband—he might catch me!

MILPHIDIPPA. But, sir, for love of you, she's thrown her husband out.

PYRGOPOLYNICES. How could she?

MILPHIDIPPA [*smiling*]. This house was in her dowry.

PYRGOPOLYNICES. Yes?

MILPHIDIPPA.   Yes, sir.

PYRGOPOLYNICES.   Then take her home—
   I'll be there in a second.

MILPHIDIPPA.   Please don't keep her waiting long—
   Don't break her heart.

PYRGOPOLYNICES.   I won't—of course. Be off!

MILPHIDIPPA.   We're off. 1280

      [MILPHIDIPPA *helps her 'fainting' mistress
        back into the old man's house*

PYRGOPOLYNICES [*looking off-stage*]. What do I see?

PALAESTRIO.   What do you see?

PYRGOPOLYNICES.   Someone's approaching, dressed
   In sailor's clothes.

PALAESTRIO. He's heading for our house—it's clear he wants
   you.
   Why, that's the skipper—

PYRGOPOLYNICES.   Come to fetch the girl, no doubt.

PALAESTRIO.   No doubt.

   Enter PLEUSICLES, *looking very uncomfortable in
   his elaborate sailor's costume. Among other items
   of apparel, he has a huge patch over his left eye*

PLEUSICLES. If I were not aware how many others have
   Done awful things because of love, I'd be afraid
   To march around dressed up like this to win my love.
   Yet, since I know of many others who committed things
   Both shady and dishonest for the sake of love . . .
   Why mention how Achilles let his Greeks be killed? . . .*
   But there's Palaestrio—he's standing with the soldier. 1290
   I'd better change my language to a different style.
   [*Affecting the accent* PALAESTRIO *demonstrated earlier*]
   Why, woman's born the daughter of Delay herself.
   For any other plain delay of equal length

Seems less of a delay than waiting for a woman.
I really do believe it's in their constitution.
But now to fetch this girl Philocomasium.
I'll knock. Hey—anybody home?

PALAESTRIO [*rushing up to him*]. Young man—what's up?
What are you knocking for?

PLEUSICLES.   I want Philocomasium.
Her mother sent me. If she's coming, let her come.
The girl's delaying everyone—we're anxious to set sail.   1300

[PYRGOPOLYNICES *dashes over nervously*

PYRGOPOLYNICES. Oh, everything's all ready. Go, Palaestrio—
Get helpers to transport her stuff onto the ship—
The gold, the jewels, the clothes and all the fancy things.
The gifts I gave her are all packed. Now let her take them!

PALAESTRIO. I'm off.

PLEUSICLES.   For heaven's sake be quick!

PYRGOPOLYNICES [*trying to placate him*]. He won't be long.
But tell me, sir, what happened to that eye of yours?

PLEUSICLES [*pointing to his unbandaged eye*]. Why, this one's
    fine.

PYRGOPOLYNICES. I mean your left one.

PLEUSICLES.   It's like this:
The *ocean* caused me to use this eye less. And yet
Were it not for *dev*-otion, I could use it now.*
But they're delaying me too long—

PYRGOPOLYNICES.   Ah—here they come!   1310

PALAESTRIO *leads a tearful* PHILOCOMASIUM
out of the soldier's house

PALAESTRIO. Will there ever be an end to all this weeping?

PHILOCOMASIUM [*woefully*].   Can I help it?
I must leave this beautiful existence . . .

PALAESTRIO.   This man's come for you
From your mother and your sister.

PHILOCOMASIUM   Yes, I see.

PYRGOPOLYNICES [*impatiently*].   Palaestrio!

PALAESTRIO. Yes?

PYRGOPOLYNICES. Command that all the stuff I gave the
    girl be carried off!

PLEUSICLES. Greetings, Philocomasium.

PHILOCOMASIUM.   The same to you.

PLEUSICLES.   Mother and sister
Also bade me tell you . . . greetings.

PHILOCOMASIUM.   Greetings to them both as well.

PLEUSICLES [*delivering his carefully memorized speech*]. They
beseech you . . . come ahead . . . the wind is fair . . . the
sails are full.

If your mother's eyes were better, she'd have come along
with me.

PHILOCOMASIUM. Though I long to stay, one must obey one's
mother.

PLEUSICLES. Very wise.

PYRGOPOLYNICES [*confidentially to* PLEUSICLES]. If she hadn't
lived with me, she'd be a half-wit to this day!   1320

PHILOCOMASIUM. That's what pains me so—the separation
from so great a man.

Why, with your abilities, you could . . . enrich . . . most
anyone.

At this moment, PALAESTRIO *appears from inside
the soldier's house, carrying a treasure chest*

And because I used to be with you, I held my head up high.
Now . . . I have to lose that one distinction.

PYRGOPOLYNICES.   Do not cry.

PHILOCOMASIUM.   I must—
When I look at you. . . .

PYRGOPOLYNICES.   Stiff upper lip.

PHILOCOMASIUM.   Oh, if you knew my feelings!

PALAESTRIO. I don't wonder, girl, that you lived happily with
him, and that his

Beauty's blaze, his noble gaze, his manly ways have held
you rapt, for

Even I—slave that I am—am brought to tears at leaving
him.

PHILOCOMASIUM [*to the soldier*]. May I hug you one more
time before I go for good?

PYRGOPOLYNICES.   You may.

[PYRGOPOLYNICES *readies himself for her*

> *embrace. She starts toward him with open*
> *arms, then staggers, wailing*

PHILOCOMASIUM. Oh, my darling . . . oh, my soul . . . oh. . . .

> [*She begins an elaborate faint.* PALAESTRIO *catches*
> *her 'just in time', and hands her to* PLEUSICLES

PALAESTRIO.   Hold this woman please; she may do 1330
  Damage to herself!

PYRGOPOLYNICES.   What's going on?

PALAESTRIO.   Because she has to leave you, the
  Poor girl's fainted dead away!

PYRGOPOLYNICES.   Well, run inside and get some water!

PALAESTRIO. Never mind the water—she needs rest.

> [*The soldier starts toward her*
>   No—don't come any closer!

  Please—let her recover.

> [PYRGOPOLYNICES *eyes* PLEUSICLES *and*
>   PHILOCOMASIUM *with suspicion*

PYRGOPOLYNICES. Say—their heads are awfully close together!
  I don't like the looks of this. Hey, sailor—take your lips
  from hers!

PLEUSICLES. I just tried to see if she was breathing.

PYRGOPOLYNICES.   Use your ear for that!

PLEUSICLES. If you'd like, I'll let her go—

PYRGOPOLYNICES.   No no—hold on!

PALAESTRIO [*weeping*].   Oh, woe is me!

PYRGOPOLYNICES [*calling inside his house*]. Men! Come out—
  bring forth her stuff—bring everything I gave the girl!

> *Various* LACKEYS *enter with* PHILOCOMASIUM'S
> *luggage and assorted gifts, as* PALAESTRIO *readies*
> *himself for an impassioned valedictory*

PALAESTRIO. Ere I go . . . let me salute you once again . . . ye
  Household Gods.
  And to you, my male and female fellow slaves . . . hail and
  farewell.   1340
  Please don't speak too badly of me 'mongst yourselves
  when I am gone.

PYRGOPOLYNICES. Come, Palaestrio, buck up!

PALAESTRIO.   Alas, I cannot help but cry—
  I must leave you.

PYRGOPOLYNICES.   Take it like a man.

PALAESTRIO.   Oh, if you knew my feelings!

       [PHILOCOMASIUM *suddenly 'regains consciousness'*

PHILOCOMASIUM. What? Where am I? What's been going
    on. Who are you?

    [*Aside*] Hello, darling!

PLEUSICLES. Ah, you have revived, [*aside*] my darling.

PHILOCOMASIUM   Goodness! Who am I embracing?
    Who's this man? I'm lost—I must have fainted.

PLEUSICLES [*aside*].   Never fear, my dearest.

      [*She puts her head on* PLEUSICLES' *chest*

PYRGOPOLYNICES. What's all this?

PALAESTRIO [*trying to cover up*]. It's nothing . . . nothing . . .
    just another fainting spell.

  Oh, I shiver and I quiver. [*To the lovers*] This is getting *far
    too public!*

PYRGOPOLYNICES. What'd you say?

PALAESTRIO.   Uh—carrying this stuff
    in public—through the city—

  It might hurt your reputation.

PYRGOPOLYNICES.   Well, it's mine to give and
                        no one else's. 1350

  I don't care what others think. Now depart—the gods be
    with you.

PALAESTRIO. I was looking out for you.

PYRGOPOLYNICES.   I know.

PALAESTRIO.   Farewell.

PYRGOPOLYNICES.   Farewell to you.

PALAESTRIO [*aside to* PLEUSICLES]. Hurry, I'll be with you in
    a second. [*Aloud*] Just two words with Master.

                [*He goes to the soldier*

  Though you have thought other servants far more faithful
    than myself,

  Still and all, I'm very grateful to you, sir . . . for everything.

  And, if you'd seen fit to, I would rather have been slave to
    you

  Than a freedman, working for another.

PYRGOPOLYNICES.   Come—stiff upper lip.

PALAESTRIO [*sudden burst of passion*]. Fond farewell to
    following a fiery, ferocious fighter!

Now I'm flunky to a frilly female ... fortitude forgot.
> [*He breaks into sobs.* PYRGOPOLYNICES *pats him on the shoulder, barely able to restrain his own tears*

PYRGOPOLYNICES. Good old fellow.

PALAESTRIO.   Oh, I can't go on—I've lost my will to live! 1360

PYRGOPOLYNICES. Go, go—follow them—no more delay.

PALAESTRIO.   Farewell.

PYRGOPOLYNICES.   Farewell to you.
> [PALAESTRIO *turns to go, then whirls back toward the soldier*

PALAESTRIO. Don't forget me, sir, for if perchance I should be freed some day,
I will send you word. You won't forsake me?

PYRGOPOLYNICES.   Ah, that's not my style.

PALAESTRIO. Always and for ever think how faithful I have been to you.
Then at last you'll know who's been a loyal slave and who has not.

PYRGOPOLYNICES. I'm aware. I've noticed often—never quite so much till now.

PALAESTRIO. Yes, today at last you'll know the kind of slave I really am.
> [PALAESTRIO *turns and starts to walk slowly off*

PYRGOPOLYNICES. I can hardly stop myself from keeping you—

PALAESTRIO [*frantically*]. Oh, don't do that!
There'd be talk—they'd say you didn't keep your word—untrustworthy.
They would say you had no faithful slaves at all—except for me.   1370
If I thought it could be done the proper way—why, I'd insist—
But you simply can't—

PYRGOPOLYNICES.   Be off then.

PALAESTRIO.   I shall bear whatever comes.

PYRGOPOLYNICES. So, farewell.

PALAESTRIO.   I'd better hurry off.

PYRGOPOLYNICES [*impatiently*]. All right—farewell already!
> [PALAESTRIO *races off-stage—with a broad smile*

PYRGOPOLYNICES [*reflecting, to the audience*]. Till today I
    always thought he was the very worst of slaves.
Now I see he was devoted to me. When I think it over,
I was foolish giving him away. But now I'll head inside,
Now's the time for love! Wait—I perceive a sound—made
    by the door.

    A SLAVE BOY *enters from the old man's house*

BOY [*to those inside the house*]. Stop coaching me, please. I
    remember what to do.
    [*Getting melodramatic*] Wheresoever in the world he be,
    I'll find him.
Yes, I'll track him down; I won't spare any effort.   1380
PYRGOPOLYNICES. This one seeks me. I'll go up and meet the
    boy.
BOY. Aha, I'm looking for you. Hail, you gorgeous creature!
O man of every hour, beyond all other men
Beloved of two gods—
PYRGOPOLYNICES.   Which two?
BOY.   Venus and Mars.*
PYRGOPOLYNICES. A clever boy.
BOY.   She begs of you to go inside.
She yearns, she burns, expectantly expecting you.
Bring solace to the lovelorn, don't wait—go!
PYRGOPOLYNICES [*hungrily*].   I will!

    [*He dashes at full speed into the old man's house*

BOY [*to the audience*]. Well, now he's trapped himself, caught
    in his own devices.
The ambush is prepared: the old man's standing staunchly
To attack this lecher who's so loud about his loveliness, 1390
Who thinks that every woman loves him at first sight,
When really they detest him, men as well as women.
Now I'll rejoin the uproar—there's a shout inside!

    [*He runs back into the house*

    Sounds of a scuffle from within, then enter
    PERIPLECTOMENUS, *followed by his servants, who*
    are carrying PYRGOPOLYNICES. *Among them is*
    CARIO, *the cook, who has a long, sharp knife*

PERIPLECTOMENUS. Bring 'im out! If he won't come, then
pick him up and throw him out!
Make a little seat for him—right in mid-air. Tear him apart!
PYRGOPOLYNICES. Please—I beg—by Hercules!
PERIPLECTOMENUS.   By Hercules, you beg in vain.
Cario, see to it that that knife of yours is sharp enough.
CARIO. Why, it's long been eager to remove this lecher's vital
parts,*
And to hang 'em like a baby's string of beads—around his
neck.
PYRGOPOLYNICES. Oh, I'm dead!
PERIPLECTOMENUS.   Not yet—you speak too soon.
CARIO [brandishing that knife].   Can I go at him now? 1400
PERIPLECTOMENUS. First let him be pummelled by your clubs
a little more.
CARIO.   Much more!
         [The SLAVES pound PYRGOPOLYNICES much more
PERIPLECTOMENUS. So! You dared to make advances to another's
wife—you pig!
PYRGOPOLYNICES. By the gods, she asked me first—she came
to me!
PERIPLECTOMENUS.   He lies—hit on.
PYRGOPOLYNICES. Wait a second—let me talk.
PERIPLECTOMENUS [to the slaves].   Why do you stop?
PYRGOPOLYNICES.   Please—may I speak?
PERIPLECTOMENUS. Speak.
PYRGOPOLYNICES.   The woman begged me—
PERIPLECTOMENUS.   But you dared to go—hit him again!
PYRGOPOLYNICES. Stop—stop—stop—I'm pounded plenty.
Please, I beg—
CARIO.   When do I cut?
PERIPLECTOMENUS. At your own convenience. Spread 'im out
and stretch 'im all the way.
PYRGOPOLYNICES. Please, by Hercules, I beg you, hear my
words before he cuts!
PERIPLECTOMENUS. Well?
PYRGOPOLYNICES.   I didn't want to—Hercules—I
thought she was divorced!
I was told as much—her maid—that little bawd—she lied
to me!   1410

PERIPLECTOMENUS. Swear that you won't harm a single person
   for this whole affair, or
   For the pounding you've received today—and will receive—
   if we now
   Let you go intact—sweet little grandson of the goddess
   Venus.
PYRGOPOLYNICES. Yes! I swear by Jupiter and Mars, I'll never
   harm a soul.
   And my beating up today—I grant it was my just reward.
   As a favour, let me leave with testimony to my manhood!
PERIPLECTOMENUS. If you break your promise after this?
PYRGOPOLYNICES.   Then may I live . . . detested.
CARIO. I suggest we wallop him a final time and let him go.
PYRGOPOLYNICES. Thank you—may the gods all bless you,
   sir, for speaking up for me.
CARIO. Also give us gold—a hundred drachmae.*
PYRGOPOLYNICES.   Why?
CARIO.   To let you go— 1420
   Without giving testimony—grandson of the goddess Venus.
   Otherwise, you'll never leave.
PYRGOPOLYNICES.   You'll get it.
CARIO.   Now you're being smart.
   And you can forget about your cloak, your tunic and your
   sword.
   [*To* PERIPLECTOMENUS] Should I pound or let him loose?
PYRGOPOLYNICES. Your pounding's made me loose already!
   Please—I beg of you—no more.
PERIPLECTOMENUS.   Release the man.
PYRGOPOLYNICES.   Oh, thank you, thank you.
PERIPLECTOMENUS. If I catch you after this, you'll never testify
   again!
PYRGOPOLYNICES. How can I object?
PERIPLECTOMENUS. Come, Cario, let's go inside.

    The OLD MAN *takes his* SLAVES *inside, just as*
    SCELEDRUS *appears, with the soldier's* LACKEYS,
      returning from the harbour

PYRGOPOLYNICES.   Look now—I
   See my slaves. Quick, tell me, has the girl set sail—well,
   has she, has she?

SCELEDRUS. Long ago—

PYRGOPOLYNICES.   Damn!!

SCELEDRUS.   If you knew what I know,
   that's not all you'd say. That
   Fellow with the woollen patch on his left eye . . . was no
      real sailor!   1430

PYRGOPOLYNICES. What? Who was he?

SCELEDRUS.   Your own sweetheart's lover.

PYRGOPOLYNICES.   How'd you know?

SCELEDRUS.   I know.
   Why, the minute they were past the city gates, right then
      and there, they
   Started kissing and embracing—constantly.

PYRGOPOLYNICES.   Oh, pity me!
   Now I see I've been bamboozled. Oh, that rogue Palaestrio!
   He enticed me into this. And yet . . . I find the verdict's just.
   [*Philosophically*]. There would be less lechery if lechers
      were to learn from this;
   Lots would be more leery and less lustful.
   [*To his slaves*] Let's go in! [*To the audience*] Applaud!
                     [*All exit into the soldier's house*

THE BROTHERS MENAECHMUS

(*Menaechmi*)

DRAMATIS PERSONAE

PENICULUS, a parasite
MENAECHMUS I
MENAECHMUS II, his twin brother (born Sosicles)
MESSENIO, slave to Menaechmus II
EROTIUM, a lady of pleasure
CYLINDRUS, a cook in Erotium's employ
MAID, also in Erotium's employ
WIFE of Menaechmus
OLD MAN, father-in-law of Menaechmus
DOCTOR

The scene is a street in Epidamnus. There are two houses. On the right (from the audience's view) is MENAECHMUS' *house; on the left,* EROTIUM'S *house. The forum is off-stage to the audience's right. The harbour is off-stage to the audience's left.*

THE BROTHERS MENAECHMUS

Enter the CHIEF ACTOR *to speak the prologue*

Now first and foremost, folks, I've this apostrophe:
May fortune favour all of you—and all of me.
I bring you Plautus. [*Pause*] Not in person, just his play.
So listen please, be friendly with your ears today.
Now here's the plot. Please listen with your whole attention
    span;
I'll tell it in the very fewest words I can.
[*A digression*] Now comic poets do this thing in every
    play:*
'It all takes place in Athens, folks,' is what they say.
So that way everything will seem *more Greek* to you.
But I reveal the real locations when I speak to you.   10
This story's Greekish, but to be exact,
It's not Athenish, it's Sicilyish, in fact.
[*Smiles*] That was a prelude to the prologue of the plot.
I now intend to pour a lot of plot for you.
Not just a cupful, fuller up, more like a pot.
Such is our storehouse, brimming full of plot!
[*Finally, to business*] There was at Syracuse a merchant
    old and worn
To whom a pair of baby boys—two twins—were born.
The babies' looks were so alike their nurse confessed
She couldn't tell to which of them she gave which breast.   20
Nor even could their own real mother tell between them.
I've learned about all this from someone who has seen
    them.
I haven't seen the boys, in case you want to know.
Their father, 'round the time the boys were seven or so,
Packed on a mighty ship much merchandise to sell—
The father also packed one of the twins as well.
They went to Tarentum to market, with each other,
And left the other brother back at home with mother.
A festival chanced to be on there when they docked there,
And piles of people for the festival had flocked there.   30

The little boy, lost in the crowd, wandered away.
An Epidamnian merchant, also there that day,
Made off with him to Epidamnus—there to stay.
The father, learning that he'd lost the lad,
Became depressed, in fact he grew so very sad
A few days later he was dead. It was that bad.

When back to Syracuse this news was all dispatched,
The grandpa of the boys learned one was snatched,
And word of father's death at Tarentum then came.
The grandpa took the other twin and changed his name.   40
He so adored the other twin, who had been snatched,
He gave the brother still at home a name that matched:
Menaechmus. That had been the other brother's name.
It was the grandpa's name as well, the very same.*
In fact, it's not a name you quickly can forget,
Especially if you're one to whom he owes a debt.*
I warn you now, so later you won't be confused:
[*Emphatically*] for both of the twin brothers one same name
    is used.

                              [*Starts to cross the stage*
Metre by metre to Epidamnus now I must wend,*
So I can chart this map unto its perfect end.   50
If any of you wants some business handled there,
Speak up, be brave, and tell me of the whole affair.
But let him give me cash, so I can take good care.
If you don't offer cash, then you're a fool, forget it.
You do—[*smiles*] then you're a bigger fool, and you'll regret
    it.
I'll go back whence I came—still standing on this floor—
And finish up the story I began before:

That Epidamnian who snatched the little lad,
He had no children; lots of cash was all he had.*
So he adopted him he snatched, became his dad.   60
And gave his son a dowried female for his bride.
And then—so he could make the boy his heir—he died.*
By chance, out in the country in a rain severe,
He tried to cross a rapid stream—not far from here.
The rapid river rapt the kidnapper, who fell,
Caught in the current, heading hurriedly to hell.

The most fantastic riches thus came rolling in
To him who lives right in the house—the kidnapped twin.
  But *now*, from Syracuse where he had always been,
Today in Epidamnus will arrive the other twin,   70
With trusty slave, in search of long-lost brother-twin.
  This town is Epidamnus, while the play is on.
But when we play another play, its name will change
Just like the actors living here, whose roles can range
From pimp to papa, or to lover pale and wan,
To pauper, parasite, to king or prophet, on and on.
[And on and on and on . . .]*

Enter the parasite PENICULUS.
He speaks directly to the audience

PENICULUS. By local boys I'm called Peniculus the sponge,
  For at the table, I can wipe all platters clean.
  [*A philosophical discourse*] The kind of men who bind
    their prisoners with chains,
  Or clap the shackles on a slave that's run away,   80
  Are acting very foolishly—in my own view.
  If you compound the wretchedness of some poor wretch,
  Why, all the more he'll long to flee and do some wrong.
  For one way or another, he'll get off those chains.
  The shackled men will wear the ring down with a file,
  Or smash the lock. This kind of measure is a joke.
  But if you wish to guard him so he won't run off,
  You ought to chain the man with lots of food and drink.
  Just bind the fellow's beak right to a well-stocked table,
  Provide the guy with eatables and drinkables,   90
  Whatever he would like to stuff himself with every day.
  He'll never flee, though wanted for a murder charge.
  You'll guard with ease by using chains that he can chew.
  The nicest thing about these chains of nourishment—
  The more you loosen them, the more they bind more tightly.
  [*End of discourse*] I'm heading for Menaechmus; he's the
    man to whom
  I've had myself condemned. I'm hoping that he'll chain me.
  He doesn't merely feed men, he can breed men and
  Indeed men are reborn through him. No doctor's better.

This is the sort of guy he is: the greatest eater,   100
His feasts are festivals. He piles the table so,*
And plants so many platters in the neatest piles
To reach the top, you have to stand up on your couch.
And yet we've had an intermission for some days
And tabled at my table, I've expended it.
I never eat or drink—except expensively.
But now my army of desserts has been deserting me.
I've got to have a talk with him. But wait—the door!
Behold, I see Menaechmus himself now coming out.

Enter MENAECHMUS, *still facing indoors, berating
someone. We will soon see that he is hiding a
lady's dress under his usual garments*

MENAECHMUS [*singing, in anger at his wife in the house*]. If
   you weren't such a shrew, so uncontrolled, ungrateful
   too,*   110
Whatever thing your husband hated, you'd find hateful
   too.
And if you act up once again, the way you've acted up
   today,
I'll have you packed up—back to Daddy as a divorcée.
However often I try to go out you detain me, delay me,
   demand such details as
Where I'm going, what I'm doing, what's my business all
   about,
Deals I'm making, undertaking, what I did when I was out.
I don't have a wife, I have a customs office bureaucrat,
For I must declare the things I've done, I'm doing, and all
   that!
All the luxuries you've got have spoiled you rotten. I want
   to live for what I give:

        Maids and aides, a pantry full,   120
        Purple clothing, gold and wool:
        You lack for nothing money buys.
        So watch for trouble if you're wise;
        A husband hates a wife who spies.

But so you won't have watched in vain, for all your diligence
   and care,

I'll tell you: 'Wench to lunch today, lovely dinner off
  somewhere.'

PENICULUS. The man now thinks he hurts his wife; it's me he
  hurts:

By eating dinner somewhere else, he won't give me my just
  desserts!

MENAECHMUS [*looks into house, satisfied, then turns to
  audience with a big grin*]. My word barrage has put the
  wife in full retreat. It's victory!

Now where are all the married 'lovers'? Pin your medals
  right on me.

Come honour me *en masse*. Look how I've battled with
  such guts,

And look, this dress I stole inside—it soon will be my little   130
  slut's.

I've shown the way: to fool a guard both hard and shrewd
  takes aptitude.

Oh, what a shining piece of work! What brilliance, glitter,
  glow and gloss!

I've robbed a rat—but lose at that, for my own gain is my
  own loss!

[*Indicates the dress*] Well, here's the booty—there's my foes,
  and to my ally—now it goes.

PENICULUS. Hey, young man! Does any of that stolen booty
  go to me?

MENAECHMUS. Lost—I'm lost—and caught in crime!

PENICULUS.   Oh, no, you're found—and found in time.

MENAECHMUS. Who is that?

PENICULUS.   It's me.

MENAECHMUS.   Oh, *you*—my Lucky
  Charm, my Nick-of-Time!

Greetings. [*Rushes to him; they shake hands vigorously*]

PENICULUS. Greetings.

MENAECHMUS.   Whatcha doing?

PENICULUS.   Shaking hands with my good-luck charm.

MENAECHMUS. Say—you couldn't come more rightly right on
  time than you've just come.

PENICULUS. That's my style: I know exactly how to pick the
  nick of time.   140

MENAECHMUS. Want to see a brilliant piece of work?

PENICULUS.   What cook concocted it?
Show me just a titbit and I'll know if someone bungled it.
MENAECHMUS. Tell me, have you ever seen those frescos
    painted on the wall—
Ganymede snatched by the eagle, Venus . . . likewise . . . with
    Adonis?
PENICULUS. Yes, but what do those damn pictures have to do
    with me?
MENAECHMUS. Just look.

    [*He strikes a pose, showing off his dress*
Notice something similar?
PENICULUS.   What kind of crazy dress is that?
MENAECHMUS [*very fey*]. Tell me that I'm so attractive.
PENICULUS.   Tell me when we're going to eat.
MENAECHMUS. First you tell me—
PENICULUS.   Fine, I'll tell you: you're
    attractive. So attractive.
MENAECHMUS. Don't you care to add a comment?
PENICULUS [*a breath*].   Also witty. Very witty.
MENAECHMUS. More!
PENICULUS.   No more, by Hercules, until I know
    what's in it for me.   150
Since you're warring with your wife, I must be wary and
    beware.
MENAECHMUS. Hidden from my wife we'll live it up and burn   152-3
    this day to ashes.
PENICULUS. Now you're really talking sense. How soon do
    I ignite the pyre?
Look—the day's half dead already, right to near its belly
    button.
MENAECHMUS. You delay me by interrupting—
PENICULUS.   Knock my eyeball through my ankle,
    Mangle me, Menaechmus, if I fail to heed a single word.
MENAECHMUS. Move—we're much too near my house.

    [*Tiptoes to centre stage, motions to* PENICULUS
PENICULUS [*follows* MENAECHMUS].   Okay.
MENAECHMUS [*moves more, motions*]. We're still too near.
PENICULUS [*follows*].   How's this?
MENAECHMUS. Bolder, let's go further from the bloody
    mountain lion's cave.

PENICULUS. Pollux! You'd be perfect racing chariots—the way
you act.   160

MENAECHMUS. Why?

PENICULUS.   You're glancing back to see if *she's*
there, riding after you.

MENAECHMUS. All right, speak your piece.

PENICULUS.   *My* piece? Whatever piece you say is fine.

MENAECHMUS. How are you at smells? Can you conjecture
from a simple sniff?

PENICULUS. Sir, my nose knows more than all the city
prophets.*

MENAECHMUS. Here now, sniff this dress I hold. What do
you smell? You shrink?

PENICULUS. When it comes to women's garments, prudence
bids us smell the *top*.

Way down there, the nose recoils at certain odours quite
unwashable.*

MENAECHMUS. All right, smell up here, you're such a fussy
one.

PENICULUS. All right, I sniff.

MENAECHMUS. Well? What do you smell? Well—

PENICULUS [*quickly*]. Grabbing, grubbing, rub-a-dub
dubbing.*   170

Hope I'm right.

MENAECHMUS.   I hope so too. . . .

Now I'll take this dress to my beloved wench, Erotium,
With the order to prepare a banquet for us both.

PENICULUS.   Oh, good!

MENAECHMUS. Then we'll drink, we'll toast until tomorrow's
morning star appears.   175

PENICULUS. Good, a perfect plan! May I proceed to pound
the portals?

MENAECHMUS.   Pound.

No no—wait!

PENICULUS.   Why wait? The flowing bowl's more than a
mile away!

MENAECHMUS. Pound politely.

PENICULUS. Why? You think the door is made of pottery?

MENAECHMUS. Wait wait wait, by Hercules. She's coming   179-80
out. Oh, see the sun!

How the sun's eclipsed by all the blazing beauty from her
body.

Grand entrance of EROTIUM *from her house*

EROTIUM [*to* MENAECHMUS]. Greetings, O my only soul!
PENICULUS.   And me?
EROTIUM [*to* PENICULUS].   Not on my list at all.
PENICULUS. Such is life for us unlisted men—in every kind of
   war.
MENAECHMUS [*to* EROTIUM]. Darling, at your house today,
   prepare a little battleground.
EROTIUM. So I will.
MENAECHMUS.   We'll hold a little drinking duel, [*indi-
   cating* PENICULUS] the two of us.
Then the one who proves the better fighter with the flowing
   bowl,
He's the one who'll get to join your company for night
   manœuvres.
[*Getting more enthusiastic*] Oh, my joy! My wife, my wife!
   When I see *you*—how I hate *her*!
EROTIUM [*sarcastically*]. Meanwhile, since you hate your wife,
   you wear her clothing, is that it?   190
What have you got on?
MENAECHMUS.   It's just a dress addressed to you,
   sweet rose.
EROTIUM. You're on top, you outtop all the other men who
   try for me.*
PENICULUS [*aside*]. Sluts can talk so sweet, while they see
   something they can snatch from you.
[*To* EROTIUM] If you really loved him, you'd have smooched
   his nose right off his face.
MENAECHMUS. Hold this now, Peniculus; religion bids me
   make redress.
PENICULUS. Fine, but while you've got a skirt on, why not
   pirouette a bit?
MENAECHMUS. Pirouette? By Hercules, you've lost your mind!
PENICULUS.   Not more than you.
Take it off—if you won't dance.
MENAECHMUS [*To* EROTIUM].

What risks I ran in stealing this!

Hercules in labour number nine was not as brave as I,   200
When he stole the girdle from that Amazon Hippolyta.

Take it, darling, since you do your duties with such diligence.*

EROTIUM. That's the spirit. Lovers ought to learn from you the way to love.

PENICULUS [to the audience]. Sure, that way to love's the perfect short cut to a bankruptcy.

MENAECHMUS. Just last year I bought my wife this dress. It cost two hundred drachmae.

PENICULUS [to the audience]. Well, there goes two hundred drachmae down the drain, by my accounts.

MENAECHMUS [to EROTIUM]. Want to know what I would like prepared?

EROTIUM.   I know, and I'll prepare it.

MENAECHMUS. Please arrange a feast at your house; have it cooked for three of us.

Also have some very special party foods bought in the forum:

Glandiose, whole-hog and a descendant of the lardly ham.   210

Or perhaps some pork chopettes, or anything along those lines.*

Let whatever's served be *stewed*, to make me hungry as a hawk.

Also hurry up.

EROTIUM.   I will.

MENAECHMUS.   Now we'll be heading to the forum.

We'll return at once and, while the dinner's cooking, we'll be drinking.

EROTIUM. When you feel like it, come. It will be all prepared.

MENAECHMUS.   And quickly too.

[To PENICULUS] Follow me—

PENICULUS.   By Hercules, I'll follow you in every way.

No, I'd lose the gods' own gold before I lose your track today.

[MENAECHMUS *and* PENICULUS
exit toward the forum

EROTIUM. Someone call inside and tell my cook Cylindrus to come out.

CYLINDRUS *enters from* EROTIUM's *house*

Take a basket and some money. Here are several coins for
   you.

CYLINDRUS. Got 'em.

EROTIUM.   Do your shopping. See that there's
   enough for three of us,   220
Not a surplus or a deficit.

CYLINDRUS.   What sort of guests, madam?

EROTIUM. I, Menaechmus, and his parasite.

CYLINDRUS.   That means I cook for *ten*:
By himself that parasite can eat for eight with greatest ease.

EROTIUM. That's the list. The rest is up to you.

CYLINDRUS.   Consider it as cooked already.
Set yourself at table.

EROTIUM.   Come back quickly.

CYLINDRUS [*starting to trot off*].   I'm as good as back.

                                                    [*He exits*

   From the exit nearer the harbour enters the boy
   *from Syracuse—*MENAECHMUS II—*accompanied by*
      his slave MESSENIO. *As chance* [*i.e. the*
      playwright] *would have it, the twin is also*
      wearing the exact same outfit as his long-lost
      brother. Several sailor types carry their luggage

MENAECHMUS II. Oh, joy, no greater joy, my dear Messenio,
   Than for a sailor when he's on the deep to see
   Dry land.

MESSENIO. It's greater still, if I may speak my mind,
   To see and then arrive at some dry land that's *home*.
   But tell me, please—why have we come to Epidamnus?* 230
   Why have we circled every island like the sea?

MENAECHMUS II [*pointedly, melodramatically*]. We are in
   search of my beloved long-lost twin.

MESSENIO. But will there ever be a limit to this searching?
   It's six entire years since we began this job.
   Through Istria, Iberia, Illyria,
   The Adriatic, up and down, exotic Greece,*
   And all Italian towns. Wherever sea went, *we* went!
   I frankly think if you were searching for a needle,

You would have found it long ago, if it existed.
We seek and search among the living for a dead man.   240
We would have found him long ago if he were living.
MENAECHMUS II. But therefore I search on till I can prove the
     fact;
If someone says he knows for sure my brother's dead,
I'll stop my search and never try an instant further.
But otherwise, I'll never quit while I'm alive,
For I alone can feel how much he means to me.
MESSENIO. You seek a pin in haystacks. Let's go home—
Unless we're doing this to write a travel book.
MENAECHMUS II [*losing his temper*]. Obey your orders, eat
     what's served you, keep from mischief!
And don't annoy me. Do things *my* way.
MESSENIO.   Yessir, yessir.   250
I get the word. The word is simple: I'm a slave.
Concise communication, couldn't be much clearer.
[*A chastened pause, then back to harping at his master*]
But still and all, I just can't keep from saying this:
Menaechmus, when I inspect our purse, it seems
We're travelling for summer—very, very light.
By Hercules, unless you go home right away,
While you search on still finding *no* kin . . . you'll be
     'bro-kin'.*
Now here's the race of men you'll find in Epidamnus:
The greatest libertines, the greatest drinkers too,
The most bamboozlers and charming flatterers   260
Live in this city. And as for wanton women, well—
Nowhere in the world, I'm told, are they more dazzling.
Because of this, they call the city Epidamnus,
For no one leaves unscathed, 'undamaged', as it were.*
MENAECHMUS II. Oh, I'll have to watch for that. Give me the
     purse.
MESSENIO. What for?
MENAECHMUS II.   Because your words make me afraid
     of you.
MESSENIO. Of me?
MENAECHMUS II.   That you might cause . . . Epidamnation
     for me.

You love the ladies quite a lot, Messenio.
And I'm a temperamental man, extremely wild.
If I can hold the cash, it's best for both of us.   270
Then you can do no wrong, and I can't yell at you.

MESSENIO [*giving the purse*]. Take it, sir, and guard it; you'll
be doing me a favour.

Re-enter cook CYLINDRUS, *his basket full of goodies*

CYLINDRUS. I've shopped quite well, and just the sort of things
I like.
I know I'll serve a lovely dinner to the diners.
But look—I see Menaechmus. Now my back is dead!*
The dinner guests are strolling right outside our door
Before I even finish shopping. Well, I'll speak.

[*Going up to* MENAECHMUS II

Menaechmus, sir . . .

MENAECHMUS II. God love you—God knows who you are.

CYLINDRUS [*thinks it's a joke*]. Who am I? Did you really say
you don't know me?

MENAECHMUS II. By Hercules, I don't.

CYLINDRUS.   Where are the other guests?   280

MENAECHMUS II. What kind of other guests?

CYLINDRUS.   Your parasite, that is.

MENAECHMUS II. My parasite? [*To* MESSENIO] The man is
simply raving mad.

MESSENIO. I *told* you there were great bamboozlers in this
town.

MENAECHMUS II [*to* CYLINDRUS, *playing it cool*]. Which
parasite of mine do you intend, young man?

CYLINDRUS. The Sponge.

MENAECHMUS II [*jocular, points to luggage*]. Indeed, my
sponge is here inside my bag.

CYLINDRUS. Menaechmus, you've arrived too early for the
dinner.
Look, I've just returned from shopping.

MENAECHMUS II.   Please, young man,
What kind of prices do you pay for sacred pigs,*
The sacrificial kind?

CYLINDRUS.   Not much.

MENAECHMUS II.   Then take this coin,   290
And sacrifice to purify your mind at my expense.
Because I'm quite convinced you're absolutely raving mad
To bother me, an unknown man who doesn't know you.

CYLINDRUS. You don't recall my name? Cylindrus, sir,
    Cylindrus!

MENAECHMUS II. Cylindrical or Cubical, just go away.
Not only don't I know you, I don't *want* to know you.

CYLINDRUS. Your name's Menaechmus, sir, correct?

MENAECHMUS II.   As far as *I* know.
You're sane enough to call me by my rightful name.
But tell me how you know me.

CYLINDRUS.   How I know you? . . . *Sir*—
[*Discreetly, but pointedly*] You have a mistress . . . she owns
    me . . . Erotium?   300

MENAECHMUS II. By Hercules, I haven't—and I don't know
    you.

CYLINDRUS. You don't know me, a man who many countless
    times
Refilled your bowl when you were at our house?

MESSENIO.   Bad luck!
I haven't got a single thing to break the fellow's skull with.
[*To* CYLINDRUS] Refilled the bowl? The bowl of one who
    till this day
Had never been in Epidamnus?

CYLINDRUS [*to* MENAECHMUS II]. You deny it?

MENAECHMUS II. By Hercules, I do.

CYLINDRUS [*points across stage*]. And I suppose that house
Is not your house?

MENAECHMUS II.   God damn the people living there!

CYLINDRUS [*to audience*]. Why, *he's* the raving lunatic—he
    cursed himself!   310
Menaechmus—

MENAECHMUS II. Yes, what is it?

CYLINDRUS.   Do take my advice,
And use that coin you promised me a while ago,
And since, by Hercules, you're certainly not sane,
I mean, Menaechmus, since you just now cursed yourself—
Go sacrifice that sacred pig to cure yourself.

MENAECHMUS II. By Hercules, you talk a lot—and you annoy
    me.
CYLINDRUS [embarrassed, to audience]. He acts this way a
    lot with me—he jokes around.
    He can be very funny if his wife is gone.
    [To MENAECHMUS] But now, what do you say?
MENAECHMUS II.   To what?
CYLINDRUS [showing basket].   Is this enough?
    I think I've shopped for three of you. Do I need more   320
    For you, your parasite, your girl?
MENAECHMUS II.   What girls? What girls?
    What parasites are you discussing?
MESSENIO [to CYLINDRUS].   And what madness
    Has caused you to be such a nuisance?
CYLINDRUS [to MESSENIO].   What do you want now?
    I don't know you. I'm chatting with a man I know.
MESSENIO [to CYLINDRUS]. By Pollux, it's for sure you're not
    exactly sane.   325
CYLINDRUS [abandons the discussion]. Well then, I guess I'll
    stew these up. No more delay.
    Now don't you wander off too far from here.
    [bowing to MENAECHMUS]. Your humble servant.
MENAECHMUS II [half aside]. If you were, I'd crucify you!
CYLINDRUS. Oh, take a cross yourself—cross over and come
    in—
    Whilst I apply Vulcanic arts to all the party's parts.*   330
    I'll go inside and tell Erotium you're here.
    Then she'll convince you you'll be comfier inside.
                                                        [Exit
MENAECHMUS II [stage whisper to MESSENIO]. Well—has he
    gone?
MESSENIO. He has.
MENAECHMUS II.   Those weren't lies you told.
    There's truth in every word of yours.
MESSENIO [his shrewd conclusion].   Here's what I think:
    I think the woman living here's some sort of slut.   335
    That's what I gathered from that maniac who left.
MENAECHMUS II. And yet I wonder how that fellow knew my
    name.

MESSENIO. Well, I don't wonder. Wanton women have this
    way:
  They send their servants or their maids to port   340
  To see if some new foreign ship's arrived in port.
  To ask around, 'Where are they from? What are their
    names?'
  Right afterward, they fasten on you hard and fast.
  They tease you, then they squeeze you dry and send you
    home.
  Right now, I'd say a pirate ship is in *this* port
  And I would say we'd better both beware of it.   345
MENAECHMUS II. By Hercules, you warn me well.
MESSENIO.   I'll know I have
  If you stay well aware and *show* I've warned you well.
MENAECHMUS II. Be quiet for a minute now; the door just
    creaked.
  Let's see who comes out now.
MESSENIO.   I'll put the luggage down.
  [*To the sailors*]. Me hearties, if you please, please guard
    this stuff for us.   350

    EROTIUM *appears, in a romantic mood, singing*

EROTIUM.

    Open my doors, let my welcome be wide,
      Then hurry and scurry—get ready inside.
See that the incense is burning, the couches have covers.
    Alluring decor is exciting for lovers.
Lovers love loveliness, we don't complain; their loss is our
    gain.
  But the cook says someone was out here—[*looks*] I see!
It's that man of great worth—who's worth so much to me.
  I ought to greet him richly—as he well deserves to be.

Now I'll go near, and let him know I'm here.   360

[*To* MENAECHMUS]. My darling-darling, it's a mite amazing
To see you standing out-of-doors by open doors.
You know full well how very much my house is yours.
All you ordered we're supplied with,

All your wishes are complied with.
So why stay here, why delay here? Come inside with . . . me.
Since dinner's ready, come and dine,   367
As soon as suits you, come . . . recline.   368

> [*To say the very least*, MENAECHMUS II *is*
> *stunned. After a slight pause, he regains his*
> *powers of speech*

MENAECHMUS II [*to* MESSENIO]. Who's this woman talking
   to?
EROTIUM. To you.
MENAECHMUS II. To me?
   What have we—?
EROTIUM. By Pollux, you're the only one of all my lovers 370
   Venus wants me to arouse to greatness. You deserve it,
      too.
   For, by Castor, thanks to all your gifts, I've flourished like
      a flower.
MENAECHMUS II [*aside to* MESSENIO]. She is surely very mad
   or very drunk, Messenio.
   Speaking to a total stranger like myself so . . . sociably.
MESSENIO. Didn't I predict all this? Why, these are only falling
   leaves.
   Wait three days and I predict the trees themselves will drop
      on you.
   Wanton women are this way, whenever they can sniff some
      silver.
   Anyway, I'll speak to her. [*To* EROTIUM] Hey, woman—
      there.
EROTIUM [*with hauteur*]. Yes, can I help you?
MESSENIO. Tell me where you know this man from.
EROTIUM.   Where? Where he knows *me* for years.
   Epidamnus.
MESSENIO.   Epidamnus, where he's never set a foot,   380
   Never been until today?
EROTIUM [*laughing*].   Aha—you're making jokes with me.
   Dear Menaechmus, come inside, you'll see that things . . .
      will pick up right.
MENAECHMUS II [*to* MESSENIO]. Pollux, look, the creature
   called me by my rightful name as well.

How I wonder what it's all about.

MESSENIO.   The perfume from your purse.

That's the answer.

MENAECHMUS II.   And, by Pollux, you did warn me
rightfully.   385

                                  [*Gives purse back to* MESSENIO

Take it then. I'll find out if she loves my person or my
purse.

EROTIUM. Let's go in, let's dine.

MENAECHMUS II [*declining*].   That's very nice of you.

                                  Thanks just the same.

EROTIUM. Why on earth did you command a dinner just a
while ago?

MENAECHMUS II. I commanded dinner?

EROTIUM.   Yes. For you, and for your parasite.

MENAECHMUS II. What the devil parasite? [*Aside*] This woman's
certainly insane.   390

EROTIUM. Your old sponge, Peniculus.

MENAECHMUS II.   A sponge—to clean
your shoes, perhaps?

EROTIUM. No, of course—the one that came along with you
a while ago.

When you brought the dress you'd stolen from your wife
to give to me.

MENAECHMUS II. Are you sane? I gave a dress I'd stolen from
my wife to you?

[*To* MESSENIO]. Like some kind of horse this woman's fast
asleep still standing up.   395

EROTIUM. Do you get some pleasure making fun of me,
denying things,

Things completely true?

MENAECHMUS II.   What do you claim I've done
that I deny?

EROTIUM. Robbed your wife and gave the dress to me.

MENAECHMUS II.   *That* I'll deny again!

Never have I had or do I have a wife, and never have I

Ever set a single foot inside that door, since I was born.   400

I had dinner on my ship, then disembarked and met you—

EROTIUM.   Oooh!

Pity me—what shall I do? What ship is this?

MENAECHMUS II.   A wooden one,
Much repaired, re-sailed, re-beamed, re-hammered and re-
    nailed and such.
Never did a navy have so numerous a nail supply.

EROTIUM. Please, my sweet, let's stop the jokes and go inside
    together . . . mmmm?   405

MENAECHMUS II. Woman, you want someone else. I mean
    . . . I'm sure you don't want me.

EROTIUM. Don't I know you well, Menaechmus, know your
    father's name was Moschus?
You were born, or so they say, in Syracuse, in Sicily,
Where Agathocles was king, and then in turn, King Phintia,* 409–10
Thirdly, King Liparo, after whom King Hiero got the crown.
Now it's still King Hiero.

MENAECHMUS II [to MESSENIO]. Say, that's not inaccurate.

MESSENIO.   By Jove—
If she's not from Syracuse, how does she know the facts so
    well?

MENAECHMUS II [getting excited]. Hercules, I shouldn't keep
    refusing her.

MESSENIO.   Oh, don't you dare!
Go inside that door and you're a goner, sir.

MENAECHMUS II.   Now you shut up!
Things are going well. Whatever she suggests—I'll just
    agree.
Why not get a little . . . hospitality? [to EROTIUM] Dear lady,
    please—
I was impolite a while ago. I was a bit afraid that   419–20
[indicating MESSENIO] He might go and tell my wife . . .
    about the dress . . . . about the dinner.
Now, when you would like, we'll go inside.

EROTIUM.   But where's the parasite?

MENAECHMUS II. I don't give a damn. Why should we wait
    for him? Now if he comes,
Don't let him inside at all.

EROTIUM.   By Castor, I'll be happy not to.
Yet [playfully] there's something I would like from you.

MENAECHMUS II.   Your wish is my command.

EROTIUM. Bring the dress you gave me to the Phrygian
    embroiderer.

Have him redesign it, add some other frills I'd like him to.

MENAECHMUS II. Hercules, a good idea. Because of all the decoration,

When my wife observes you in the street, she won't know what you're wearing.

EROTIUM. Therefore take it with you when you leave.

MENAECHMUS II. Of course, of course, of course. 430

EROTIUM. Let's go in.

MENAECHMUS II. I'll follow you. [Indicates MESSENIO]
I want a little chat with him.
[Exit EROTIUM

Hey, Messenio, come here!

MESSENIO. What's up?

MENAECHMUS II. Just hop to my command.

MESSENIO. Can I help?

MENAECHMUS II. You can. [Apologetically] I know you'll criticize—

MESSENIO. Then all the worse.

MENAECHMUS II. Booty's in my hands. A fine beginning. You continue, fast—

Take these fellows [indicating sailors] back to our lodging tavern, quicker than a wink,

Then be sure you come to pick me up before the sun goes down.

MESSENIO [protesting]. Master, you don't know about these sluts—

MENAECHMUS II. Be quiet! Just obey.

If I do a stupid thing, then I'll be hurting, not yourself.

Here's a woman stupid and unwitting, from what I've just seen. 440

Here's some booty we can keep.

MESSENIO. I'm lost. [Looks] Oh, has he gone? He's lost!

Now a mighty pirate ship is towing off a shipwrecked skiff.

I'm the fool as well. I tried to argue down the man who owns me.

But he bought me only as a sounding board, not to sound off.

Follow me, you men [to the sailors], so I can come on time—as I've been ordered.

[They exit

Stage empty for a moment [musical interlude?].
Enter PENICULUS—*all upset*

PENICULUS. More than thirty years I'm on this earth and
during all that time
Never till today have I done such a damned and dopey
deed!
Here I had immersed my whole attention in a public
meeting.
While I stood there gaping, that Menaechmus simply stole
away,
Went off to his mistress, I suppose, and didn't want me
there.   450
Curse the man who was the first to manufacture public
meetings,
All designed to busy men already busy with their business.
They should choose the men who have no occupation for
these things,
Who, if absent when they're called, would face fantastic
fines—and fast.
Why, there's simply gobs of men who only eat just once a
day,
Who have nothing else to do; they don't invite, they're not
invited.
Make *these* people spend their time at public meetings and
assemblies.
If this were the case today, I'd not have lost my lovely
feast.   460
Sure as I'm alive, that man had really wished to feed me
well.
Anyhow, I'll go. The thought of scraps left over lights my
soul.
But—what's this? Menaechmus with a garland, coming from
the house?
Party's over, I'm arriving just in time to be too late!
First, I'll spy how he behaves and then I'll go accost the
man.

MENAECHMUS II *wobbles happily out of*
EROTIUM'*s house, wearing a garland, and carrying*
the dress earlier delivered by his brother

MENAECHMUS II [*to* EROTIUM]. Now, now, relax, you'll get
    this dress today for sure,
Returned on time, with lovely new embroidery.
I'll make the old dress vanish—it just won't be seen.

PENICULUS [*indignant, to the audience*]. He'll decorate the
    dress now that the dinner's done,
The wine's been drunk, the parasite left in the cold.   470
No, Hercules, I'm not myself, if not revenged,
If I don't curse him out in style. Just watch me now.

MENAECHMUS II [*drunk with joy—and a few other things*]. By 473-4
    all the gods, what man in just a single day
Received more pleasures, though expecting none at all:
I've wined, I've dined, I've concubined, and robbed her
    blind—
No one but me will own this dress after today!

PENICULUS. I just can't bear to hide and hear him prate like
    this.
Smug and satisfied, he prates about *my* party.

MENAECHMUS II. She says I gave her this—and tells me that
    I stole it.   480
I stole it from my *wife*! [*Confidentially*] I knew the girl was
    wrong,
Yet I pretended there was some affair between us two.
Whatever she proposed, I simply said, 'Yes, yes,
Exactly, what you say.' What need of many words?
I've never had more fun at less expense to me.

PENICULUS. Now I'll accost the man, and make an awful
    fuss.

MENAECHMUS II. Now who's this fellow coming toward me?

PENICULUS [*in a fury*].   Well, speak up!
You lighter than a feather, dirty, rotten person,
You evil man, you tricky, worthless individual!
What did I ever do to you that you'd destroy me?   490
You stole away from me, when we were in the forum;
You dealt a death blow to the dinner in my absence!

How could you dare? Why, I deserved an equal part!

MENAECHMUS II. Young man, please indicate precisely what
   you want from me.

And why you're cursing someone you don't know at all.

Your dressing-down of me deserves a beating-up!

PENICULUS. By Pollux, you're the one who beat me out, just
   now.

MENAECHMUS II. Now please, young man, do introduce
   yourself at least.

PENICULUS. And now insult to injury! You don't know *me*?

MENAECHMUS II. By Pollux, no, I don't, as far as I can tell. 500
   I've never seen you, never met you. Whoever you are—

At least behave, and don't be such a nuisance to me.

PENICULUS. Wake up, Menaechmus!

MENAECHMUS II.   I'm awake—it seems to me.

PENICULUS. And you don't recognize me?

MENAECHMUS II.   Why should I deny it?

PENICULUS. Don't recognize your parasite?

MENAECHMUS II.   My dear young man,

It seems to me your brain is not so very sane.

PENICULUS. Just answer this: did you not steal that dress
   today?

It was your wife's. You gave it to Erotium.

MENAECHMUS II. By Hercules, I have no wife. Erotium?

I gave her nothing, didn't steal this dress. You're mad. 510

PENICULUS [*to audience*]. Total disaster! [*To* MENAECHMUS
   II] But I saw you wear that dress

And, wearing it, I saw you leave your house.

MENAECHMUS II.   Drop dead!

You think all men are fags because *you* are?

You claim I actually put on a woman's dress!

PENICULUS. By Hercules, I do.

MENAECHMUS II.   Oh, go where you belong!

Get purified or something, raving lunatic!

PENICULUS. By Pollux, all the begging in the world won't
   keep me

From telling every single detail to your wife.

Then all these present insults will rebound on you. 520

You've gobbled up my dinner—and I'll be revenged!

[He storms into MENAECHMUS' *house*

MENAECHMUS II. What's going on? Everyone I run across
Makes fun of me . . . but why? Oh, wait, the door just
creaked.

Enter EROTIUM'S MAID, *a sexy little thing.*
She carries a bracelet

MAID. Menaechmus, your Erotium would love a favour—
Please, while you're at it, take this to the goldsmith for her 525
And have him add about an extra . . . ounce . . . of gold,
So that the bracelet is remodelled, shining new.

MENAECHMUS II [*ironically*]. I'm happy to take care of both
these things for her,
And any other thing that she'd like taken care of.

MAID. You recognize the bracelet?

MENAECHMUS II.   Uh—I know it's gold.   530

MAID. This very bracelet long ago was once your wife's,
And secretly you snatched it from her jewel box.

MENAECHMUS II. By Hercules, I never did.

MAID.   You don't recall?
Return the bracelet, if you don't remember.

MENAECHMUS II.   Wait!
I'm starting to remember. Why, of course I gave it.   535
Now where are those two armlets that I gave as well?

MAID. You never did.

MENAECHMUS II.   Of course, by Pollux—this was all.

MAID. Will you take care of things?

MENAECHMUS II [*ironically*].   I said I'd take good care.
I'll see that dress and bracelet are both carried back together. 539 –

MAID [*the total coquette*]. And, dear Menaechmus, how about 40
a gift for me?
Let's say four drachmae's worth of jingly earrings?
Then when you visit us, I'll really welcome you.

MENAECHMUS II. Of course. Give me the gold, I'll pay the
labour costs.

MAID. Advance it for me, afterwards I'll pay you back.

MENAECHMUS II. No, you advance it, afterwards I'll double
it.

MAID. I haven't got it.

MENAECHMUS II.   If you ever get it—give it.

MAID [*frustrated, she bows*]. I'm at your service.

[*Exit*

MENAECHMUS II.   I'll take care of all of this
As soon as possible, at any cost—I'll sell them.
Now has she gone? She's gone and closed the door behind
     her.   550
The gods have fully fostered me and favoured me unfailingly!
But why do I delay? Now is the perfect chance,
The perfect time to flee this prostitutish place.
Now rush, Menaechmus, lift your foot and lift the pace!
I'll take this garland off, and toss it to the left,
So anyone who follows me will think I'm thataway.
I'll go at once and find my slave, if possible,
And tell him everything the gods have given me today.*

[*Exit*

From MENAECHMUS' *house enter* PENICULUS
and MENAECHMUS' *wife*

WIFE [*melodramatic, a big sufferer*]. Must I keep suffering
     this mischief in my marriage?
Where husband sneaks and steals whatever's in the house 560
And takes it to his mistress?

PENICULUS.   Can't you quiet down?
You'll catch him in the act, if you just follow me.
He's drunk and garlanded—at the embroiderer's,
Conveying that same dress he stole from you today.
Look—there's the garland. Do I tell you lies or truth?
He's gone in that direction; you can follow clues.
But wait—what perfect luck—he's come back right now!
Without the dress.

WIFE.   What should I do? How should I act with him?

PENICULUS. The very same as always: make him miserable.
But let's step over here—and spread a net for him.   570

Enter MENAECHMUS I

MENAECHMUS [*singing*]. We have this tradition, we have this
     tradition,*
An irksome tradition, and yet it's the best

Who love this tradition much more than the rest.
They want lots of clients, all want lots of clients.
Who cares if they're honest or not—are they rich?
Who cares if they're honest, we'll take them with zest—
    If they're rich.

If he's poor but he's honest—who cares for him?
He's dishonest but rich? Then we all say our prayers for
    him.
So it happens that lawless, corrupting destroyers   580
    Have overworked lawyers.
Denying what's done and delivered, this grasping and
    fraudulent sort
Though their fortunes arise from exorbitant lies
    They're all anxious to step into court.*   584a
When the day comes, it's hell for their lawyer as well,
For we have to defend things unjust and unpretty
To jury, to judge, or judicial committee.

So I just was delayed, forced to give legal aid, no evading
    this client of mine who had found me.
I wanted to do you know what—and with whom—but he
    bound me and tied ropes around me.
Facing the judges just now, I had countless despicable deeds
    to defend.   590
Twisting torts with contortions of massive proportions,
I pleaded and pleaded right down to the end.
But just when an out-of-court settlement seemed to be
    sealed—*my client appealed!*
I never had seen someone more clearly caught in the act:
For each of his crimes there were three who could speak to
    the fact!

        By all the heavens, cursed be he
        Who just destroyed this day for me.   596
        And curse me too, a fool today,
        For ever heading forum's way.   597
        The greatest day of all—destroyed.
        The feast prepared, but not enjoyed   598

The wench was waiting too, indeed.
The very moment I was freed   599
I left the forum with great speed.
She's angry now, I'm sure of it.   600
The dress I gave will help a bit,

Taken from my wife today . . . a token for Erotium.

> [*A pause.* MENAECHMUS *catches his breath, still not noticing his* WIFE *or the* PARASITE, *who now speaks*

PENICULUS. Well, what say you to that?

WIFE.   That I've married a rat.

PENICULUS. Have you heard quite enough to complain to him?

WIFE. Quite enough.

MENAECHMUS.   Now I'll go where the pleasures will flow.

PENICULUS. No, remain. Let's be flowing some *pain* to him.

WIFE. You'll be paying off at quite a rate for this!

PENICULUS [*to wife*].   Good, good attack!

WIFE. Do you have the nerve to think you'd get away with secret smuggling?

MENAECHMUS. What's the matter, Wife?

WIFE.   You're asking me?

MENAECHMUS [*indicating* PENICULUS]. Should I ask him instead?

WIFE. Don't turn on the charm.

PENICULUS.   That's it!

MENAECHMUS.   But tell me what I've done to you. Why are you so angry?

WIFE.   You should know.

PENICULUS.   He knows—and can't disguise it.

MENAECHMUS. What's the matter?

WIFE.   Just a dress.

MENAECHMUS.   A dress?

WIFE.   A dress.

PENICULUS [*to* MENAECHMUS].   Aha, you're scared.

MENAECHMUS. What could I be scared of?

PENICULUS.   Of a dress—and of a dressing-down. 610
You'll be sorry for that secret feast. [*To* WIFE] Go on, attack again!

MENAECHMUS. You be quiet.

PENICULUS. No, I won't. He's nodding to me not to speak.

MENAECHMUS. Hercules, I've never nodded to you, never winked at you! 613

PENICULUS. Nothing could be bolder: he denies it while he's doing it!

MENAECHMUS. By Jove and all the gods I swear—is that enough for you, dear Wife?—

Never did I nod to him.

PENICULUS [*sarcastically*]. Oh, she believes you. Now go back!

MENAECHMUS. Go back to what?

PENICULUS. Go back to the embroiderer's—and get the dress!!

MENAECHMUS. Get what dress?

PENICULUS. I won't explain, since he forgets his own . . . affairs. 619

WIFE. What a woeful wife I am.

MENAECHMUS [*playing very naïve*]. Woeful wife? Do tell me why? 614

Has a servant misbehaved, or has a maid talked back to you? 620

Tell me, dear, we'll punish misbehavers.

WIFE. Oh, is *that* a joke.

MENAECHMUS. You're so angry. I don't like to see you angry.

WIFE. *That's* a joke!

MENAECHMUS. Someone from the household staff has angered you.

WIFE. Another joke!

MENAECHMUS. Well, of course, it isn't me.

WIFE. Aha! At last he's stopped the jokes!

MENAECHMUS. Certainly I haven't misbehaved.

WIFE. He's making jokes again!

MENAECHMUS. Tell me, dear, what's ailing you?

PENICULUS. He's giving you a lovely line.

MENAECHMUS. Why do you annoy me? Did I talk to you?

[*Throws a punch at* PENICULUS

WIFE [*to* MENAECHMUS]. Don't raise your hand!

PENICULUS [*to* WIFE]. Let him have it! [*To* MENAECHMUS] Now go eat your little feast while I'm not there.

    Go get drunk, put on a garland, stand outside, and mock
    me now!

MENAECHMUS. Pollux! I've not eaten any feast today—or been
    in there.   630

PENICULUS. You deny it?

MENAECHMUS.   I deny it all.

PENICULUS.   No man could be more brazen.
    Didn't I just see you here, all garlanded, a while ago?
    Standing here and shouting that my brain was not exactly
    sane?
    And you didn't know me—you were just a stranger here in
    town!

MENAECHMUS. I've been absolutely absent, since the second
    we set out.

PENICULUS. I know you. You didn't think that I could get
    revenge on you.
    All has been recounted to your wife.

MENAECHMUS.   What 'all'?

PENICULUS.   Oh, I don't know.
    Ask her for yourself.

MENAECHMUS.   Dear Wife, what fables has this man
    been telling?
    What's the matter? Why are you so silent? Tell me.

WIFE.   You're pretending,*
    Asking what you know.

MENAECHMUS.   Why do I ask, then?

PENICULUS.   What an evil man! 640
    How he fakes. But you can't hide it, now the whole affair
    is out.
    Everything's been publicized by me.

MENAECHMUS.   But *what*?

WIFE.   Have you no shame?
    Can't you tell the truth yourself? Attend me and please pay
    attention:
    I will now inform you what he told, and why I'm angry at
    you.
    There's a dress been snatched from me.

MENAECHMUS.   There's a dress been snatched from me?

PENICULUS. Not from *you*, from *her*. [*To* WIFE] The evil man
    resorts to every dodge.

[*To* MENAECHMUS] If the dress were snatched from you, it *really* would be lost to us.

MENAECHMUS. You're not anything to me. [*To* WIFE] Go on, my dear.

WIFE.   A dress is gone.

MENAECHMUS. Oh—who snatched it?

WIFE.   Pollux; who'd know better than the man himself?

MENAECHMUS. Who is this?

WIFE.   His name's Menaechmus.

MENAECHMUS.   Pollux, what an evil deed! 650
What Menaechmus could it be?

WIFE.   Yourself.

MENAECHMUS.   Myself?

WIFE.   Yourself.

MENAECHMUS.   Who says?

WIFE. *I* do.

PENICULUS. I do, too. And then you gave it to Erotium.

MENAECHMUS. *I* did?

WIFE.   You, you, you!

PENICULUS.   Say, would you like an owl for a pet—
Just to parrot 'you you you'? The both of us are all worn out.

MENAECHMUS. By Jove and all the gods, I swear—is that enough for you, dear Wife?—
No, I didn't give it to her.*

PENICULUS.   No, we know *we* tell the truth.

MENAECHMUS [*backing down*]. Well . . . that is to say . . . I didn't *give* the dress. I loaned it to her.

WIFE. Oh, by Castor, do I give your tunics or your clothes away—
Even as a loan? A woman can give women's clothes away. Men can give their own. *Now will you get that dress back home to me?* 660

MENAECHMUS [*cowed*]. Yes, I'll . . . get it back.

WIFE.   I'd say you'd better get it back, or else. Only with that dress in hand will you re-enter your own house.
Now I'm going in.

PENICULUS [*to* WIFE]. But what of me—what thanks for all my help?

WIFE [*sweetly bitchy*]. I'll be glad to help you out—when
someone steals a dress from you.

PENICULUS. That'll never happen. I don't own a single thing
to steal.

Wife and husband—curse you both. I'll hurry to the forum
now.

I can very clearly see I've been expelled from this whole
house.

[*He storms off*

MENAECHMUS. Hah—my wife thinks that she hurts me, when
she shuts the door on me.

But, as far as entering, I've got another, better place.

[*To* WIFE'*s door*] You don't like me. I'll live through it
since Erotium here does.   670

She won't close me out, she'll close me tightly in her arms,
she will.

I'll go beg the wench to give me back the dress I just now
gave,

Promising another, better one. [*Knocks*] Is there a doorman
here?

Open up! And someone ask Erotium to step outside.

EROTIUM *steps outside her house*

EROTIUM. Who has asked for me?

MENAECHMUS.   A man who loves you
more than his own self.

EROTIUM. Dear Menaechmus, why stand here outside? Come
in.

MENAECHMUS. Wait just a minute.

Can you guess what brings me here?

EROTIUM.   I know—you'd like some . . . joy with me.

MENAECHMUS. Well . . . indeed, by Pollux. But—that dress I
gave to you just now.

Please return it, since my wife's discovered all in full detail.

I'll replace it with a dress that's twice the price, and as you
like it.   680

EROTIUM. But I gave it to you for embroidery a moment
back,

With a bracelet you would bring the goldsmith for re-
modelling.

MENAECHMUS. What—you gave me dress and bracelet? No,
you'll find that isn't true.

No—I first gave *you* the dress, then went directly to the
forum.

Now's the very second I've returned.

EROTIUM.   Aha—I see what's up.

Just because I put them in your hands—you're out to swindle
me.

MENAECHMUS. Swindle you? By Pollux, no! Why, didn't I
just tell you why?

Everything's discovered by my wife!

EROTIUM [*exasperated*].   I didn't ask you for it.

No, you brought it to me of your own free will—and as a
gift.

Now you want the dress right back. Well, have it, take it,
wear it!   690

You can wear it, or your wife—or lock it in your money
box.

But from this day on you'll never set a foot inside my
house.

After all my loyal service, suddenly you find me hateful,

So you'll only have me now by laying cash right on the
line.

Find yourself some other girl to cheat the way you've cheated
me!

MENAECHMUS. Hercules, the woman's angry! Hey—please
wait, please listen to me—

                              [EROTIUM *exits, slamming her door*

Please come back! Please stay—oh, won't you do this favour
for me?

Well, she's gone—and closed the door. I'm universally kicked
out.*

Neither wife nor mistress will believe a single thing I say.

What to do? I'd better go consult some friends on what
they think.   700

                              [*Exit* MENAECHMUS

A slight pause [musical interlude?]. Then enter
MENAECHMUS II *from the opposite side of the
stage. He still carries the dress*

MENAECHMUS II. I was a fool a while ago to give that purse
  With all that cash to someone like Messenio.
  I'm sure by now the fellow's 'oozing' in some dive.

WIFE *enters from her house*

WIFE. I'll stand on watch to see how soon my husband comes.
  Why, here he is—I'm saved! He's bringing back the dress.

MENAECHMUS II. I wonder where Messenio has wandered
  to....

WIFE. I'll go and greet the man with words that he deserves.
  [*To* MENAECHMUS II] Tell me—are you not ashamed to
  show your face,
  Atrocious man—and with that dress?

MENAECHMUS II.   I beg your pardon,
  What seems to be the trouble, madam?

WIFE.   Shame on you!   710
  You dare to mutter, dare to speak a word to me?

MENAECHMUS II. Whatever have I done that would forbid
  my talking?

WIFE. You're asking me? Oh, shameless, brazen, wicked man!

MENAECHMUS II [*with quiet sarcasm*]. Madam, do you have
  any notion why the Greeks
  Referred to Hecuba as ... female dog?

WIFE.   I don't.

MENAECHMUS II. Because she acted just the way you're acting
  now.
  She barked and cursed at everyone who came in sight,
  And thus the people rightly called her ... female dog.

WIFE. I simply can't endure all this disgracefulness—
  I'd even rather live my life ... a divorcée   720
  Than bear the brunt of this disgracefulness of yours.

MENAECHMUS II. What's it to me if you can't stand your
  married life—
  Or ask for a divorce? Is it a custom here
  To babble to all foreigners who come to town?

WIFE. 'To babble'? I won't stand for that. I won't! I won't!
  I'll die a divorcée before I'd live with you.

MENAECHMUS II. As far as I'm concerned you can divorce
  yourself,

And stay a divorcée till Jupiter resigns his throne.

WIFE. Look—you denied you stole that dress a while ago,
And now you wave it at me. Aren't you ashamed?   730

MENAECHMUS II. By Hercules, you are a wild and wicked
woman!

You dare to claim this dress I hold was stolen from you?
Another woman gave it to me for . . . repairs.

WIFE. By Castor—no, I'd better have my father come,
So I can tell him all of your disgracefulness.

[*Calls in to one of her slaves*] Oh, Decio—go find my
father, bring him here.
And tell my father the entire situation.

[*To* MENAECHMUS II]. I'll now expose all your disgracefulness.

MENAECHMUS II. You're sick!
All what disgracefulness?

WIFE.   A dress—and golden bracelet.
You rob your legal wife at home and then you go   740
Bestow it on your mistress. Do I 'babble' truth?

MENAECHMUS II. Dear Madam, can you tell me please what
I might drink
To make your bitchy boorishness more bearable?
I've not the slightest notion who you think I am.
I know you like I know the father-in-law of Hercules!*   745

WIFE. You may mock me, by Pollux, but you can't mock
him.
My father's coming. [*To* MENAECHMUS II] Look who's
coming, look who's coming;
You do know *him*.

MENAECHMUS II [*ironically*]. Of course, a friend of Agamemnon.*
I first met him the day I first met you—*today*.

WIFE. You claim that you don't know me, or my father?   750

MENAECHMUS II. And how about your grandpa—I don't know
him either.

WIFE. By Castor, you just never change, *you never change!*
                    [*Enter the* OLD MAN, MENAECHMUS' *father-
                    in-law, groaning and wheezing*

OLD MAN [*to the audience, in halting song*].

Oh, my old age, my old age, I lack what I need,
I'm stepping unlively, unfast is my speed,
But it isn't so easy, I tell you, not easy indeed.
For I've lost all my quickness, old age is a sickness.
My body's a big heavy trunk, I've no strength.
Oh oh, old age is bad—no more vigour remains.
Oh, when old age arrives, it brings plenty of pains.
I could mention them all but I won't talk at length.   760
But deep in my heart is this worry:
My daughter has sent for me now in a hurry.
She won't say what it is,
What it is I've not heard.
She just asked me to come, not explaining a word.

And yet I've a pretty good notion at that:
That her husband and she are involved in a spat.
Well, that's how it is always with big-dowry wives,*
They're fierce to their husbands, they order their lives.
But then sometimes the man is . . . let's say . . . not so pure.
There's limits to what a good wife can endure.
And, by Pollux, a daughter won't send for her dad.   770
Unless there's some cause, and her husband's been bad.
Well, anyway I can find out since my daughter is here.
Her husband looks angry. Just what I suspected, it's clear.   733-4

                    [*The song ends. A brief pause*

  I'll address her.
WIFE.   I'll go meet him. Many greetings, Father dear.
OLD MAN. Same to you. I only hope I've come when all is
    fine and dandy.
  Why are you so gloomy, why does he stand off there,
    looking angry?
  Has there been some little skirmishing between the two of
    you?
  Tell me who's at fault, be brief. No lengthy arguments at
    length.
WIFE. *I've* done nothing wrong, dear Father, you can be
    assured of that.   780
  But I simply can't go on and live with him in any way.
  Consequently—take me home.

OLD MAN.   What's wrong?

WIFE.   I'm made a total fool of.

OLD MAN. How and who?

WIFE.   By him, the man you signed and
  sealed to me as husband.

OLD MAN. Oh, I see, disputing, eh? And yet I've told you
  countless times
  Both of you beware, don't either one approach me with
  complaints.

WIFE. How can I beware, when he's as bad as this?

OLD MAN.   You're asking me?

WIFE. Tell me.

OLD MAN.   Oh, the countless times I've preached on duty
  to your husband:
  Don't check what he's doing, where he's going, what his
  business is.*

WIFE. But he loves a fancy woman right next door.

OLD MAN.   He's very wise! 790
  Thanks to all your diligence, I promise you, he'll love her
  more.

WIFE. But he also boozes there.

OLD MAN.   You think you'll make him booze the less,
  If he wants to, anywhere he wants? Why must you be so
  rash?
  Might as well go veto his inviting visitors to dine,
  Say he can't have guests at home. What do you women
  want from husbands?
  Servitude? Why, next you'll want him to do chores around
  the house!
  Next you'll order him to sit down with the maids and card
  the wool!

WIFE. Father dear, I called you to support my cause, not help
  my husband.
  You're a lawyer prosecuting your own client.

OLD MAN.   If *he's* wrong,
  I'll attack him ten times harder than I'm now attacking
  you.   800
  Look, you're quite well dressed, well jewelled and well
  supplied with food and maids.

Being well off, woman, why, be wise, leave well enough
    alone.

WIFE. But he filches all the jewels and all the dresses from the
    house.

Stealing on the sly, he then bestows the stuff on fancy
    women.

OLD MAN. Oh, he's wrong if he does that, but if he doesn't,
    then you're wrong,

Blaming blameless men.

WIFE.   He has a dress this very moment, Father,

And a bracelet he's brought from her because I've found
    him out.

OLD MAN. Well, I'll get the facts, I'll go accost the man, and
    speak to him.

               [*He puffs over to* MENAECHMUS II

Say, Menaechmus, tell me why you're muttering. I'll
    understand.

Why are you so gloomy? Why is she so angry over there? 810

MENAECHMUS II. Whatever your name is, old man, and
    whoever you are, I swear by Jove supreme,

Calling all the gods to witness—

OLD MAN.   Witness for what, about what in the world?

MENAECHMUS II. Never ever did I hurt this woman now
    accusing me of

Having sneaked into her house and filched this dress.

WIFE.   He's telling lies!

MENAECHMUS II. If I've ever set a single foot inside that house
    of hers,   815–16

Anxiously I long to be the very saddest man on earth.

OLD MAN. No, you can't be sane too long for that, to claim
    you've not set foot

In the house you live in. Why, you're the very *maddest*
    man on earth!

MENAECHMUS II. What was that, old man? You claim I live
    right here and in this house?   820

OLD MAN. You deny it?

MENAECHMUS II.   I deny it.

OLD MAN.   Your denial isn't true.

That's unless you moved away last night. Daughter, come
over here.

> [*Father and daughter walk aside;*
> OLD MAN *whispers confidentially*

Tell me—did you move away from here last night?

WIFE.   Where to? What for?

OLD MAN. *I* don't know, by Pollux.

WIFE.   He's just mocking you—or don't you get it?

OLD MAN. That's enough, Menaechmus, no more joking, now
let's tend to business.

MENAECHMUS II. Tell me, sir, what business do you have
with me? Just who *are* you?

What have I to do with you or—[*points to* WIFE] that one,
who is such a bother?

WIFE. Look—his eyes are getting green, a greenish colour's
now appearing

From his temples and his forehead. Look, his eyes are 829–30
flickering!

MENAECHMUS II [*aside, to the audience*]. Nothing could be
better. Since they both declare that I'm raving mad

I'll pretend I am insane, and scare them both away from
me.

> [MENAECHMUS *begins to 'go berserk'*

WIFE. What a gaping mouth, wide open. Tell me what to do,
dear Father.

OLD MAN. Over here, dear Daughter, get as far as possible
from him.

MENAECHMUS II [*caught up in his own act, 'hearing' divine
words*]. Bacchus! Yo-ho, Bacchus, in what forest do you
bid me hunt?

Yes, I hear you, but I can't escape from where I am just
now:

On my left I'm guarded by a very rabid female dog.

Right behind her is a goat who reeks of garlic, and this
goat has

Countless times accused a blameless citizen with perjury.*

OLD MAN [*enraged*]. You you you, I'll—

MENAECHMUS II [*'hearing'*]. What, Apollo? Now your oracle
  commands me: 840
  Take some hotly blazing torches, set this woman's eyes on
  fire.
WIFE. Father, Father—what a threat! He wants to set my
  eyes on fire!
MENAECHMUS II [*aside, to audience*]. They both say I'm crazy;
  I know they're the really crazy ones!
OLD MAN. Daughter—
WIFE.   Yes?
OLD MAN.   Suppose I go, and send some
  servants here at once.
  Let them come and take him off, and tie him up with ropes
  at home.
  Now—before he makes a bigger hurricane!
MENAECHMUS II.   I'm caught!
  I'll be taken off unless I find myself a plan right now.
  [*'Hearing oracle,' aloud*] Yes, Apollo, 'Do not spare thy
  fists in punching in her face?
  That's unless she hurries out of sight and quickly goes to
  hell!'
  Yes, Apollo, I'll obey you.
OLD MAN.   Run, dear Daughter—quickly home! 850
  Otherwise, he'll pound you.
WIFE.   While I run, please keep an eye on him.
  See he doesn't get away. [*A final groan*] What wifely woe
  to hear such things!
                                                    [*Exit*
MENAECHMUS II. Hah, not bad, I got *her* off. And now I'll
  get *this*—poisoned person,
  White-beard, palsied wreck. Tithonus was a youth compared
  to him.*
  [*To 'Apollo'*] What's my orders? Beat the fellow limb from
  limb and bone from bone?
  Use the very stick he carries for the job?
OLD MAN.   I'll punish you—
  If you try to touch me, if you try to get much closer to me!
MENAECHMUS II [*to 'Apollo'*]. Yes, I'll do thy bidding: take
  a double axe and this old fogey,
  Chop his innards into little pieces, till I reach the bone?

OLD MAN [*panicked*]. Goodness, now's the time for me to be
    on guard and very wary.   860

I'm afraid he'll carry out his threats and cause some harm
    to me.

MENAECHMUS II [*to 'Apollo' again*]. Dear Apollo, you com-
    mand so much. I now must hitch up horses,

Wild, ferocious horses, and then mount up in my chariot,

Then to trample on this lion—creaking, stinking, toothless
    lion?

Now I'm in the chariot, I've got the reins, I've got the
    whip.   865

Up up up, ye steeds, now let us see the sound of horses'
    hoofbeats.*

Quickly curve your course with splendid speed and swifty
    swoop of steps.

OLD MAN. Threatening me with hitched-up horses?

MENAECHMUS II.   Yea, Apollo, once again,

Now you bid me charge and overwhelm the man who's
    standing here.

[*Fakes Homeric divine intervention*] But what's this? Who
    takes me by the hair and hauls me from the car?*   870

Look, Apollo, someone's changing your command as spoke
    to me!

OLD MAN. By Hercules, he's sick, he's very sick. Ye gods!

And just a while ago, the man was very sane,

But suddenly this awful sickness fell on him.

I'll go and get a doctor—fast as possible.

                            [*Exit at a senile sprint*

MENAECHMUS II. Well, have they disappeared from sight, the
    two of them,

Who forced a normal, healthy man to act insane?

I shouldn't wait to reach my ship while things are safe.

[*To the audience*] But, everybody, please—if that old man 879–80
    returns,

Don't tell him, please, which street I took to get away.

               [*He dashes off-stage, toward the harbour*

      Enter OLD MAN,* *tired, annoyed, complaining*

OLD MAN. My limbs just ache from sitting and my eyes from
    looking,

While waiting for that doctor to leave office hours.
At last, unwillingly, he left his patients. What a bore!
He claims he'd set Asclepius' broken leg,
And then Apollo's broken arm. I wonder if
The man I bring's a doctor or a carpenter!
But here he's strutting now. [*Calling off*] Why can't you hurry up?

Enter DOCTOR, *the superprofessional*

DOCTOR [*right to the point*]. What sort of illness does he have? Speak up, old man.
Is he depressed, or is he frantic? Give the facts.*   890
Or is he in a coma? Has he liquid dropsy?
OLD MAN. But that's precisely why I've brought you—to tell *me*—
And make him well again.
DOCTOR.   Of course. A snap.
He shall be well again. You have my word on that.
OLD MAN. I want him to be cared for with the greatest care.
DOCTOR. I'll sigh a thousand sighs, I'll take great pains with him.
For you—I'll care for him with all the greatest care.
But here's the man himself; let's see how he behaves.

[*They step aside to eavesdrop*

From the forum side enter MENAECHMUS,
addressing himself in soliloquy

MENAECHMUS. Pollux, what a day for me: perverted and inverted too.
Everything I plotted to be private's now completely public. 900
My own parasite has filled me full of fearful accusations!
My Ulysses, causing so much trouble for his royal patron!*
If I live, I'll skin him live. I'll cut off all his livelihood.
What a foolish thing to say. What I call his is really mine.
My own food and fancy living nurtured him. I'll starve him now.
And my slut has been disgraceful. Typical of slutitude.
All I did was ask her to return the dress to give my wife.
She pretends she gave it to me. Pollux, I'm in awful shape!

OLD MAN [*To* DOCTOR]. Did you hear his words?

DOCTOR [*nods*].   Admits his 'awful shape'.

OLD MAN.   Go up to him.

DOCTOR [*aloud*]. Greetings, dear Menaechmus. Do you realize
    that your cloak has slipped   910
  Don't you know how dangerous that sort of thing is for
  your health?

MENAECHMUS. Why not hang yourself?

OLD MAN [*whispers to* DOCTOR].   You notice anything?

DOCTOR.   Of course I do!
  This condition couldn't be relieved with tons of hellebore.
  [*To* MENAECHMUS, *again*]. Tell me now, Menaechmus.

MENAECHMUS.   Tell what?

DOCTOR.   Just answer what I ask.
  Do you drink white wine or red?

MENAECHMUS.   And why don't you go straight to hell?

DOCTOR. Hercules, I notice teeny traces of insanity.

MENAECHMUS.   Why not ask
  Do I favour purple bread, or pink or maybe even mauve?
  Do I eat the gills of birds, the wings of fishes—?

OLD MAN.   Oh, good grief!
  Listen to his ravings, you can hear the words. Why wait at   919–20
  all?
  Give the man some remedy before the madness takes him
  fully.

DOCTOR. Wait—I have more questions.

OLD MAN.   But you're killing him with all this blab!

DOCTOR [*to* MENAECHMUS]. Tell me this about your eyes: at
  times do they get glazed at all?

MENAECHMUS. What? You think you're talking to a lobster,
  do you, rotten man!

DOCTOR [*unfazed*]. Tell me, have you ever noticed your
  intestines making noise?

MENAECHMUS. When I've eaten well, they're silent; when I'm
  hungry, they make noise.

DOCTOR. Pollux, that's a pretty healthy answer he just gave
  to me.
  [*To* MENAECHMUS]. Do you sleep right through till dawn,
  sleep easily when you're in bed?

MENAECHMUS. I sleep through if all the debts I owe are paid. 929–30
    But listen you, you

Question-asker, you be damned by Jupiter and all the gods! 931–3

DOCTOR. *Now* I know the man's insane, those final words
    are proof.

[*To* OLD MAN] Take care!

OLD MAN. He speaks like a Nestor now, compared to just a
    while ago.*

Just a while ago he called his wife a rabid female dog.

MENAECHMUS. *I* said that?

OLD MAN.   You're mad, I say.

MENAECHMUS.   I'm mad?

OLD MAN.   And do you know what else? You
    Also threatened that you'd trample over me with teams of
    horses!

Yes, I saw you do it. Yes, and I insist you did it, too.   939–40

MENAECHMUS [*to* OLD MAN]. *You*, of course, have snatched
    the sacred crown of Jove, that's what I know.

Afterwards, they tossed you into prison for this awful crime.

When they let you out, while you were manacled, they beat
    you up.

Then you killed your father. Then you sold your mother as
    a slave.

Have you heard enough to know I'm sane enough to curse
    you back?

OLD MAN. Doctor, please be quick and do whatever must be
    done for him.

Don't you see the man's insane?

DOCTOR.   I think the wisest thing for you's to
Have the man delivered to my office.

OLD MAN.   Do you think?

DOCTOR.   Of course.

There I'll treat him pursuant to diagnosis.

OLD MAN.   As you say.

DOCTOR [*to* MENAECHMUS]. Yes, I'll have you drinking
    hellebore for twenty days or so.   950

MENAECHMUS. Then I'll have *you* beaten hanging upside down
    for thirty days.

DOCTOR [*to* OLD MAN]. Go and call for men who can deliver
    him.

OLD MAN. How many men?

DOCTOR. From the way he's acting, I'd say four, none less could do the job.

OLD MAN [exiting]. They'll be here. You watch him, Doctor.

DOCTOR [anxious to retreat]. No, I think I'd best go home. Preparations are in order for the case. You get the slaves. Have them carry him to me.

OLD MAN.   I will.

DOCTOR.   I'm going now.

OLD MAN.   Goodbye.

MENAECHMUS. Doctor's gone, father-in-law's gone. I'm now alone. By Jupiter!—

What does all this mean? Why do these men insist that I'm insane?

Really, I have not been sick a single day since I've been born.

Nor am I insane, nor have I punched or fought with anyone. 960

Healthy, I see healthy people, only talk with folks I know.

Maybe those who wrongly say I'm mad are really mad themselves.

What should I do now? My wife won't let me home, as I would like.

[Pointing to EROTIUM's house] No one will admit me there. All's well—well out of hand, that is.*

Here I'm stuck. At least by night—I think—they'll let me in my house.

> [MENAECHMUS sits dejectedly in front of his
> house, all wrapped up in his troubles
>
> From the other side of the stage, enter MESSENIO
> singing about How to Succeed in Slavery

MESSENIO. If you should seek the proof of whether someone's slave is good,

See, does he guard his master's interest, serve right to the letter

When Master is away   the way he should

If Master were at hand   or even better.

For if the slave is worthy, and he's well brought up,   971

He'll care to keep his shoulders empty—not to fill his cup. 970

His master will reward him. Let the worthless slave be told

The lowly, lazy louts get whips and chains,
And millstones, great starvation, freezing cold.
The price for all their misbehaviours: pains.
I therefore fully fear this fate and very gladly
Remain determined to be good—so I won't turn out badly.
I'd so much rather be bawled out than sprawled out on a
    pillory,
I'd so much rather eat what's cooked than have some work
    cooked up for me.
So I follow Master's orders, never argue or protest.   980
Let the others do it their way; I obey; for me, that's best. . . .*
But I haven't much to fear; the time is near for something
    nice.*
My master will reward his slave for 'thinking with his
    back'—and thinking twice.

Enter OLD MAN, *leading four burly servants*

OLD MAN. Now, by all the gods and men, I bid you all obey
    my orders.   990
Be most careful so you'll follow what I've ordered and will
    order.
Have that man picked up aloft, and carried to the doctor's
    office.
That's unless you're not a bit concerned about *your* back
    and limbs.
Every man beware. Don't pay attention to his threats of
    violence.
But why just stand? Why hesitate? It's time to lift the man
    aloft!
[*Not very brave himself*] And I'll head for the doctor's
    office. I'll be there when you arrive.
MENAECHMUS [*notices the charging mob*]. I'm dead! What's
    this? I wonder why these men are rushing swiftly toward
    me?
Hey, men, what do you want? What are you after? Why
    surround me now?

                    [*They snatch up* MENAECHMUS
Where are you snatching me and taking me? Won't someone
    help me, please?

O citizens of Epidamnus, rescue me! [*To slaves*] Please let
   me go!   1000

MESSENIO. By the immortal gods, what am I seeing with my
   very eyes?

Some unknown men are lifting Master in the air. Out-
   rageously!

MENAECHMUS. Won't someone dare to help?

MESSENIO.   Me, me! I'll dare to help with derring-do!

O citizens of Epidamnus, what a dirty deed to Master!

Do peaceful towns allow a free-born tourist to be seized in
   daylight?

[*To slaves*] You let him go!

MENAECHMUS [*to* MESSENIO]. Whoever you may be, please
   help me out!

Don't allow this awful outrage to be perpetrated on me.

MESSENIO. Why, of course I'll help, and hustle hurriedly to
   your defence.

Never would I let you down. I'd rather let myself down
   first.   1010

[*To* MENAECHMUS] Grab that fellow's eye   the one who's
   got you by the shoulder now.

I can plough the other guys and plant a row of fists in them.

[*To slaves*] Hercules, you'll lose an awful lot by taking
   him. Let go!

                        [*A wild mêlée ensues*

MENAECHMUS [*while fighting, to* MESSENIO]. Hey, I've got his
   eye.

MESSENIO. Then make the socket in his head appear!

Evil people! People snatchers! Bunch of pirates!

SLAVES [*together*].   Woe is us!

Hercules! No—please!

MESSENIO.   Let go!

MENAECHMUS.   What sort of handiwork is this?

Face a festival of fists.

MESSENIO.   Go on, be gone, and go to hell!

[*Kicking the slowest slave*] You take that as your reward
   for being last to get away.

                 [*They are all gone.* MESSENIO *takes*
                 a deep breath of satisfaction

Well, I've really made my mark on every face I've faced
today.

Pollux, Master, didn't I come just in time to bring you aid! 1020

MENAECHMUS. Whoever you are, young man, I hope the gods
will always bring you blessings.

If it hadn't been for you, I'd not have lived to see the sunset.

MESSENIO. If that's true, by Pollux, then do right by me and
free me, Master.

MENAECHMUS. Free you? I?

MESSENIO.   Of course. Because I saved you, Master.

MENAECHMUS.   Listen here, you're
Wand'ring from the truth—

MESSENIO.   I wander?

MENAECHMUS.   Yes, I swear by Father Jove
I am not your master.

MESSENIO [stunned].   Why proclaim such things?

MENAECHMUS.   But it's no lie.
Never did a slave of mine serve me as well as you just did.

MESSENIO. If you're so insistent and deny I'm yours, then I'll
go free.

MENAECHMUS. Hercules, as far as I'm concerned, be free. Go
where you'd like.

MESSENIO.   Am I really authorized?

MENAECHMUS.   If I've authority for you. 1030

MESSENIO [dialogue with himself]. 'Greetings, patron.'— 'Ah,
Messenio, the fact that you're now free

Makes me very glad.'—'Well, I believe that's true.' [To
MENAECHMUS] But, patron dear,

You can have authority no less than when I was a slave.

I'll be glad to live with you, and when you go, go home
with you.

MENAECHMUS [doesn't want some strange person in his house].
Not at all, no thank you.

MESSENIO [jubilant]. Now I'll get our baggage at the inn—

And, of course, the purse with all our money's sealed up in
the trunk

With our travel cash. I'll bring it to you.

MENAECHMUS [eyes lighting up at this]. Yes! Go quickly,
quickly!

MESSENIO. I'll return it just exactly as you gave it to me.
Wait right here.

[MESSENIO *dashes off toward the harbour*

MENAECHMUS [*soliloquizing*]. What unworldly wonders have
occurred today in wondrous ways:
People claim I'm not the man I am and keep me from their
houses.   1040
Then this fellow said he was my slave   and that I set him
free!   1041
Then he says he'll go and bring a wallet full of money to
me.   1043
If he does, I'll tell him he can go quite freely where he'd
like
That's so when he's sane again he won't demand the money
back.
[*Musing more*] Father-in-law and doctor said I was insane.
How very strange.
All this business seems to me like nothing other than a
dream.
Now I'll go and see this harlot, though she's in a huff with
me.
Maybe I'll convince her to return the dress, which I'll take
home.

[*He enters* EROTIUM's *house*

Enter MENAECHMUS II *and* MESSENIO

MENAECHMUS II [*angry with* MESSENIO]. Effrontery in front
of me! You dare to claim we've seen each other   1050
Since I gave you orders that we'd meet back here?
MESSENIO.   But didn't I just
Snatch and rescue you from those four men who carried
you aloft
Right before this house? You called on all the gods and
men for aid.
I came running, snatched you from them, though with fists
they fought me back.
For this service, since I saved your life, you made a free
man of me.

[*Ruefully*] Now just when I said I'd get the cash and
    baggage, you sped up and
Ran ahead to meet me, and deny you've done the things
    you've done.

MENAECHMUS II. Free? I said you could go free?

MESSENIO.   For sure.

MENAECHMUS II.   Now look, for *super*-sure
I would rather make *myself* a slave than ever set you free.

MENAECHMUS I *is pushed by* EROTIUM
out of her house

MENAECHMUS I. If you would like to swear by your two eyes,
    go right ahead, but still   1060
You'll never prove that I absconded with your dress and
    bracelet—[*door slams*] hussy!

MESSENIO [*suddenly seeing double*]. By the gods, what do I
    see?

MENAECHMUS II. What do you see?

MESSENIO.   Why—your reflection!

MENAECHMUS II. What?

MESSENIO.   Your very image just as like yourself
    as it could be.

MENAECHMUS II. Pollux—he's not unlike me . . . I notice . . .
    similarities.

MENAECHMUS I [*to* MESSENIO]. Hey, young man, hello! You
    saved my life—whoever you may be.

MESSENIO. You, young man, if you don't mind, would you
    please tell me your name?

MENAECHMUS I. Nothing you could ask would be too much
    since you have helped me so.
My name is Menaechmus.

MENAECHMUS II.   Oh, by Pollux, so is mine as well!

MENAECHMUS I. Syracuse-Sicilian—

MENAECHMUS II.   That's my city, that's my country too!

MENAECHMUS I. What is this I hear?

MENAECHMUS II.   Just what is true.

MESSENIO [*to* MENAECHMUS II]. I know you—*you're* my
    master!   1070

[*To audience*] I belong to this man though I thought that
    I belonged to that man.

[*To* MENAECHMUS I, *the wrong man*] Please excuse me, sir,
    if I unknowingly spoke foolishly.

For a moment I imagined he was you—and gave him
    trouble.

MENAECHMUS II. Madness, nothing but! [*To* MESSENIO] Don't
    you recall that we were both together,

Both of us got off the ship today?

MESSENIO [*thinking, realizing*]. That's right. You're very right.

You're my master. [*To* MENAECHMUS I] Find another slave,
    farewell. [*To* MENAECHMUS II] And you, hello!

[*Pointing to* MENAECHMUS II] Him, I say, this man's
    Menaechmus.

MENAECHMUS I. So am I!

MENAECHMUS II.   What joke is this?

You're Menaechmus?

MENAECHMUS I.   That I say I am. My father's name
    was Moschus.

MENAECHMUS II. You're the son of my own father?

MENAECHMUS I.   No, the son of *my* own father.

I'm not anxious to appropriate your father or to steal him
    from you.   1080

MESSENIO. Gods in heaven, grant me now that hope unhoped-
    for I suspèct.

For, unless my mind has failed me, these two men are both
    twin brothers.

Each man claims the selfsame fatherland and father for his
    own.

I'll call Master over. O Menaechmus

MENAECHMUS I and II [*together*].   Yes?

MESSENIO.   Not both of you.

Which of you two travelled with me on the ship?

MENAECHMUS I.   It wasn't me.

MENAECHMUS II. Me it was.

MESSENIO.   Then you I want. Step over here [*motioning*].

MENAECHMUS II [*following* MESSENIO *to a corner*]. I've
    stepped. What's up?

MESSENIO. That man there is either one great faker or your
lost twin brother.

Never have I seen two men more similar than you two
men:

Water isn't more like water, milk's not more alike to milk

Than that man is like to you. And what's more he named
your father.   1090

And your fatherland. It's best to go and question him still
further.

MENAECHMUS II. Hercules, you do advise me well. I'm very
grateful to you.

Please work on, by Hercules. I'll make you free if you
discover

That man is my brother.

MESSENIO.   Oh, I hope so.

MENAECHMUS II.   And I hope so too.

MESSENIO [to MENAECHMUS I]. Sir, I do believe you've just
asserted that you're named Menaechmus.

MENAECHMUS I. That is so.

MESSENIO.   Well, his name is Menaechmus,
too. You also said

You were born is Sicily at Syracuse. Well, so was he.

Moschus was your father, so you said. That was *his* father,
too.

Both of you can do yourselves a favour—and help me as
well.*

MENAECHMUS I. Anything you ask me I'll comply with, I'm
so grateful to you.   1100

Treat me just as if I were your purchased slave—although
I'm free.

MESSENIO. It's my hope to prove you are each other's brothers,
twins in fact,

Born of the selfsame mother, selfsame father, on the selfsame
day.

MENAECHMUS I. Wonder-laden words. Oh, would you could
make all your words come true.

MESSENIO. Well, I can. But, both of you, just give replies to
what I ask you.

MENAECHMUS I. Ask away. I'll answer. I won't hide a single
thing I know.

MESSENIO. Is your name Menaechmus?

MENAECHMUS I.   Absolutely.

MESSENIO [to MENAECHMUS II].   Is it yours as well?

MENAECHMUS II. Yes.

MESSENIO.   You said your father's name was Moschus.

MENAECHMUS I.   Yes.

MENAECHMUS II.   The same for me.

MESSENIO. And you're Syracusan?

MENAECHMUS I.   Surely.

MESSENIO [to MENAECHMUS II].   You?

MENAECHMUS II.   You *know* I am, of course.

MESSENIO. Well, so far the signs are good. Now turn your
minds to further questions.   1110

[*To* MENAECHMUS I] What's the final memory you carry
from your native land?

MENAECHMUS I [*reminiscing*]. With my father . . . visiting
Tarentum for the fair. Then after that . . .
Wandering among the people, far from Father . . . Being
snatched—

MENAECHMUS II [*bursting with joy*]. Jupiter above, now help
me—!

MESSENIO [*officiously*]. What's the shouting? You shut up.
[*Turning back to* MENAECHMUS I] Snatched from father
and from fatherland, about how old were you?

MENAECHMUS I. Seven or so. My baby teeth had barely started
to fall out.
After that, I never saw my father.

MESSENIO.   No? Well, tell me this:
At the time how many children did he have?

MENAECHMUS I.   I think just two.

MESSENIO. Which were you, the older or the younger?

MENAECHMUS I.   Neither, we were equal.

MESSENIO. Do explain.

MENAECHMUS I.   We were both twins.

MENAECHMUS II [*ecstatic*]. Oh—all the gods are with me
now!   1120

MESSENIO [*sternly, to* MENAECHMUS II]. Interrupt and I'll be
    quiet.

MENAECHMUS II [*obedient*].   I'll be quiet.

MESSENIO [*to* MENAECHMUS I].   Tell me this:
    Did you both have just one name?

MENAECHMUS I.   Oh, not at all. My name is mine,
    As it is today—Menaechmus. Brother's name was Sosicles.

MENAECHMUS II [*mad with joy*]. Yes, I recognize the signs. I
    can't keep from embracing you!

    Brother, dear twin brother, greetings! I am he—I'm Sosicles!

MENAECHMUS I. How is it you afterward received the name
    Menaechmus, then?

MENAECHMUS II. When we got the news that you had
    wandered off away from Father

And that you were kidnapped by an unknown man, and
    Father died,

Grandpa changed my name. The name you used to have he
    gave to me.

MENAECHMUS I. Yes, I do believe it's as you say. [*Goes to* 1129–30
    embrace him, suddenly stops] But tell me this.

MENAECHMUS II.   Just ask.

MENAECHMUS I. What was Mother's name?

MENAECHMUS II.   Why, Teuximarcha.

MENAECHMUS I.   That's correct, it fits.
    Unexpectedly I greet you, see you after so much time!

MENAECHMUS II. Brother, now I find you after so much
    suffering and toil,

Searching for you, now you're found, and I'm so very, very
    glad.

                     [*They embrace*

MESSENIO [*to* MENAECHMUS II]. *That's* the reason why the
    slut could call you by your rightful name,

Thinking you were he, I think, when she invited you to
    dinner.

MENAECHMUS I. Yes, by Pollux, I had ordered dinner for
    myself today,

Hidden from my wife—from whom I filched a dress a while
    ago—and

Gave it to her. [*Indicates* EROTIUM'*s house*]

MENAECHMUS II. Could you mean this dress I'm holding,
   Brother dear?

MENAECHMUS I. That's the one. How did you get it?   1140

MENAECHMUS II.   Well, the slut led me to dinner.
   There she claimed I gave it to her. *Wonderfully* have I just
   dined,
   Wined as well as concubined, of dress and gold I robbed
   her blind.

MENAECHMUS I. O by Pollux, I rejoice if you had fun because
   of me!
   When she asked you in to dinner, she believed that you
   were me.

MESSENIO [*impatient for himself*]. Is there any reason to delay
   the freedom that you promised?

MENAECHMUS I. Brother, what he asks is very fair and fine.
   Please do it for me.

MENAECHMUS II [*to* MESSENIO, *the formula*]. 'Be thou free.'

MENAECHMUS I. The fact you're free now makes me glad,
   Messenio.

MESSENIO [*broadly hinting for some cash reward*]. Actually,   1149-50
   I need more facts, *supporting* facts to keep me free.

MENAECHMUS II [*ignoring* MESSENIO, *to his brother*]. Since
   our dreams have come about exactly as we wished, dear
   Brother,
   Let us both return to our homeland.

MENAECHMUS I.   Brother, as you wish.
   I can hold an auction and sell off whatever I have here.
   Meanwhile, let's go in.

MENAECHMUS II.   That's fine.

MESSENIO [*to* MENAECHMUS I].
               May I request a favour of you?

MENAECHMUS I. What?

MESSENIO.   Please make me do the auctioneering.

MENAECHMUS I.   Done.

MESSENIO.   All right. Then please inform me:
   When should I announce the auction for?

MENAECHMUS I.   Let's say—a week from now.

     [*The brothers go into* MENAECHMUS' *house,*
     leaving MESSENIO *alone on stage*

MESSENIO [*announcing*]. In the morning in a week from now
    we'll have Menaechmus' auction.

Slaves and goods, his farm and city house, his everything
    will go.

Name your prices, if you've got the cash in hand, it all will
    go.

Yes, and if there's any bidder for the thing—his wife will
    go.   1160

Maybe the entire auction will enrich us—who can tell?

For the moment, dear spectators, clap with vigour. Fare ye
    well!

THE HAUNTED HOUSE

(*Mostellaria*)

DRAMATIS PERSONAE

TRANIO, slave to Philolaches
GRUMIO, a slave
PHILOLACHES, a young man
PHILEMATIUM, a girl of joy
SCAPHA, her maid, an old hag
CALLIDAMATES, a young man
DELPHIUM, a girl of joy to Callidamates
THEOPROPIDES, an old man, father to Philolaches
MISARGYRIDES, a moneylender
SIMO, an old man, neighbour to Theopropides
SLAVES
WHIPPERS in the employ of Theopropides

The scene is a street in Athens. There are two houses on stage, with an alley between them. One house belongs to THEOPROPIDES, *the other to* SIMO. *The latter has an altar before it.*

THE HAUNTED HOUSE

Enter GRUMIO, *a puritanical slave from one
of* THEOPROPIDES' *farms. In a huff, he storms up
to the door of* THEOPROPIDES' *house, and
shouts inside*

GRUMIO. Come out here from the kitchen, will you, whipping
    post?
You show such cleverness amidst the pots and pans.
Come out here, come outside, you master's ruination!
I'll get revenge on you some day, out at the farm.
Come out, you kitchen stink-up; don't you hide from me!

From inside the house saunters TRANIO

TRANIO [*smiling and calm*]. Why all this shouting here outside
    the house, you wretch?
You think you're in the country? Go away from here.
Go to the country, go to hell—but go away.
[*Throws a flurry of punches*] Do you want *this*?
GRUMIO [*cringing*].   Oh no! Why beat *me* up? 9–10
TRANIO. Because you live.
GRUMIO.   All right. If our old master comes—
    [*Melodramatically, to heaven*] Oh, let him come back safe,
    the man you're eating up!
TRANIO. Your symbols and your similes are terrible.
How can a person eat a person who's not here?
GRUMIO. Terrific city wit! The people love your jokes.
You mock my country ways, but you wait, Tranio.
I'll see you there, and very soon—chained to the mill.
Know what awaits you in a while or two, my boy?
Irons on the fire for you, in the country.
Now, while you still can do it, booze and bankrupt us,   20
And keep corrupting Master's wonderful young son.
Keep drinking day and night, and Greek-it-up like mad!*
Buy mistresses and free 'em, feed your flatterers,
Buy groceries as if you all were caterers!
Did Master bid you do this when he went abroad?

Did he expect to come back finding things like this?
And did you think this is the way good slaves behave—
By ruining Master's wealth and Master's son as well?
For ruined he is, to judge by his behaviour now.
That boy, who out of all the boys in Attica   30
Was once so chaste, so frugal, once so well behaved,
Now takes the prizes in completely different sports,
Thanks to all your tutoring and all your talent.

TRANIO. Why do you give a damn for me? Why do you care?
  Can't you go find some country cows to care for?
  It's fun to drink, to love, to have a lot of whores.
  I'm risking my own back, you know, not risking yours.

GRUMIO. How bold he talks! [*To* TRANIO] Well, 'foo' to you!

TRANIO.   By Jupiter
  And all the gods, the hell with you—you reek of garlic!
  Of home-made country mud, of goats and pigs combined—   40
  All scum and scatologic.

GRUMIO.   Well, what do you want?
  Not all of us can smell of fancy foreign perfumes,
  Or have the place of honour at a banquet table,
  Or live as high and mighty off the hog as you do.
  You keep your doves, the fancy fish and fancy birds,
  And let me live my life the way I like—with garlic.
  Right now you're very high, I'm very low. I'll wait.
  As long as in the end we end up in reverse.   49–50

TRANIO. Why, Grumio, it seems to me you're acting jealous!
  But things are best when best for me and worst for you;
  For I was made for wooing—you were made for . . . mooing.
  Thus I live very high and you, of course, live low.

GRUMIO. Oh, torture-target—which I know you'll soon
    become,
  When whippers prod you manacled right through the streets
  With goads—[*reverently*] if ever our old master does return.

TRANIO. Can you be sure your turn won't come before my
    own?

GRUMIO. I've not deserved it. *You* deserve it, always have.

TRANIO. Oh, save your efforts, save your words as well,   60
  Unless you'd like a lot of lashing for yourself.

GRUMIO [*to business*]. Look, are you going to give me feed
    to feed the cows?

Unless you eat *that*, too. Go on and gallivant
The way you've started, drink and Greek-it-up like mad,
Eat on and stuff yourselves, destroy the fatted calf.
TRANIO. Shut up, back to the sticks! I'm off to the Piraeus*
To buy myself a little fish for this night's dinner.
I'll have someone deliver you the feed tomorrow.
[*Starts to go off, notices* GRUMIO *glaring at him*] What's
up? What is it now you want, you gallows bird?
GRUMIO. I think *you'll* be the gallows bird—and very soon. 70
TRANIO. I have my 'now,' let 'very soon' come when it comes.
GRUMIO. Oh, yes? Remember this one thing: 'What comes in
life
Is not so much what you would like, but what you don't.'
TRANIO. Right now you bother me. Go back to farming,
move!
By Hercules, I want no more delays from you!

[TRANIO *skips off-stage*

GRUMIO. Well, has he gone and treated my words just as
straws?
[*Fervently, to heaven*] O ye immortal gods, I call on you
and pray,
Do let our senior master come back home to us—
Although he's gone three years. And let him come before
It all is lost, the house and holdings. If not now, 80
In little time, there'll only be remains remaining.
I'm for the farm. [*Notices off-stage*] But look—here comes
our junior master.
Behold—a most corrupted youth—once oh so fine.

[GRUMIO *walks sadly off-stage in the opposite
direction to that in which* TRANIO *left*
Young PHILOLACHES *enters. This lad is typical of
Plautus' young men, wide-eyed and handsome,
but not very bright. In fact,* PHILOLACHES *is
rather an imbecile. When he reaches centre stage,*
PHILOLACHES *sings a doleful lament**

PHILOLACHES. I've been pounding my head a lot, pondering.
Deep in me, words have been wandering.
Things roll around in my mind—if I do have a mind—
And I've thought and I've sought many answers to find.

[*A breath*] What is a man when he's born?
I mean, what is he like?
After looking around, here's the answer I've found: 90
[*A breath, then a profound conclusion*]

> Like a house. Like a newly built house.
> That's a man when he's born, and it's true.
> Perhaps you don't quite see the likeness,
>   I'll see that you do.
> And my words will confirm and convince you.
> I'm sure when you hear what I say,
> You will see things my way.

So hark to my argument, folks, and you'll be
Just as smart in this matter as . . . me.   100
   A house when it's steady and ready, all straight with no
      tilt,
   A house when it's perfectly built,
Both the building and builder are praised; the approval's
    immense.
People all want the same sort of house; they won't spare
    the expense.
But then—suppose some lax and lazy lout moves in
And brings a filthy laggard group along. Your cares begin.
For even one mistake can make a good house . . . break.
You know what also happens often? Storms.
   Tiles and gutters shatter,
Then suffer from the lazy man's neglect.   110

Rain blows right through and flows right through the walls.
The timber goes. A good construction job is wrecked.
It grows still worse with wear, as you'd expect.
Of course it's not the builder's fault at all.
Repairs are costly, people are so cheap.
The less they spend, the more they have to keep.

They wait till it must be rebuilt completely, all is in a heap.
So far I've talked of houses. Now I shall proceed
To state why men are similar to houses—till you've all
    agreed.
Now, first of all, a parent is a builder of a child.   120

He lays the groundwork, as it were, sees that he's styled.
He brings him up, prepares him to grow tall and straight,
In hopes that what he builds may some day serve the state—
Or stand alone at least. In all events,
They spare no pains, and they spare no expense.
Then it's lots of schooling: arts and letters, legal lore to
    build his brain.
Expensive. Parents strain
To raise a son who'll show the level others might attain.
Then it's off to the army, prepared he is sent
To serve as some relative's reinforcement.   130
It's goodbye to the builders, he's out of their hands,
And now people see if the building still stands!
Speaking now for myself, I used to be one of the top,
A genuine model—at least while I stayed in the shop.
But when left to my own sweet devices at last,
The builder's whole structure began to slip fast.

> Laziness came like a storm.
> There was raining and hailing.
> The next thing I knew all my virtues were failing.
> A sudden unroofing caught me unaware,   140
> Unroofing I was a bit slow to repair.

Then in place of the rain a swift new storm would start:
For then *love* billowed in, and it drenched my whole heart.
Then, all at once, my name, my fame, my fortune, all that
    once was fair
Had fled the camp. Now day by day, it grows still worse
    with wear.
My roof, it leaks, and it so creaks
My house can't be repaired now, it's a total wreck for
    good.
The whole foundation's finished. Nothing helps—and
    nothing could.
What pain to see me now, and know what once I used to
    be:
There never was a cleaner-living youth than me.   150
No greater athlete in the arts gymnastic,
In throwing, riding, running, fighting—I was just fantastic.

It nourished me with joy
To be a model of restraint and ruggedness to every boy.
All the noblest people looked to me for discipline,
But now, it's all my fault, I'm nothing—see the awful shape
   I'm in.

After his song, PHILOLACHES *hears the sounds*
   of someone approaching from the back
   [the women's quarters] of his house. He steps
   to the side of the stage to observe, as
   PHILEMATIUM *and* SCAPHA *enter. The first is*
   a dazzling young girl of joy,
recently freed by PHILOLACHES, *the second a wise*
   and wizened ex-whore, now serving as
   PHILEMATIUM's *personal maid.* SCAPHA *carries*
   a sort of make-up table and a stool on which
   her mistress can sit to perform her toilette.*
      PHILEMATIUM *and* SCAPHA *converse,*
      as young PHILOLACHES *observes from the*
         sidelines, and comments

PHILEMATIUM. By Castor, it's a while since I have had a
   fresher bath,
   Or a better one, dear Scapha. Why, I feel all scrubbed and
   polished.
SCAPHA [*the hard pragmatist*]. Well, time will tell. You know,
   just like the recent harvest stored away.*
PHILEMATIUM. What does the recent harvest have to do with
   my own bathing?   160
SCAPHA. As much as your own bathing has to do with it.
PHILOLACHES [*aside, ecstatic*].   O queen of Venus!
   [*To the audience, pointing at the girl*] Look, there's my
   storm, the one that unroofed all my reputation.
   I used to have a roof, but Love and Cupid showered on
   me.
   Love soaked right through my heart, and it's beyond repair.
   My walls are oozing and my house is losing its whole
   structure.
PHILEMATIUM. Do look me over, Scapha. Is my costume nice
   enough?

I long to please my darling benefactor Philolaches.

SCAPHA. No need for lovely ornaments when you yourself
    can glitter.
The lovers don't love women's clothes; [*with a leer*] they
    love what's stuffed inside them.

PHILOLACHES [*aside*]. By all the gods, that Scapha's charming;
    she knows all the tricks!   170
How charmingly she speaks of love affairs and lovers'
    thoughts!

PHILEMATIUM. And now?

SCAPHA.   My dear?

PHILEMATIUM.   Please look me over. Am I nice enough?

SCAPHA. You're beautiful inside and so you beautify your
    clothes.

PHILOLACHES [*aside*]. For that nice thought, dear Scapha,
    you shall get a gift today.
You won't have complimented my sweet love without
    reward.

PHILEMATIUM. I don't want simply flattery.

SCAPHA.   You're such a silly girl.
I think you'd rather have false criticism than true praise.
By Pollux, I myself would much prefer false flattery.
Who wants true criticism? People laughing at my looks?   180

PHILEMATIUM. Not I. I much prefer the truth. I can't abide
    a liar.

SCAPHA. I swear, by Philolaches' love for you, you're simply
    lovely.

PHILOLACHES [*aside*]. What's that you swear, you bitch? By
    all my love for her?
But what of hers for me? You left that out. Forget the gift.
You're finished, fully finished, now that gift has flown away.

SCAPHA. And yet I'm quite amazed. I thought that you were
    shrewd and wise.
You're being foolish foolishly.

PHILEMATIUM.   What's this? Have I done wrong?

SCAPHA. By Castor, yes. You're wrong to put your hopes in
    just one lover,
To be so dutiful to him, rejecting other men.*
Fidelity's for wives, but not for mistresses.   190

PHILOLACHES [*aside*]. By Jupiter, what sort of evil earthquake
    shakes my house?
May all the gods and goddesses destroy me with distress
If I don't kill that hag with hunger, thirst and freezing cold!

PHILEMATIUM. But, Scapha, I don't want to learn such wicked
    things.

SCAPHA.   You're foolish
To think that man will always be your friend and benefactor.
I warn you, someday he'll be jaded—you'll be faded—then
    he'll leave.

PHILEMATIUM. I *hope* not.

SCAPHA.   'Things unhoped-for come more
    often than things hoped.'
Well, I suppose I never will convince you with my words,
But learn from my example, what I am and what I was:
For once I was a charming beauty just as you are now   200
And, loved as you are now, was dutiful to just one man. 200a
He loved me, yes, by Pollux, till with time my hair turned
    grey,
Then left me in the lurch. [*A sigh*] I know the same will
    come to you.

PHILOLACHES [*aside, furious*]. I'm barely in control, I'd fly
    right at the evil bitch's eyes.

PHILEMATIUM. He freed me—spent such sums to be my single
    swain.
I only think it's right I stay . . . monogamous to him.*

PHILOLACHES [*aside*]. By the immortal gods, a lovely girl—
    and ladylike.
By Hercules, it's worth it to be bankrupt all for her.

SCAPHA. By Castor, are you so unshrewd?

PHILEMATIUM.   But why?

SCAPHA.   To care for him,
To hope he really loves you.

PHILEMATIUM.   Why should I *not* care?

SCAPHA.   You're free.
You've got what you desired now. If he won't love you
    still,   210
He really would be suffering a loss from his investment.

PHILOLACHES [*aside*]. I'm dead, by Hercules, if I don't chop
that bitch to bits!

That vicious, ill-advising villainess corrupts my love!

PHILEMATIUM. How can I ever show my gratitude for what
he's done?

Don't ever bid me love him less, stop all this trying.

SCAPHA. I will, but do remember this: if you serve one man
now

While you're in full bloom, then when you're old, you'll
look for men.

PHILOLACHES [*aside*]. I wish I could transform into a rope to
choke that poisoner,

By winding round her evil, ill-advising throat—and kill
her.

PHILEMATIUM. But since I have my freedom, I should show
the same affection,   220

And be as lovey-dovey to him as I was before.

PHILOLACHES [*aside*]. Whatever heaven does, now that I've
heard those little words,

I'd free you ten times over—and kill Scapha twice as dead.

SCAPHA. If you feel that your contract spells eternal love,

And he's to be your only lover for your whole life long,

Then honour and obey—put on a wifely hairdo.*

PHILEMATIUM. Your reputation gets you what you earn in
life.

If I preserve my reputation, then the cash will come.

PHILOLACHES [*aside*]. Why, if I had to sell my father, I would
rather sell him*

Than let this lovely girl lack anything while I'm alive.   230

SCAPHA. But what of other men who love you?

PHILEMATIUM.   Well, they'll love me more

To see how I show gratitude in paying back a kindness.

PHILOLACHES [*berserk with joy*]. Oh, someone bring the news
right now—the news my father's dead!

I'll disinherit myself, and make *her* heir to all my goods!

SCAPHA. His cash will soon be gone, through dining, drinking
day and night.

He never saves a single thing. It's clear-cut gluttonizing.

PHILOLACHES [*aside*]. By Hercules, for you I'll change my
style and start to save.

I won't give *you* a thing to eat or drink for ten whole days!

PHILEMATIUM. If you have anything that's nice to say of him,
then say it.

But if you keep abusing him . . . I'll beat you up.   240

PHILOLACHES [*aside*]. If I had used that cash to sacrifice to
Jove supreme

Instead of buying her, I couldn't be more blessed than now.

Look how she loves me—deep, in depth. Oh, what a lucky
man I am!

I freed a girl protector; she defends me masterfully.

SCAPHA. Although I see you spurn all other men for Philolaches,

I won't be beaten up because of him. I'll say he's nice,

If you're so assured your contract is eternal with him,

PHILEMATIUM. Quickly, Scapha, now my mirror, and my box
of jewellery.*

I must be completely dressed before my darling Philo comes.

SCAPHA. Mirrors are for women who have doubts and need
a glass to cling to.*   250

You don't need a glass; why, you're a really first-rate glass
yourself.

PHILOLACHES [*aside*]. Lovely words, dear Scapha—and they
won't be unrewarded either.

I'll be sure and give a little bonus thing to—Philematium.*

PHILEMATIUM. Everything in order? How's my hairdo, coiffed
with quality?

SCAPHA. *You* have quality, my dear, and so how could your
coif be otherwise?

PHILOLACHES. What on earth could be more awful than that
wicked woman there?

Now she's full of compliments, when she was all complaints
before.

PHILEMATIUM. Powder, please.

SCAPHA.   But why on earth do you need powder?

PHILEMATIUM.   For my cheeks, of course.

SCAPHA. That would be like white-on-white; no need to gild
the lily, dear.

PHILOLACHES [*aside*]. Very nicely put, the gilding and the
   lily, Scapha, good!   260

PHILEMATIUM. All right, pass the rouge to me.

SCAPHA.   I won't. You know, you're not too bright.

   Do you want to overpaint an absolutely perfect picture?

   Blooming girls like you should never ever use false colouring.

   Never rouge, or cream from Melos, never any paint at all.

PHILEMATIUM [*pleased, looks at herself, kisses the mirror,
   hands it to* SCAPHA]. Take the mirror then.

PHILOLACHES.

              She kissed it! Oh, my god, she kissed the glass!

   Oh, I want a rock; I want to knock a piece of glass right
   off!

SCAPHA. Here's a towel; better wipe your hands off very well.

PHILEMATIUM.   But why?

SCAPHA [*ironically*]. You've just held the mirror—and your
   hands might smell of silver now.*

   Philolaches might suspect you've taken silver from a man.

PHILOLACHES. I don't think I've ever seen a shrewder bitch
   than that old bag!   270

   What a neat and clever thing—to prick her mind about the
   glass.

PHILEMATIUM. Do you think perfuming with some perfumes
   might be—?

SCAPHA.   Not at all.

PHILEMATIUM. Why?

SCAPHA. The perfect women smell of absolutely nothing, dear.

   Only hags try renovation, perfuming themselves with
   perfume,

   Youthless, toothless hags who try to hide their faults with
   false aromas.

   Ah, but when their body sweat at last commingles with the
   perfume—

   What a smell, just like those soups in which the cooks put
   everything!

   What you're smelling there's no telling, you just know they
   smell like hell!

PHILOLACHES. What a woman, worldly-wise in everything.
   Who could be wiser?

And she speaks the truth, as many people in this theatre
    know.*   280

[*To audience, grinning*] Haven't you got smelly wives whose
    only perfume is their dowry?

PHILEMATIUM. Scapha, please inspect my dress and jewels.
    Are they nice enough?

SCAPHA. *I* can't answer that.

PHILEMATIUM.   Who can?

SCAPHA.   Philolaches, of course.

After all, would he have bought you jewels he didn't like
    himself?

And besides, he doesn't need displays of what he doesn't
    want.   287

Pretty girls are prettier without their clothes—however lush. 289

Any dress is overdressing for a beauty.

PHILOLACHES.   I can't wait!   292
                    [*Dancing out to meet his beloved*

Hi, what are you doing?

PHILEMATIUM.   Dressing up to please you.

PHILOLACHES.   Don't dress more.

[*To* SCAPHA]. You be off and take those trinkets with you.
    [*To* PHILEMATIUM] You, my joy,

Philematium darling, I would love to booze it up with you.

PHILEMATIUM. I would like to do so with *you*; everything
    you love, I love.

Darling—

PHILOLACHES. Ah, that single word is cheaply bought at
    twenty minae.*

PHILEMATIUM. Give me ten, my darling. For my love I give
    a lovely discount.

PHILOLACHES. Fine. You're holding ten—and yet the price
    for you was thirty minae.

[*Leaning over to kiss her*] Balance my account.

PHILEMATIUM. Oh, why assail me with those thirty minae? 300

PHILOLACHES. I assail my very self about those thirty minae,
    love.

That's the best investment deal I ever made in my whole
    life.

PHILEMATIUM. Where could I have found a better place to
    place my loving in?

PHILOLACHES. Look at our accounts: income and outgo
balance perfectly.

You love me and I love you. Our two appraisals are the
same.

PHILEMATIUM. Come and lie beside me. [*Calls inside*] Water!
Put a cocktail table here.

Bring the dice! [*To* PHILOLACHES] Sweet perfume, dear?

PHILOLACHES [*puts his arm around her*]. No, I've got sweet-
ness right beside me.

[*Looks off-stage*]. Say—isn't that my pal right there—
approaching with his lovely mistress?   310

Yes—Callidamates with his mistress! Goody! [*Calling*]
Darling boy!

Soldiers are assembling, seeking shares in all the beauty
booty.*

> *Enter young* CALLIDAMATES, *incredibly drunk.*
> *He is leaning heavily on his mistress,* DELPHIUM.
> *A* SLAVE *follows behind them*

CALLIDAMATES [*singing*].

Philolaches told me to meet him here,
Told me to meet him on time.

[*To* SLAVE]. Listen, I've given you orders.

[SLAVE *goes*

I'm here, I'm on time.
I fled from the party I was at before.
I didn't have fun there,
It was a big bore.
With Philolaches, I'll have a great revel,
He'll welcome me then, and we'll both raise the devil
And spirits will soar.   316

[*To* DELPHIUM] Do I seem to be—[*eyes her bosom*] titititit-
tipsy to you?*

DELPHIUM [*smiling*]. Always . . . always . . . always.   320
And always delays. Here's the place we should go.

CALLIDAMATES. Wanna hug and embrace you all over the
place. You wanna hug too?

DELPHIUM. If it will make you glad—

CALLIDAMATES [*drunkenly embracing her*]. It'll make me and
make me!

Now take me to them.

> [*His knees buckle*

DELPHIUM [*holding him up*].   Oh, don't fall, baby, stand.

CALLIDAMATES. Dadadadadadada-darling, my honey,   325
I'm yours—to lead by the hand.   325a

DELPHIUM. Oh, baby, don't fall in the street—
We can lie by and by where the mattress is sweet.

CALLIDAMATES. Let me fall. I like falling and falling and
falling. . . .

DELPHIUM. If you fall, I fall with you—

CALLIDAMATES. 'It's falling that binds you—till somebody finds
you.'   330

DELPHIUM [*to the audience*]. He's tipsy.

CALLIDAMATES [*gazing at her bosom again*]. I'm tititit-tipsy,
you say?

DELPHIUM. Do give me your hand, don't get hurt on the
way.

CALLIDAMATES [*operatically*]. Take my hand!

DELPHIUM.   Come along.

CALLIDAMATES.   Where we going?

DELPHIUM.   Where do you think?

CALLIDAMATES. Oh, now I recall—going home for a drink.

DELPHIUM. Well, you're on the right track.

CALLIDAMATES.   Yes, it's all coming back!   335

> [*They stagger along a bit.* PHILOLACHES,
> *who has been watching all this with
> amusement, now turns to* PHILEMATIUM

PHILOLACHES. Shall I meet them and greet them, my darling?
He's my best pal of all, and our friendship is strong.

> [*Stands up to go*

I'll be back in a jiffy.

PHILEMATIUM.   A jiffy's too long.

CALLIDAMATES. Hey, anyone home?

PHILOLACHES.   Me.

CALLIDAMATES. Philo! [*To* DELPHIUM] It's Philo, it's Philo!
That marvellest, wonderf'lest, friendliest fellow!   340

PHILOLACHES. Hello!

CALLIDAMATES.   Hello!

DELPHIUM.   Hello!

PHILEMATIUM.   Hello!
  Where do you come from?
CALLIDAMATES.   Where roses are red—and the
  rose wine is mellow.
PHILEMATIUM. Sit down, dear Delphium, let's all drink
  deep.
CALLIDAMATES [*suddenly collapsing*]. I'm going to sleep.
PHILOLACHES [*smiling*]. It's not something new. . . .   345
DELPHIUM. But what should we do?
PHILEMATIUM.   Let him get forty winks,
  While meanwhile the rest of the party has—drinks!

> [*Music. Laughter. They revel for
> at least a few seconds*

> TRANIO *runs on-stage, in a great panic*

TRANIO. Jupiter supreme with his supremest might and mighty
  main
  Surely wants to kill me and my master Philolaches, too.
  Hope is absolutely gone—we have no refuge we can trust
  in.   350
  Safety couldn't save us if she wanted—safety's unsafe, too!
  Terrors and titanic tides of troubles have just touched the
  harbour—
  And I saw them. Master's back from foreign fields—and
  now I'm finished!
  Anybody in the audience would like to make a little money?
  All you have to do today is take my place—for crucifixion.
  Come, speak up, you whip-resisters, iron glad-men, raise
  your hands.
  Where are you—you men who'd storm a city wall for next
  to nothing?*
  And get paid with ten or twenty . . . javelins, right in the
  gut.
  You can have a talent if you win the race to bear my cross.
  Nailing down your fee as soon as arms and legs are nailed
  down twice.   360
  [*Smiles*] After crucifixion, then present yourself—and I'll
  pay up.

[*Then reflects*] Am I not a tragic fool? I should be sprinting
home with speed!

> [*At this moment*, PHILOLACHES *notices
> that* TRANIO *has appeared*

PHILOLACHES. Ah, he's back from shopping. Look—there's
Tranio, back from the harbour.

> [TRANIO *now runs up to his master*

TRANIO. Philolaches—!

PHILOLACHES.   Hi!

TRANIO.   Both you and me—

PHILOLACHES.   Both you and me?

TRANIO.   We're finished!

PHILOLACHES. What?

TRANIO.   Your father's here!

PHILOLACHES.   What's that you say?

TRANIO.   I say we're both destroyed!
Father's here, your father's here!

PHILOLACHES.   He's where?

TRANIO.   He's here, arrived!

PHILOLACHES. What? Who says so? Who has seen him?

TRANIO.   I myself.

PHILOLACHES.   Oh, woe is me!
Gad—I'm lost—where am I now?

TRANIO.   You're lying down, that's where you are.

PHILOLACHES. Did you really see him?

TRANIO.   Yes.

PHILOLACHES.   For sure?

TRANIO.   For sure.

PHILOLACHES.   For sure—I'm dead!
Dead—if what you say is true.

TRANIO.   But why on earth would I tell lies? 370

PHILOLACHES. Tell me what to do—what should I do?

TRANIO [*pointing to the party stuff*]. Have this mess cleaned
up.
Who's the guy asleep?

PHILOLACHES.   Callidamates. [*To* DELPHIUM] Delphie,
wake him up.

DELPHIUM [*shaking* CALLIDAMATES]. Dear Callidamates, do
wake up.

CALLIDAMATES [*drunkenly*]. I am awake. [*Quickly*] I want a
  drink.

DELPHIUM. Do wake up now—Philolaches' father's back!

CALLIDAMATES [*toasting drunkenly*].   Welcome, Father!

PHILOLACHES. Welcome Father, goodbye me!

CALLIDAMATES [*drunkenly, half hearing*]. Who'd buy me? Buy
  me? What for?

PHILOLACHES. Please, by Pollux, do stand up—my father's
  here!

CALLIDAMATES [*drunkenly*].   Your father's here?
  Tell him to go off again. Why did he have to come back
  here?

PHILOLACHES [*terribly upset*]. What can I do now, when
  Father comes and finds me drunk like this,
  Finds his house is overflowing full of girls and party guests?
  What a thing—to start to dig a well when you're already
  thirsty.   380
  That's my problem—what to do. My father's here and I'm
  in trouble.

TRANIO [*indicating* CALLIDAMATES]. Look, your friend has
  fallen off asleep again. Do shake him up.

PHILOLACHES. Hey—wake up, my father's come back home.

CALLIDAMATES.   What's that? Your father?
  Get my sandals and my weapons, then I'll go and kill your
  father!*

PHILOLACHES. You'll destroy us!

DELPHIUM.   Do be quiet.

PHILOLACHES [*to slaves*].   Carry this guy in at once.

CALLIDAMATES [*drunkenly, to one of the slaves carrying him
  inside*]. Hey—are you a chamber pot? You will be in
  another second.

                                    [*They carry* CALLIDAMATES *inside*

PHILOLACHES. Oh, we're dead!

TRANIO.   Be brave. I'll medicate your misery . . . with wit.

PHILOLACHES. Oh, I'm finished.

TRANIO.   Quiet, will you? I'll dream up some remedy.
  Look—will it suffice you if I see your now-arriving father
  Doesn't set foot in this house and even rushes far from it?   390
  For the moment, go inside and clear the party stuff away.

PHILOLACHES. Where will I be?

TRANIO.   Where you like it best: with
her. And Cal with Del.

DELPHIUM. Wouldn't it be better if we left?

TRANIO.   Don't even budge, my dear.
If you stay inside, you can drink up no less than right out
here.

PHILOLACHES. Oh, ye gods, what will your sweet words bring?
I'm drunk with fear!

TRANIO. Look—can you keep calm and follow all my orders?

PHILOLACHES.   Yes, I think.

TRANIO. First and foremost, girls, I want the two of you to
go inside.

DELPHIUM. Both of us will be most dutiful to you.*

                              [*The girls slink off into the house*

TRANIO.   Jove make it so.
[*Playing commander in chief, to* PHILOLACHES]
All right, pay attention now; I'll tell you what I want from
you:

First and foremost, have the house completely closed and
locked up tight.*   400

Be on guard inside; don't let a single person mumble—

PHILOLACHES [*nods*].   Yes.

TRANIO. Make it look like no one really lives here.

PHILOLACHES [*repeating*].   'No one lives here.'

TRANIO.   Right.
When the old man knocks, nobody answers. Not a living
soul.

PHILOLACHES. Yes, what else?

TRANIO.   The front-door key, that locks
you in from here outside,

Get it to me, then I'll lock the house and close it up
completely.

PHILOLACHES [*getting emotional*]. Tranio, it's in your hands—
my welfare and my wealth as well.

                              [*He goes into the house*

TRANIO [*much bravado*]. If a man has talent, it's no different   407–8
if he's a slave or master.

                              [TRANIO *goes to the front of the
                              stage to address the audience*

The man who has no bit of boldness in his breast,
It doesn't matter if he's high or low in life,   410
He fails as fast as anyone—if he's a failure.
And yet you have to seek out someone super-smart
To take a bungled business that is in hot water
And see that everything calms down, no damage done,
While he himself is not ashamed of anything.
Now *that's* what *I* intend! I'll take our sea of troubles
And soothe them down to absolute tranquillity,
No single bit of pain produced for anyone.

> *At this moment, a* BOY SLAVE *steps out of the*
> *house, carrying a huge key*

TRANIO. But why have you come out here, Sphaerio? [*Sees
key*] Ah, good!
You fully followed my instructions.

BOY [*carefully repeating a message*].   Master orders—   420
And begs you please—to chase his father off somehow.
Don't let him come inside.

TRANIO.   You tell our master this:
His dad will feel such terror just to *see* the house
He'll flee completely panicked, with a shrouded head.
I'll take the key. Go in and lock the doors up tight.
I'll also lock them up out here.

> [*Boy exits*

                    We're ready for him.
The games we hold today, while this old man's alive,
Will far outmatch whatever games he'll get when dead.*
I'll leave the door and set a lookout post up here.

> [*He skips to a corner of the stage, peers off*

And when the old man comes, I'll fill him full of it.*   430

> [*A pause—musical interlude?*

> *Finally, enter old* THEOPROPIDES,
> *dressed in his travelling clothes*

THEOPROPIDES. O Neptune, what a debt of gratitude I owe
thee!
For thou allowed me, half alive, to reach my home.
Indeed, if after this you learn I've gone to sea,
Or set a single foot upon a wave, proceed

To do me in the way you almost did me now.
Away with you, away, away forevermore!
I've trusted you with everything I'll ever trust.

TRANIO [*aside*]. By Pollux, Neptune, thou hast really blundered
    badly:
For thou allowed the perfect chance to slip right by.

THEOPROPIDES. I'm coming home from Egypt after three long
    years.   440
My people surely are most anxious to receive me.

TRANIO [*aside*]. The man your people are most anxious to
    receive
Is someone who would bring them news that you were dead!
                       [THEOPROPIDES *has gone up to his house*

THEOPROPIDES. I say, what's this? The doors are all locked
    up in daytime?
I'll knock. [*He knocks*] Hello—is someone home? Hey—
    open up!

TRANIO [*revealing himself to* THEOPROPIDES, *melodramatic-
    ally*]. What man is this who now approaches our front
    door?

THEOPROPIDES. It's Tranio, my slave!

TRANIO.   O Theopropides!
Dear master, greetings! Great to see you safe and sound.
Have you been well?

THEOPROPIDES.   As well as now.

TRANIO [*a bit uneasy*].   That's nice to hear.

THEOPROPIDES. And you—are you unwell?

TRANIO.   Unwell?

THEOPROPIDES.   Well, look at you—   450
You stroll while not a living soul stays in the house.
No guard, no janitor, no one to open up.
I nearly broke both doors from knocking on and on.

TRANIO [*in mock shock*]. What's that—you touched the
    house???

THEOPROPIDES.   You have to touch to knock.

TRANIO. You touched it?

THEOPROPIDES.   Yes, I knocked it too.

TRANIO.   Oh, god!

THEOPROPIDES.   What's wrong?

TRANIO. A dirty deed.

THEOPROPIDES.   What's going on?

TRANIO.   Impossible
  To say how horrible, horrendous—also bad.

THEOPROPIDES. But what?

TRANIO.   Just flee! Flee far from this most foul front
  door!   460
  Flee hither, flee to me. [THEOPROPIDES approaches TRANIO]
  Sir, did you really touch?

THEOPROPIDES. You tell me how to knock and still not touch
  a door.

TRANIO. By Hercules, you killed—

THEOPROPIDES [quivering].   I killed?

TRANIO.   Your near and dear ones.

THEOPROPIDES. Oh, what an omen—gods and goddesses
  forbid!

TRANIO. I tremble . . . Can you purify yourself and kin?

THEOPROPIDES. But why? What is this unexpected shock you
  bring?

> Two of THEOPROPIDES' PORTERS now come
> on-stage, to deliver the old man's baggage to
> his house. TRANIO watches them approach
> with trepidation

TRANIO. Oh no, hey, hey! [To THEOPROPIDES] Please tell those
  two to both retreat.

THEOPROPIDES. You two—retreat!

TRANIO [to PORTERS].   Don't touch the house
  oh no!
  Go quickly—touch the ground!

THEOPROPIDES.   But tell me what's so wrong
  with touching?

    [TRANIO sighs a deep sigh, as if to say, 'This is it'

TRANIO. It's seven months now since we haven't gone in there. 470
  It's seven months since we have all moved out.

THEOPROPIDES. But why? Speak up!

TRANIO.   First look around for other people.
  Does someone try to catch our conversation?

THEOPROPIDES [looks high and low. Sees nothing]. All clear.

TRANIO [stalling for time—to dream up a story]. Uh—look
  around again.

THEOPROPIDES [*looks high and low*]. There's no one. Speak
   up, will you?

TRANIO. The sin . . . was murder.

THEOPROPIDES.   Huh? I don't quite understand.

TRANIO. A sin committed long ago in ancient times.

THEOPROPIDES. In ancient times?

TRANIO.   We just found out in modern times.

THEOPROPIDES. What sort of sin? And who committed it?
   Tell, tell!

TRANIO. A guest was taken unawares by a host—and
   slaughtered.

   I think it was the man who sold the house to you.   480

THEOPROPIDES. S-slaughtered?

TRANIO. Yes. And robbed his own guest's gold, and then—
He buried his own guest right in this house of yours.

THEOPROPIDES [*trembling*]. But how—how did you know of
   it—did you suspect?

TRANIO. I'll tell you. Listen carefully: he had dined out—
Your son, that is—and after dinner he came home.
We went to bed. We all of us were sleeping tight.
By chance, I had forgotten to put the lantern out.
And suddenly he screamed. An awful scream he screamed!

THEOPROPIDES. Who screamed? My son?

TRANIO.   Be quiet, will you? Listen closely.
He told me that the corpse came to him in a dream.   490

THEOPROPIDES. So it was in a dream?

TRANIO.   It was, but listen closely.
He told me that the corpse addressed him in this manner—

THEOPROPIDES. Within a dream?

TRANIO.   How could he talk to him awake?
The man was murdered over sixty years ago!
At times you can be rather silly, sir. . . .   495

THEOPROPIDES [*chastened*]. I'll shut my mouth.

TRANIO.   And then within the dream, he spake:
'My name's Transoceanus from . . . across the sea.*
I'm housèd in this house where I must house myself—
The King of Hades has refused to let me in
Because I died . . . too early. And I was deceived   500
By someone's word of honour: my host slaughtered me,

And buried me in secret—here—unfuneralled.
A sin. A sin for gold. Now, boy, move out of here!
The house is full of sin, the habitation cursed.'
[*To* THEOPROPIDES] I'd need at least a year to tell you all
   the horrors, sir.

      [*Suddenly, noise filters out from the closed house*
TRANIO [*whispering loudly to those within*].   Sh, sh!
THEOPROPIDES. By Hercules, what's happened now?
TRANIO.   The door has creaked.
   It's *he* who tapped.
THEOPROPIDES [*in terror*]. I haven't got a drop of blood left!
   The dead can carry me alive right down to Hades!
TRANIO [*to himself*]. I'm lost! Those folk inside perturb my
   perfect story!   510
I greatly fear he'll catch me in the act of lying!
THEOPROPIDES. What are you saying to yourself?
TRANIO [*stirring up panic again*].   Retreat, retreat!
   And flee, by Hercules!
THEOPROPIDES.   Flee where? Why don't *you* flee?
TRANIO. I have no fear. I've made my peace with all the
   dead.

      [*From inside the house, young* PHILOLACHES' *voice*
PHILOLACHES. Hey, Tranio!
TRANIO [*whispering through the door*]. Take care—don't call
   me by my name!
   [*Now aloud, a statement to 'the ghost'*] I'm wholly
   blameless. *I've* not tapped these sinful walls.   516
THEOPROPIDES. Who *are* you talking to?
TRANIO [*to* THEOPROPIDES, *pretending surprise*]. Oh, was that
   you who called?   519
Dear gods above, I thought it was the dead man speaking,
Perhaps to ask me why you dared to touch the door.
But why do you still stand there? What of my advice?
THEOPROPIDES. What should I do?
TRANIO.   Flee! Don't look back—and shroud your head!
THEOPROPIDES. And you don't flee?
TRANIO   I told you, I'm at peace with them.
THEOPROPIDES. But just a while ago you were in fear and
   trembling.   525

TRANIO. Don't worry, please, I'll look out for myself.
But you go on—go flee and fly with utmost speed.
And call 'Sweet Hercules!'
THEOPROPIDES [*obeys completely, starts running*]. I call 'Sweet
Hercules!'

[*He scurries off-stage*

TRANIO. I'll call on him as well—to give you awful trouble.
Immortal gods above, I bid you all draw near   530
To see the splendid trouble I've created here!

[TRANIO *ecstatically skips off—to
the back of the 'haunted' house**
From the exit nearer the forum, enter
*MISARGYRIDES, *the moneylender, a miser-of-
misers. As he begins to address the audience,*
TRANIO *re-enters from inside the house*

MISARGYRIDES. It's been a cursed year for lending cash at
interest.
I've never seen a season worse than this has been.
I'm in the forum all day long from dawn till dusk
Unable to find customers to lend a bit.
TRANIO [*noticing* MISARGYRIDES, *aside*]. Oh, now we're fully
finished off forevermore!
The broker's here, who lent us cash on interest
To buy the girl and pay for our expensive parties.
We're caught red-handed if I don't do something fast
To keep this from our senior master. I'll go meet him.   540

And now enter THEOPROPIDES *as well!*
TRANIO *sees the old man and is struck by yet
another blow*

What's this? What brings *that* fellow back so soon?
I tremble—has he got a hint of what we've done?
I'd better greet him too! Am I in awful shape!
There's nothing worse than *knowing* that you've done a
wrong.
And do I know! But since I've stirred things up already,
I'll go on stirring. That's the order of the day.

[*He goes to* THEOPROPIDES

What a surprise!

THEOPROPIDES.   I met the chap I bought the house from.

TRANIO [*taken aback*]. Uh—did you mention anything—of
    what I told you?

THEOPROPIDES. By Hercules, I told him everything!

TRANIO [*aside*].   Oh no!
    I tremble—all my tricks have permanently perished!   550

THEOPROPIDES [*to* TRANIO]. What are you mumbling?

TRANIO.   Nothing, nothing. Tell me this:
    What did you say?

THEOPROPIDES.   Why, everything from start to finish.

TRANIO. Did he confess about his guest?

THEOPROPIDES.   No, he denied it.
    [*A new topic*] What's your advice for now?

TRANIO.   You're asking my advice?
    By Hercules, I'd take the thing to arbitration.
    [*Aside*] But get a judge who'd swallow anything I say.
    You'd win as easily as foxes eat a pear.*

MISARGYRIDES. But look—there's Philolaches' slave man
    Tranini.*   560
    Those fellows never pay me principal or interest.

            [TRANIO *starts toward* MISARGYRIDES, *who is on*
            one side of the stage, while THEOPROPIDES
            stands at the opposite end

THEOPROPIDES [*to* TRANIO]. But where're you going?

TRANIO [*to himself*].   Nowhere. I'm in no condition.
    Oh, am I cursed, born under inauspicious stars.
    The man will dun me while my master's here. It's tragic.
    On either side of me an awful time awaits.
    I'll seize the situation.

MISARGYRIDES.   He approaches. All is saved.
    There's hope for money yet.

TRANIO [*aside*].   He's happy—but he's wrong.
    [*Calling*] Hello, Misargyrides, hope you're feeling well.

MISARGYRIDES. Well, what about my money?

TRANIO.   Do behave yourself.
    The minute I arrive, you throw your javelins.   570

MISARGYRIDES. A worthless man!

TRANIO [*ironically*]. Now there's a truthful prophecy.

MISARGYRIDES. Don't start some dodge with me.

TRANIO.   Then speak—what's on your mind?

MISARGYRIDES. Where's Philolaches?

TRANIO [too, too friendly]. Ah, dear friend, you couldn't have
   Arrived more opportunely than you've just arrived.

MISARGYRIDES. How come?

TRANIO. Come over here . . . [beckons MISARGYRIDES to a quiet
   corner]

MISARGYRIDES [loudly]. When do I get my interest?

TRANIO. I know you've got a healthy voice; please don't shout.

MISARGYRIDES. By Hercules, why not?

TRANIO.   Do me a little favour.

MISARGYRIDES. What sort of little favour?

TRANIO.   Won't you please . . . go home?

MISARGYRIDES. Go home?

TRANIO.   Come back here sometime after midday, please.

MISARGYRIDES. But will I get my interest then?

TRANIO.   You will. Now go. 580

MISARGYRIDES ['adding' things up in his miserly mind]. But
   why expend the effort and exhaust myself?
   I think I'll wait around right here till midday.

TRANIO. Oh no, go home. By Hercules, it's better home.

MISARGYRIDES. Why don't I get my interest? Why these jokes
   with me?

TRANIO. By Hercules, I wish you would . . . go home for now.

MISARGYRIDES. By Hercules, I'll call my client—

TRANIO [ironically].   Loud, I'm sure!
   Your greatest joy is loudness.

MISARGYRIDES.   I just want what's mine.
   For days and days you've held me off with tricks like this.
   If I annoy you, pay me, then I'll go away.   590
   The single phrase 'I'll pay' will end all complications.

TRANIO [a sudden thought—to faze MISARGYRIDES]. Well—
   take your principal.

MISARGYRIDES.   I want my interest first!

TRANIO. What's that? You lowest, basest, vilest man on earth!
   You're practising extortion? No, go do your worst.
   He owes you zero.

MISARGYRIDES [flabbergasted]. Owes me zero?

TRANIO.   Now you won't get
  A single spot of dust from us. Are you afraid
  He'll leave the city, just to dodge your interest?
  He's offering the principal.
MISARGYRIDES.   But I don't want it!
  I first and foremost want to get some interest paid me.   599–600
TRANIO. Look, don't annoy us. Nothing you can do will help.
  You think that you're the only moneylender here?
MISARGYRIDES [*starting to foam at the mouth*]. My interest
      now, my interest, interest; pay me interest!
  Will you please pay my interest to me right away?
  I want my interest!
TRANIO.   'Interest' here and 'interest' there,
  The only interest this man has in life is 'interest'.
  Do go away. I think in all my years on earth
  I've never seen a fouler, viler beast than you.
MISARGYRIDES. By Pollux, you don't scare me with those
      words of yours!
                              [*Across the stage, old* THEOPROPIDES
                                has been waiting quasi-patiently
THEOPROPIDES. Hot talk! Why, even over here I feel the heat. 609a
  [*A bit louder*] I wonder what that interest is the man is
      after.   610
TRANIO [*to* MISARGYRIDES, *indicating* THEOPROPIDES]. Look,
      there's his father, just returned from overseas.
  He'll give you back your principal and interest too,
  So stop your bearing down and shady practices.
  That man won't make you wait.
MISARGYRIDES.   I'll take what I can get.
THEOPROPIDES [*to* TRANIO]. Hey, Tranio!
TRANIO.   Yes, sir?
                              [*Dashes over to* THEOPROPIDES
THEOPROPIDES.   Who's that? What is he claiming?
  Why does he seem to mention my son Philolaches?
  Why does he make this sort of hue and cry to you?
  What's owed the man?
TRANIO.   By Hercules, give orders, sir,
  To smash this rotten fellow's face with all his cash.
THEOPROPIDES. Give orders?

TRANIO.   Yes—to knock his block off with hard currency. 620

MISARGYRIDES. I'd gladly suffer any knocks for blocks of
cash. 621

TRANIO. Did you hear that? The perfect moneylender speaks. 625
A moneylender—vilest, foulest breed there is.

THEOPROPIDES. Don't tell me what he is; I don't care where
he's from.

I really want to know and long to be informed. 628

What is this sum that Philolaches owes this man? 622

TRANIO. A teeny bit.

THEOPROPIDES.   How teeny?

TRANIO.   Forty thousand drachmae.
That isn't very much.

THEOPROPIDES [*ironically*].   Oh no, it's tiny. 624

I hear there's interest due as well. So what's the total? 629

TRANIO. Our total debt to him is—[*quickly*] forty-four thousand drachmae. 630
Just say you'll pay—and send him off.

THEOPROPIDES.   Just say I'll pay??? 633

TRANIO. Just say you'll pay.

THEOPROPIDES.   Myself?

TRANIO.   In person. Listen, sir,
Go on and say it, I command you.

THEOPROPIDES.   Tell me this:
That money—what'd you do with it?

TRANIO.   It's solid.

THEOPROPIDES.   Solid?
Then pay him back yourself, if that's the case.

TRANIO [*coming up with a big idea, makes a big announce-
ment*].   Your son—
Has bought a house.

THEOPROPIDES.   A house?

TRANIO.   A house.

THEOPROPIDES [*ecstatic*].   Oh, goody, goody!
His father's son he is, he is, he's going into business!*
A house, you say?

TRANIO [*nods*].   A house. And do you know what kind? 640

THEOPROPIDES. How could I know?

TRANIO.   Oh, boy!

THEOPROPIDES.   *What kind?*
TRANIO.   Don't even ask!
THEOPROPIDES. Oh, tell!
TRANIO.   A splendiddifferiffic, brilliant building!
THEOPROPIDES. By Hercules, well done! What did he pay for
   it?
TRANIO. Two silver talents. One plus one—like you and me.
  He gave as cash deposit forty thousand drachmae.   645
  [*Indicating the moneylender*] We borrowed cash from him
    to pay the owner—understand?
  The moment we discovered that our house was . . . cursed
  Your son made haste to buy himself another house.
THEOPROPIDES. By Hercules, well done!   649–51
MISARGYRIDES [*to himself*]. The day is fast collecting noon.
TRANIO [*to* THEOPROPIDES]. Let's rid ourselves of him—before
  he pukes on us.
  Our total debt to him is forty-four thousand drachmae   652a
  Both principal and interest—   631
MISARGYRIDES.   And that's all I seek.
TRANIO. I'd like to see you dare demand a penny more!   632
THEOPROPIDES [*to* MISARGYRIDES]. Young man, you'll deal
  with me.
MISARGYRIDES [*to* THEOPROPIDES].   So I collect from you?
THEOPROPIDES. Collect tomorrow.
MISARGYRIDES.   Good. Tomorrow. Good, good, good.
      [*Rubbing his greedy hands in anticipation,*
      MISARGYRIDES *shuffles off*
TRANIO [*at* MISARGYRIDES, *as he goes*]. May all the gods and
  goddesses give trouble to you!   655
  You missed destroying all my plans by half-a-hair's breadth.
  [*To audience*] By Pollux, you won't find a fouler class of
  men
  Or men less lawful than the moneylending breed!
THEOPROPIDES. What sort of neighbourhood did my boy buy
  this house in?
TRANIO [*aside*]. I'm lost again!
THEOPROPIDES.   Speak up, I asked you something.   660
TRANIO. I can't—I just forgot the former owner's name.
THEOPROPIDES. Come on, just use your wits, my lad.

TRANIO [*aside*].   What can I do?
Unless I choose our neighbour's house . . .
And claim this is the house his son just bought. I've heard
That lies taste best when served up piping hot. All right, 665
Whatever hodgepodge heaven hints, I'll hand to him. 667

THEOPROPIDES. Well, have you thought it out?

TRANIO [*to* THEOPROPIDES]. That goddamned owner, sir—
[*Aside*] My goddamned master! [*Aloud*] Sir . . . it is your
neighbour's house.

[*Indicating* SIMO's *home*] Your son just bought this house.

THEOPROPIDES [*wide-eyed with joy*]. I can't believe it's true! 670

TRANIO. Well, if you pay whatever cash is due, it's true.
If you don't pay the cash, then what I'm saying isn't true.

THEOPROPIDES. And not just in a goodly part of town—

TRANIO [*feeding his enthusiasm*].   The very best!

THEOPROPIDES. By Hercules, I'd love to look inside. Please
knock.
Yes, Tranio. Go summon someone from inside.

TRANIO [*aside*]. I'm lost again—I really don't know what to
say!
Another time the tide has turned me on the rocks!

THEOPROPIDES. What now?

TRANIO [*aside*]. By Hercules, I don't know what to do.
I'm caught red-handed.

THEOPROPIDES.   Call somebody out at once.
I want a tour.

TRANIO [*nervously*]. But, sir . . . there are the women, sir. 680
We ought to ask permission—if they are presentable.

THEOPROPIDES. The proper thing to do. You go ahead and
ask.
And while you do, I'll wait outside right here.

TRANIO [*aside to the audience*]. May all the gods and goddesses destroy this old man—
For giving all my plans attacks from every side!

*At this very moment, the door of the 'new' house
opens, and out comes* SIMO, *a chubby old man,
who is slightly drunk from dinner.*

TRANIO. What luck! The owner of the house is stepping out.

Old Simo in the flesh. I'll step aside to watch,
And call a senate assembly inside my interior soul.
I'll broach the man as soon as I think up a plan.

    [*As* TRANIO *slinks into the alley to eavesdrop,*
      SIMO *steps down-stage to sing a solo*

SIMO [*singing*].

> That was the best meal of the year.   690
> Never have I eaten better.
> What a fine dinner prepared by my wife.
> But after she wanted to 'sleep' and I wouldn't let her.
> That old hag made a dinner better than usual,
> Simply a plot to get me to bed.
> 'Sleep isn't good after dinner,' I said.
> Secretly, quietly, I have slipped out.
> Wife will be wild at me, I have no doubt.

TRANIO [*aside*]. What a bad evening's preparing for that old
    duffer.   700
    In sleep and at supper he'll suffer.

SIMO.

> The more I reflect, as I think very deep,
> I see wedding a hag for some gold in a bag
> Means you won't oversleep.
> The bedroom is torture, so I'd rather roam.
> Better work in the forum than bed her at home.   706–7

[*Winks at the audience*] By Pollux, I don't know of your
    wives—are their ways diverse?
I know my case is bad and it's bound to get worse.   709–10

TRANIO [*aside*]. It's your own ways, old man, that have made
    your life worsen.
Blame no god in the sky, blame your own very person.   712–13
But it's time now for me to deceive that old man.
For I've just had a thought and I've just found a plan,
A ruse that will fend off a bruise just as far as I can.
I'll approach him and broach him. Hi, Simo—the gods
    make you glad.

SIMO. Ah, Tranio!

TRANIO.   How have you been?

SIMO.   Not too bad.

[*They shake hands warmly*
Doing what?

TRANIO.   Shaking hands with a wonderful guy.

SIMO [*smiles*].   Thank you, lad.
I would like to requite those nice words you just gave:
[*With a smile*] I am now shaking hands with a wonder-
ful . . . rogue of a slave.   720

THEOPROPIDES [*calling from across the stage*]. Hey, you
whipping post, come over here.

TRANIO [*calling over, nervously*]. One minute, one minute! 721a

SIMO [*to* TRANIO, *confidentially*]. How's the house?

TRANIO.   Sir?

SIMO.   The house. What is now going on in it?
I approve! Life is short.
We must live every minute!

TRANIO. Uh, sir? Beg your pardon?
I scarcely can grasp what you're saying.

SIMO. I'm saying—keep playing. Live life as a song—
Keep wining and dining, keep rolling in clover—

TRANIO [*confidentially, to* SIMO].   That life is . . . all over. 729–30

SIMO. What?

TRANIO.   All of us, one great big fall of us, Simo.

SIMO. It was all going well for you.

TRANIO.   I can't deny that's a fact.
We lived it, we loved it, there's nothing we lacked.
But, Simo, a storm came, our good ship is racked.

SIMO. But your ship was so sound, pulled right up on dry
ground.

TRANIO. But another ship rammed. Now we're damned—and
we're drowned!   740

SIMO. I'm on your side, but what's the problem? Tell me,
please.

TRANIO. Master—back from overseas.

[*End of musical moment. A
pause.* SIMO *gets the picture*

SIMO [*to* TRANIO, *with a wry smile*]. For you a slight *ironic*
twist. You're in a kind of cruci—fix?

TRANIO. I beg you, please don't tell my master.

SIMO.   He won't get a thing from me.

TRANIO. Thank you, you're my patron.

SIMO.   I don't need your kind of client, thank you.

TRANIO. But now the reason Master sent me here to you—

SIMO. No, first you answer something I would like to ask:
  How much of your affairs does he already know?

TRANIO. Why—not a thing.

SIMO.   He hasn't shouted at his son?   750

TRANIO. His sky is blue and calm and balmy. All is clear.
  But now he's asked me to convey a strong request.
  He'd like to take a look around inside your house.

SIMO. It's not for sale.

TRANIO.   I know, of course. But the old man
  Is anxious to build women's quarters in his own house,
  And baths and paths and porticoes, a big construction.

SIMO. Whatever made him dream of doing this?

TRANIO.   I'll tell you, sir.
  He's very anxious that his son now take a wife
  As soon as possible. And so—the women's quarters.
  He said he heard some architect, I don't know who,   760
  Discuss your house design. The man was mad with praise.
  And so he'd like to copy from it, do you mind?
  The special thing he wants to copy from your house is this:
  He's heard you have terrific shade, all summer through,
  And all day long, and even if it's awfully bright.

SIMO [surprised]. But listen here—when shadows fall all over
    town
  There's *never* shade in here. It's sunny all day long.
  The sun just stays—as if it were a bill collector.
  The only shade I have at all is down my well.

TRANIO [with a weak laugh]. Well . . . shady things are shady,
    sun is . . . nice and bright.*   770

SIMO. Look, don't annoy me. Things are as I've just explained.

TRANIO. But still, he'd like to look around.

SIMO.   Well, let him look!
  If he sees anything he likes and wants to copy,
  Why, let him build it.

TRANIO.   Can I call him?

SIMO.   Go and call him.

[TRANIO *struts across the stage and shares
his satisfaction with the audience*

TRANIO. They say Kings Alexander and Agathocles*
Were two who did big things. Now would you say *I'm*
third—
Who solo does so many memorable things?
I've saddled up both old men like a pair of mules.
This latest ploy I've started isn't bad at all!
For just as muleteers have saddled mules to ride,   780
I've got two saddled men to act as mules for me.
They're loaded up—and what a load they're carrying!

[*Music begins*

[*Singing*] Now I must talk to him, walk up and talk to
him.
Hey, Theo, hey!

THEOPROPIDES.   Who's calling, I say?

TRANIO. Your multi-faithful servant.

THEOPROPIDES.   Say, where have you been?

TRANIO. Your mission, sir, is, sir, accomplished. You now
can begin.

THEOPROPIDES. But what on earth caused such a delay?

TRANIO. The man was engaged in some business, so I had to
wait.

THEOPROPIDES. I know you—the slow you—you've always
been late.

TRANIO. The ancient proverb, sir, still bears repeating: 790
'No one can whistle the same time he's eating.'
I couldn't be with you right here—and also be there too.

THEOPROPIDES. What now?

TRANIO.   You can visit his house just as
long as you care to.

THEOPROPIDES. Go on, lead the way.

TRANIO.   Am I causing delay?

THEOPROPIDES.   Lead the way.

TRANIO [*confidentially to* THEOPROPIDES]. Look at the old
boy just standing there—sad to behold it,
He's very unhappy—regrets having sold it.

THEOPROPIDES. Why so?

TRANIO.   He's been constantly begging, pursuing
And pleading to cancel the sale.

THEOPROPIDES [*the tough businessman*].   Nothing doing!
  'A man sows his crop, and the man must then reap it.'   800
  If *we* were complaining, he'd force us to keep it.
  No, 'All sales are final', 'What's been done, don't undo',
  'Pity's a luxury', 'Eat what you chew'.
TRANIO. Your words of wisdom slow me down. Please follow
  me.
THEOPROPIDES.   That's what I'll do.
  Faithfully I'll follow you.

                          [*They cross the stage to* SIMO

TRANIO [*to* THEOPROPIDES]. Look—there's the old man. [*To*
  SIMO] Here's your man....
SIMO. Greetings, Theopropides, I'm glad you're back both
  safe and sound.
THEOPROPIDES. Greetings.
SIMO.   Your man told me that you'd like to look around.
THEOPROPIDES. If you wouldn't mind.
SIMO.   I wouldn't mind. Go in and look around.
THEOPROPIDES. But of course, the women—
SIMO.   Women? Don't you care a hoot for them!
  Stroll around in any room you'd like; pretend the house is
  yours.
THEOPROPIDES [*whispers to* TRANIO]. What—'pretend'?
TRANIO [*whispers back*]. Oh, let's not put the gentleman
  through further pain,   810
  Throwing up the fact you've bought his place. You see
  how sad he looks.
THEOPROPIDES. Yes, I see.
TRANIO. Well, let's not make it worse by making fun of him.
  Let's not mention that you've bought it any more.
THEOPROPIDES.   I see your point.
  Well advised. I think that's very sensitive of you, my boy.*
  Now what, Simo?
SIMO.   Go inside, just take your time and look around.
THEOPROPIDES. Very nice, considerate. I thank you kindly.
SIMO.   You're quite welcome.

                  [TRANIO *further 'sells' his master
                    the qualities of the house*

TRANIO. Look at what a vestibule it has; observe the wonderful
  front path.

THEOPROPIDES. Splendid, splendid, oh, by Pollux—

TRANIO.   Take a good look at those pillars.

   [*Ironically gestures to the audience that he means the two old men*]

   Solid, strong, and oh so thick. Oh yes, dear Master, oh so thick!

THEOPROPIDES. Never have I seen more pretty pillars.

SIMO.   And the price I paid— 820
   Pretty penny, even long ago.

TRANIO [*to* THEOPROPIDES].   You hear that 'long ago'?
   He can scarcely keep from weeping.

THEOPROPIDES [*to* SIMO]. How much did you pay for them?

SIMO. Paid three hundred drachmae for them both; delivery was extra, too.

THEOPROPIDES [*examining more closely*]. Hercules! I see they're not as good as what I first believed.

TRANIO. Why?

THEOPROPIDES. Because, by Pollux, they've got termite trouble, both of them.

TRANIO [*again, ironically to the audience, suggesting the old men*]. Past their prime is what I'd say's the major trouble with them both.

   Still and all, they'd do quite well, if we'd just throw some tar on them.

   They're well built. No pasta-eating *foreign* workmen did the job.*

   Also, sir, observe the door joint.

THEOPROPIDES.   Yes, I see.

TRANIO.   Terrific dolts!

THEOPROPIDES. Dolts, what dolts?

TRANIO.   Excuse me, sir, I meant 'terrific bolts', of course. 830
   Seen enough?

THEOPROPIDES.

                The more I see, the more I really like the house!

TRANIO. [*to mock them still further, points above the doorway*]. See the picture painted there—the crow who's mocking two old vultures?

THEOPROPIDES. I don't see a thing.

TRANIO.   But *I* do. I can see the crow is standing

Right between the vultures and by turns he twits at each of
  them.
Look at me, just look at me, and tell me if you see the crow.

                              [THEOPROPIDES *turns*
See the crow?

THEOPROPIDES [*confused*]. Why, no, I see no crow of any
  kind at all.
TRANIO. Look in your direction, then, although the crow's
  not in your sight.
Maybe if you glance about, you'll catch a glimpse of those
  two vultures.
THEOPROPIDES [*frustrated*]. Stop this, will you, I can't see a
  painted bird of any sort!
TRANIO. Well, forget it, I forgive you. At your age, it's tough
  to spot.   840
THEOPROPIDES. What I can see I adore, I'll tell you that. I
  just adore it!
SIMO. Look some more; you'll find it worth the effort.
THEOPROPIDES.   Pollux, good advice!
SIMO [*calling to a slave inside his house*]. Boy, come here and
  take this fellow round the house and all the bedrooms.
[*To* THEOPROPIDES] Can't take you around myself. I've
  got some business in the forum.
THEOPROPIDES [*feeling very smart*]. Never mind a run-around
  from anyone; I need no leading.
When it comes to being taken in, I'm taken in by no one. 846–7
SIMO. Even into houses?
THEOPROPIDES [*smiles*]. No one ever takes me in.
SIMO.   Then go!
THEOPROPIDES. In I go.
TRANIO.   But wait—beware the dog!
THEOPROPIDES [*unbrave*].   Y-you beware for me!
TRANIO [*now an impromptu dog act*]. Dog! Hey, dog! Go
  'way! Go kill yourself! Go right to hell!   850
Dog, go, dog! [*to* THEOPROPIDES] The dog won't go. [*to*
  '*dog*'] Go, dog!
SIMO.   That little thing can't hurt you.*
She's as harmless as all other pregnant pooches. Go, be
  brave!

Forum for myself for now. Farewell.

> [*He walks off*

THEOPROPIDES [*calling after* SIMO].   Farewell—and many
thanks.

Tranio, be good enough to get someone to take that dog
off.

Even though she isn't . . . fearsome.

TRANIO [*peeking at the 'dog' again*]. Look at her—so sweetly
sleeping.

You don't want to have the people think you're frightened.

THEOPROPIDES [*half-heartedly*].   No—you're right.

Follow me inside now.

TRANIO [*grandiloquent*]. Sir, there's nothing can deter me
from you.

> [*They both enter* SIMO'S *house*
> *After a pause* [*musical interlude?*],
> *enter* PHANISCUS, *slave to young* CALLIDAMATES.
> *He sings of the joys of good slave behaviour*

PHANISCUS. It's the slaves who are fault-free and *still* fear the
whips

Who serve masters best.

The slaves who fear nothing, they earn themselves something.   860

They'll pay for their folly—they'll soon be distressed.

All they're doing is training for sprinting. They run. When
they're caught,

They see it's a nest egg of torture they've bought.*

For the sake of my skin is how I always act.   868

So I keep it intact.

If my hand is commanded, my roof will stay strong.   870

Let it rain in on others, let others do wrong.

For however the slaves treat their master, that treatment
they see:

He's good if they're good; if .hey're bad, bad he'll be.

Our own slaves at home are the worst on this earth;

Their 'goods' are expended, bad treatment is all that they're
worth.

Just now we were commanded to meet Master here,

But not one volunteer!
They all mocked me for going, the duties I'm showing,
  I've gone out and my goodness will pay:
I'm the one single slave to fetch Master today,   880
  So that breakfast for them will be cowhide to eat.
[*Smiles*] I am one slave who's too good to be beat.
I don't really care about *their* backs, I just care for mine.
They'll be drawn and quartered, *I'll* do what I'm ordered
  . . . and be fine.

  Another slave, PINACIUM, *rushes in after* PHANISCUS

PINACIUM. Wait, Phaniscus!

  Stop a mite!
PHANISCUS [*haughtily*]. Don't annoy me!
PINACIUM. What a monkey!
  Won't you wait—you parasite?
PHANISCUS. I, a parasite?
PINACIUM [*sarcastically*]. Wherever you see food—you bite.
PHANISCUS. Well, *I* enjoy it. You drop dead.
PINACIUM. Talk tough—you share the master's bed!*   890
PHANISCUS. You're blurring my eyes. Whenever you talk, there
  are fumes that arise!
PINACIUM. You're a maker of counterfeit coins and counterfeit
  groins.*
PHANISCUS. Nothing you do, boy, will make me lose tether.
  Our master knows me.
PINACIUM.   But, of course! You've been sleeping together!
PHANISCUS. Sober up, and don't curse me.
PINACIUM.   I know you can't bear me,
  I feel quite the same about you.
PHANISCUS.   Kindly spare me.
  Your lecture's a bore.
PINACIUM.   Well, I'll knock on the door.
  [*Knocks at the 'haunted' house, calls grandiloquently*]
Is there a mortal to halt my great fistic assault on this 899–900
  portal?
[*To audience*] Not a soul at the door.
Suitable for disreputable people—they simply ignore.
But I'd better take care

Not to get myself singed in their flaming affair.

> [PINACIUM *and* PHANISCUS *stand at the door,*
> *periodically knocking* [*in pantomime*] *while*
> *the next dialogue takes place*

> TRANIO *and* THEOPROPIDES *come out of* SIMO'S
> *house. The slave is really baiting his master*

TRANIO. Tell me how the deal seems to you now.

THEOPROPIDES.   I'm overjoyed with it!

TRANIO. Too expensive, do you think?

THEOPROPIDES.   Expensive? Oh, by Pollux, never
Ever have I seen a house just tossed away!

TRANIO.   So then you're pleased.

THEOPROPIDES. 'Pleased' you ask me? Hercules, I'm more
  than that, I'm super-pleased!

TRANIO. How about the women's quarters? What a portico—

THEOPROPIDES.   Fantastic!
I don't think you'd find a public portico that's any bigger.

TRANIO. Actually, your son and I, we personally toured the
  city,   910
Measuring the public porticoes.

THEOPROPIDES.   You did?

TRANIO.   And ours *is* biggest.

THEOPROPIDES. What a luscious, lovely deal. By Hercules, if
  someone offered
Half a dozen silver talents, cash in hand, to buy this house
  here,
I'd refuse it.

TRANIO.   Even if you tried to take it, *I'd* prevent you.

THEOPROPIDES. I would say our capital is well invested in
  this deal.

TRANIO. I don't blush to say how much I prompted and
  promoted this,
Forcing him to borrow cash on interest from the moneylender,
Giving it to Simo as deposit. . . .

THEOPROPIDES.   Lad, you saved the ship!
And we owe the moneylender eighty minae?

TRANIO.   Nothing more.

THEOPROPIDES. He'll be paid today.

TRANIO.   You're smart. That way,
   there'll be no complications.   920

   Or—you could give me the cash, and I'll go pay the man
   myself.

THEOPROPIDES [*warily*]. Give the cash to you? Some little
   trick is lurking in that thought.

TRANIO [*irony-clad protestation*]. Would I ever dare to fool
   you for a fact—or even just for fun?

THEOPROPIDES. Would I ever dare to *not* distrust you, or be
   off my guard?

TRANIO. Since I've been your slave, have I bamboozled you
   in any way?

THEOPROPIDES. That's because I've been on guard. So thank
   me and my wits for that.

Being on my guard with you is proof I'm smart.

TRANIO [*aside*].   I quite agree.

THEOPROPIDES [*an order to* TRANIO]. To the country now,
   and tell my son I'm back.*

TRANIO.   At your command.

THEOPROPIDES. Have him sprint with you back to the city —
   at full speed.

TRANIO.   Yessir.   930

             [TRANIO *starts off, then stops*
                to address the audience

Now I'll join my fellow fighters by arriving through the
   rear guard

To report the situation's calmed—and he's been beaten
   back.

             [TRANIO *now skips down the alley between*
                the two houses to get into the 'haunted' one
                through the back door

   Our attention now returns to the two slaves,
   who have kept knocking at the 'haunted' front door
   in pantomime all during the TRANIO–THEOPROPIDES
                conversation

PHANISCUS. Not a sound of merrymaking, as there used to
   be.

I can't hear the singing of a musical girl—or anyone.

THEOPROPIDES [*finally noticing the two servants*]. Now what
is this? Whatever do those people seek at my old house?
Wonder what they want, what they are peeking at.

PINACIUM.   I'll knock again.
Open up! Hey, Tranio, come loose the locks!

THEOPROPIDES.   What farce is this?

PHANISCUS. Open up—we've come to fetch our master, we
were ordered to.

THEOPROPIDES [*calls over*]. Hey, you boys, what are you
doing, what's this beating on the house?

PINACIUM. Hey, old man, why do you ask about what's no
concern of yours?   940

THEOPROPIDES. No concern of mine?

PINACIUM.   Unless you've just been made a new official,*
Authorized to make interrogations and to spy and eavesdrop.

THEOPROPIDES. Where you stand is my own house.

PINACIUM.   Has Philolaches sold the place?

PHANISCUS [*to* PINACIUM]. Maybe that old geezer's simply
trying to bamboozle us.

THEOPROPIDES [*firmly*]. Look, I speak the truth. Now tell
me what's your business here.

PHANISCUS.   It's this:
Here is where our master's boozing.

THEOPROPIDES.   Boozing here?

PHANISCUS.   That's what I said.

THEOPROPIDES. I don't like your cheekiness, my boy.

PHANISCUS.   We're here to pick him up.

THEOPROPIDES. Pick who up?

PINACIUM.   Our master. Must we tell you
all this twenty times?

THEOPROPIDES [*to* PHANISCUS, *ignoring* PINACIUM]. Since you
seem a decent chap, I'll tell you: no one lives here now.

PHANISCUS. Doesn't that young Philolaches live right here
inside this house?   950

THEOPROPIDES. *Used* to live here. He moved out of this house
quite a while ago.

PHANISCUS [*whispers to* PINACIUM]. This old geezer's mad

for sure. [*To* THEOPROPIDES] You're very wildly wrong,
  kind sir.

For, unless he moved last night—or earlier today—I'm
  certain Philolaches lives here.

THEOPROPIDES.   No one's lived here for six months.

PINACIUM.   You're dreaming.

THEOPROPIDES. Dreaming?

PINACIUM.   Dreaming.

THEOPROPIDES [*to* PINACIUM].   Don't butt in. Allow
  me to converse with him.

[*Now to* PHANISCUS] No one lives here.

PHANISCUS.   Someone lives
here now, and also yesterday...

And the day before, the day before, the day before, et
  cetera.

Since his father went abroad, the party's been continuous.

THEOPROPIDES. What is this?

PHANISCUS.   No intermission in the wining or the dining,

Or the wenching, Greeking-up, inviting women skilled in
  music.   960

THEOPROPIDES. Who's been doing this?

PHANISCUS.   Why, Philolaches, sir.

THEOPROPIDES.   What Philolaches, boy?

PHANISCUS. Son of, I believe, one Theopropides.

THEOPROPIDES [*aside*].   He's killing me!

If he tells the truth, he kills me. First I ought to follow
  further.

[*To* PHANISCUS] So you say this person Philolaches has
  been boozing here—

With your master?

PHANISCUS.   Yessir.

THEOPROPIDES.   Boy, you're more a fool than
  you first seemed.   965

Are you sure you didn't stop to have a little snack somewhere,

Having just a teeny-weeny bit too much to drink?

PHANISCUS.   Why so?

THEOPROPIDES. Maybe it's an error and you chose the wrong
  house by mistake.

PHANISCUS. Sir, I'm well aware of where I'm going, and the
place I'm at.

Philolaches lives here—he's the son of Theopropides.   970
When his father went abroad on business, then the young
man freed a
Music girl.

THEOPROPIDES. What? Philolaches?

PHANISCUS.   Philematium—the girl.

THEOPROPIDES [*almost afraid to ask*]. How much?

PHANISCUS.   Only thirty.

THEOPROPIDES.   Thirty talents?

PHANISCUS.   Thirty minae, sir.*

THEOPROPIDES [*in a state of shock*]. So . . . he freed the girl . . .

PHANISCUS [*nodding*]. For thirty minae, yes, indeed, sir.

THEOPROPIDES [*still in disbelief*]. Thirty minae . . . really
. . . spent by Philolaches for a woman?

PHANISCUS. Really.

THEOPROPIDES.   Then he freed her?

PHANISCUS.   Really.

THEOPROPIDES.   Following his father's faring
Forth for foreign fields, the fellow fell to full-time festive
frolicking*
With your master?

PHANISCUS.   Really.

THEOPROPIDES [*almost too afraid to ask*]. Tell me, has he
bought the house next door?

PHANISCUS. No, not really.

THEOPROPIDES.   Was there a down payment to the
man who lives there?

PHANISCUS. No, not really.

THEOPROPIDES.   That's the finish!

PHANISCUS.   Yes—he finished his own father.

THEOPROPIDES. So—your tale is truth.

PHANISCUS. Would it were fiction! You his father's friend?   980

THEOPROPIDES [*nods 'yes'*]. How do you foretell his father's
fall in fortune?

PHANISCUS.   That's not all.
Thirty minae is a straw compared to other wild expenses.

THEOPROPIDES [*half aside*]. Father's fully finished.

PHANISCUS.   And from one slave, one unholy terror:
    Tranio, a sinful rogue who'd even bankrupt Hercules!*
    Oh, by Pollux, how I pity pitifully that boy's poor father. 985
    When he finds this out, the fellow's little heart will fall
        apart!

THEOPROPIDES [agonized]. If the things you say are true—

PHANISCUS.   What profit, sir, would lying get me?

PINACIUM [knocking].   Hey, will someone open up?

PHANISCUS [to PINACIUM]. Why are you knocking—no one's
        there!
    I suppose they've moved the party to another place. Let's
        go . . .

                            [The two slaves start to exit

THEOPROPIDES [calling]. Boy—

PHANISCUS [to PINACIUM]. . . . and search some more for
    Master. Follow me.

PINACIUM.   I'll follow you. 990

THEOPROPIDES. Boy—you can't just go.

PHANISCUS [going].   You have your free-
    dom to protect your back.*
    I have no protection for my own . . . unless I serve my
        master.

                            [With this, PHANISCUS and
                            PINACIUM leave the stage

THEOPROPIDES [in total consternation]. By Hercules, I'm
    finished. Why, from what I hear,
    I haven't travelled back and forth from Egypt,
    But through the vastest reaches, farthest beaches too.   995
    I've circled so, I don't know where I am right now.
    [Looks off-stage] I'll soon find out, for here's the man who
        sold my son
    The house. [To SIMO] How are you?

SIMO [entering].   Coming from the forum home.

THEOPROPIDES. Did anything that's new transpire in the
    forum?

SIMO. Why, yes.

THEOPROPIDES.   Well, what?

SIMO.   I saw a funeral.*

THEOPROPIDES.   And so?   1000

SIMO. The corpse was new: he'd just transpired recently.
   At least, that's how I heard it told.
THEOPROPIDES.   Oh, go to hell!
SIMO. It's your own fault, you busybodied me for news.
THEOPROPIDES. But look, I've just come back from overseas.
SIMO [*sarcastically*].   I'm sorry
   I can't ask you to dinner. I'm invited out.*   1005
THEOPROPIDES. Look, I'm not hinting—
SIMO [*jocular*].   But tomorrow's dinner, then—
   I'll let you ask me—if nobody else does first.
THEOPROPIDES. Look, I'm not hinting for that, either. If you're
   free,
   Please give me your attention now.
SIMO.   Of course, of course.
THEOPROPIDES. From what I know, you've gotten forty minae
   from   1010
   My son.
SIMO.   From what *I* know, I've got no such thing.
THEOPROPIDES. From Tranio, his slave?
SIMO.   That's *more* impossible.
THEOPROPIDES. The first deposit that he gave to you?
SIMO.   You're dreaming!
THEOPROPIDES [*now suspicious of* SIMO's *motives*]. Oh no—
   you're dreaming if you hope this is the way
   You'll cancel our negotiation by some masquerade.
SIMO. I'd cancel what?
THEOPROPIDES.   The deal concluded with my son
   While I was gone.
SIMO [*surprised*]. Negotiations with your son—
   While you were gone? What were the terms? What was the
   date?   1020
THEOPROPIDES. To start with, I still owe you eighty minae . . .
   cash.
SIMO. Oh no, you don't—[*stops, thinks*] Well, if you say so,
   then . . . pay up!
   A deal's a deal, don't try to duck out with a dodge.
THEOPROPIDES. I don't deny the debt at all. I'll gladly pay.
   But you behave, and don't deny you got the forty.

SIMO. By Pollux, look me in the eye and tell me this:
  What did they say you bought with all the cash?
THEOPROPIDES.   Your house.
  [That's why I toured your portico and women's quarters.
SIMO. Why, Tranio told me a wholly different story:]*
  He said you were about to give your son a wife   1027
  And wanted to add women's quarters to your house.
THEOPROPIDES. I wanted to build . . . over *there*?
SIMO.   That's what he said.
THEOPROPIDES. Oh no, I'm lost, I'm absolutely speechless.   1030
  Oh, neighbour, I'm for ever finished.
SIMO [*suspecting*].   Tranio
  Has started something?
THEOPROPIDES.   No, he's finished everything!
  He flim-flammed me today in a disgraceful way.
SIMO. What's this?
THEOPROPIDES.   The situation can be summarized:
  He flim-flammed me today for good, forevermore.
  But now, I beg you, Simo, aid me and abet me.
SIMO. In what?
THEOPROPIDES. Please let me go with you back to your house.
SIMO. I will.
THEOPROPIDES. Then give me several slaves and several whips.
SIMO. They're yours.
THEOPROPIDES. And while you do I'll tell you everything—
  The many-splendoured ways he put me in a haze!   1040

         [*The two old men exit into* SIMO's *house*
     A pause [*musical interlude?*]. TRANIO *struts*
         happily out of THEOPROPIDES' *house*

TRANIO. Any man who trembles in a crisis isn't worth a
    pittance.
  [*Aside*] Actually I wonder what a 'pittance' means—I'd love
    to know.
  [*To the audience*] Anyway, when Master sent me country-
    ward to get his son,
  I sneaked off in secret down the alley to our own back
    garden,

Flinging open wide the garden gate we have there in the
  alley,
Leading out my whole entire legion, boy and girl divisions.
When I led my troops out of the siege conditions into
  safety,*
Then I thought it time to summon all my soldiers in a
  senate.
But no sooner summoned than the senate moved—to move
  me out!   1050
Seeing how they planned to sell me out in my own forum,
  quickly,
I reacted as men should whenever storms of trouble stir:
Stir the storm up even further. Not a thing could calm it
  now.
It's for certain there's no way to keep this all from my old
  master.   1054
So I'll seek him out to sign a treaty. I delay myself!   1061
Wait, what's this? I hear the door creak in our neighbour's
  neighbourhood.
It's my master! I would like to drink in what he has to say.

> [TRANIO *sneaks back towards
> the alley to eavesdrop*
>
> THEOPROPIDES *enters from* SIMO's *house, giving
> instructions to the slave whippers he has enlisted*

THEOPROPIDES. Stand inside the doorway there, all ready to
  be called to action,
Then be quick to leap right out and manacle the man with
  speed.
I'll just linger here until my flim-flam man comes on the
  scene,
Then I'll flim and flam his hide as sure as I'm alive today!
TRANIO [*to audience*]. All is out! Now, Tranio, think up a
  plan to save yourself!
THEOPROPIDES. I'll be wise and wily if I want to catch him
  when he comes,
Won't show him my hook at once; I'll play him out with
  lots of line.*   1070
I'll pretend I'm ignorant of everything.

TRANIO [*sarcastically*].　　　　　　　　O tricky man!
No one in all Athens could be shrewder than that fellow is.
Fooling him's as hard a task as fooling some great—hunk
of stone.*
Now I'll broach him and approach. . . .

THEOPROPIDES.　　　I just can't wait till that man comes.

TRANIO. Looking for me, sir? I'm present to present myself to
you.

THEOPROPIDES [*barely able to conceal his satisfaction that
the victim's here*]. Tranio—hel-*lo*! What's new?

TRANIO.　　　　　The hicks are coming from the sticks.*
Philolaches is *en route*.

THEOPROPIDES [*still welcoming* TRANIO]. By Pollux, what a
nice arrival.*
Say, our neighbour there is very bold and cunning, as I see
it.

TRANIO. Why?

THEOPROPIDES. Denies he ever dealt with you.

TRANIO.　　　　　　　　　　　　　　Denies?

THEOPROPIDES.　　　　　　　　And what is more—
Claims you never paid a thing.

TRANIO.　　　　　Oh no, you're joking. He denies it? 1080

THEOPROPIDES. Well?

TRANIO.　　　　　I know you're joking; it's not possible
that he denies it.

THEOPROPIDES. Still, he does deny it, and he claims he never
sold the house.

TRANIO. Unbelievable! And he denies we paid him cash for
it?

THEOPROPIDES. He'd be willing to go under oath, if I would
like him to,
Swearing that he's never sold the house or got any cash.
Still, I claimed he had.

TRANIO.　　　　　What did he answer?

THEOPROPIDES.　　　　　　　　Offered all his slaves—
All of them to me for trial by torture.*

TRANIO.　　　　　　　　Oh, he'll never give them.

THEOPROPIDES [*portentously*]. Yes, he will.

TRANIO.　　　　　I'll go inside and look for him.

[*Starts to exit*]

THEOPROPIDES.   No—stay, stay, stay.
Let's investigate the matter.

TRANIO [*stops*].   Why not leave the man to me? 1090

THEOPROPIDES. Let me get the slaves out here.

TRANIO.   You should have done that long ago.
Or at least have made a legal claim.

THEOPROPIDES.   What I want first of all is—
[*heavy irony*] Trial by torture for the slaves.

TRANIO.   Indeed, by Pollux, good idea.
[*Leaps onto altar*]* While you do, I'll sit up on this altar.

THEOPROPIDES.   Why?

TRANIO.   Why, don't you see?
While I'm here no other slave can flee for refuge from the
torture.

THEOPROPIDES [*extra sweetly*]. Do get up.

TRANIO.   Oh no.

THEOPROPIDES.   Not on the altar, please.

TRANIO.   Why not?

THEOPROPIDES. Actually . . . I'd *like* the slaves to flee for refuge
on the altar.
Then I'll have a stronger case in court and win more money
too.

TRANIO. Don't keep switching plans of action. Why sow seeds
for further trouble?   1100
After all, these legal things are very tricky, you know that.

THEOPROPIDES. Do get up. Come over here. I'd like to ask
for some advice.

TRANIO. *Here* I'll be a fine adviser. Sitting down, I'm so much
wiser.
Speaking from a holy spot, I can advise with greater strength.

THEOPROPIDES. Do get up, no joking. Look at me.

TRANIO.   I'm looking.

THEOPROPIDES.   Do you see?

TRANIO. Well, I see if someone came between us, he would
starve to death.

THEOPROPIDES. Why?

TRANIO [*smiles*].   We're both so tricky that we give no
food for honest thought.

[*Now* THEOPROPIDES *sees that* TRANIO
knows. He drops his friendly pose

THEOPROPIDES. Go to hell!

TRANIO.   What's up?

THEOPROPIDES.   You tricked me!

TRANIO.   Did I?

THEOPROPIDES.   Oh, and what a way you
　　Egged me on.

TRANIO [*naïvely*]. Let's see your face: is any egg still on it now?

THEOPROPIDES. No, of course not, since you egged me out of
　　every brain I had!   1110
　　Every evil deed of yours is now discovered—and in depth.
　　And from this discovery there's one recovery—in death!

TRANIO. Well, you'll never get me up from where I sit.

THEOPROPIDES.   But I'll command that
　　Fire and firewood be put around you, gallows bird. You'll
　　roast!

TRANIO. Don't do that. I'm so much sweeter when I'm boiled,
　　not roasted up.

THEOPROPIDES. I'll make an example of you—

TRANIO [*smiling*].   Ah, so I'm exemplary.

THEOPROPIDES [*angry*]. Speak—when I went off abroad, what
　　sort of son did I leave here?

TRANIO. Normal type—two eyes, two ears, two hands, two
　　feet, et cetera.

THEOPROPIDES. That was not the question.

TRANIO.   Sorry, that was what I felt like saying.
　　[*Peering off-stage*] Look—I see your son's best friend,
　　Callidamates, coming here.
　　Why not wait till he arrives and deal with me when he's at
　　hand?   1120

　　Enter CALLIDAMATES, *now clear-headed and sober*

CALLIDAMATES [*to audience*]. After the effects of all my
　　boozing were slept off and under,
　　Philolaches told me that his father's back from overseas,
　　Also how that slave had fooled his father as he just arrived.
　　Philo's too ashamed right now to step into his father's
　　sight.

So our little social circle chose me as ambassador to
Seek the sire and sue for peace. [*Sees* THEOPROPIDES] But
   look who's here—how wonderful!
[*Calls*] Greetings, Theopropides, I'm glad to see you safe
   and sound,
Back from overseas. Do come to dinner at our house tonight.
THEOPROPIDES. Hail, Callidamates. Many thanks for dinner—
   I can't come.   1130
CALLIDAMATES. Oh, why not?
TRANIO [*to* THEOPROPIDES].   Go on—or else I'll take the
   invitation for you.
THEOPROPIDES. Whipping post—you mock me still?
TRANIO.   Because I'd go to dinner for you?
THEOPROPIDES. Well, you won't. I'll see you go where you
   deserve—right on a cross!
CALLIDAMATES [*to* THEOPROPIDES]. Never mind all this; just
   say you'll come to dinner.
TRANIO.   Well, speak up!
CALLIDAMATES [*to* TRANIO]. Hey, why are you refugeeing on
   that altar—that's so stupid!*
TRANIO [*indicating* THEOPROPIDES]. His arrival frightened me.
   [*To* THEOPROPIDES] But tell me what you claim I've done.
Now we have an arbitrator for us both, so state your case.
THEOPROPIDES. I say you corrupted my young son.
TRANIO.   Now just a minute, please.
   Yes, I will confess: he sinned while you were gone. He
      freed a girl,
   Drew a lot of cash on interest, threw the lot of cash away. 1140
   Yet do other boys of noble families do otherwise?*
THEOPROPIDES. Hercules, I must be careful of you; you're a
   tricky advocate.
CALLIDAMATES. Let me be the judge. [*To* TRANIO] Get up,
   and I'll sit on the altar now.
THEOPROPIDES. Yes, that's good, get closer to the case.
TRANIO [*as* CALLIDAMATES *sits next to him*]. I fear some trick
   in this.
   [*To* CALLIDAMATES] If you want to sit in my position, take
      my fear from me.
THEOPROPIDES. All the rest I rate at nothing. I'm just angry
   at the way he

Made a fool of me.

TRANIO.   Well done it was, and I rejoice in it!

Old men with a hoary head should act their age in brains
  as well.

THEOPROPIDES [to CALLIDAMATES]. What do I do now?

TRANIO.   Well, if you know Diphilus or Philemon*

Go and tell them every way your slave bamboozled you
  today.   1150

You'll provide the finest flim-flam plot for any comedy.

CALLIDAMATES [to TRANIO]. Quiet, will you? Let me talk a
  bit. [To THEOPROPIDES] Do listen, sir.

THEOPROPIDES.   All right.

CALLIDAMATES. You know well that I'm the very closest friend
  your son has got.

Since he's too ashamed to set a single foot in sight of you,

Knowing that you know all that's been done, he came and
  asked my help.

Now I beg of you, forgive his youth and folly—he's your
  son.

Boys are boys, you know, and when they're young, they
  play so playfully.

What's been done, we did it both together, and we both
  were wrong.

All the principal and interest, all the cash we paid to free
  the girl,   1160

We'll both pay it back, we'll share the cost, and you won't
  pay a thing.

THEOPROPIDES. No more eloquent ambassador could come
  to me on his behalf.

You succeed. I'm now not angry or annoyed at what he
  did.

Even while I'm here let him drink up, make love, do what
  he'd like!

If he feels ashamed at what he's done, that's punishment
  enough.

CALLIDAMATES. Very, very shamed he is.

TRANIO.   Now what about forgiving *me*?

THEOPROPIDES. I'm for—giving you a thousand lashes.

TRANIO.   Even if I'm shamed?

THEOPROPIDES. Hercules, I'll kill you if I live!

CALLIDAMATES.   Oh, can't you pardon *all*?
  Let him go for my sake. Please forgive whatever wrong he's
  done.

THEOPROPIDES. Anything but that—I would do *anything* for
  you but that!   1170
  No—for every dirty deed, I'll make that dirty fellow bleed.

CALLIDAMATES. Can't you let him go?

THEOPROPIDES.   But look how insolent he's posing there!

CALLIDAMATES. Tranio, behave yourself.

THEOPROPIDES [*to* CALLIDAMATES].   And you behave—
  forget all this.

  Don't annoy me, while I *beat* this fellow into deadly silence.

TRANIO. Not a chance of that!

CALLIDAMATES.   Please don't take the trouble!

THEOPROPIDES. Please don't beg.

CALLIDAMATES.   I beg.

THEOPROPIDES.   Don't beg me, please.

CALLIDAMATES.   Don't beg me not to beg.
  Just this once, I beg you, sir, forgive his wrong—at my
  request?

TRANIO [*to* THEOPROPIDES]. Why persist? You *know* tomorrow I'll commit some fresh new wrong.

  Then you'll get revenge for both—for what I've done and
  what I'll do.

CALLIDAMATES. Please.

THEOPROPIDES [*won over*]. All right, no punishment. [*To*
  TRANIO] But you be grateful to your friend.   1180
  [*Turning to spectators*] Now I ask the audience to clap
  their hands. This is—the end!

THE POT OF GOLD

(*Aulularia*)

DRAMATIS PERSONAE

LAR FAMILIARIS, divine guardian of Euclio's household
EUCLIO, an old miser
STAPHYLA, his slave, an ancient housekeeper
EUNOMIA, a matron
MEGADORUS, her brother, Euclio's next-door neighbour
PYTHODICUS, his slave
CONGRIO, ANTHRAX, cooks
PHRYGIA, ELEUSIUM, flute girls
STROBILUS, slave of Megadorus
LYCONIDES, an Athenian young man, son of Eunomia
SLAVE OF LYCONIDES*
PHAEDRIA, off-stage character, daughter of Euclio
VARIOUS SLAVES

The entire action takes place on a street in Athens. There are two houses separated by a shrine to Fides *(Trust). The dwelling to the spectators' right (nearer the exit to the forum) belongs to* MEGADORUS. *The one to the spectators' left (nearer the exit to the countryside) belongs to* EUCLIO. *There is also a small altar in front of the rich man's house.*

THE POT OF GOLD

The LAR FAMILIARIS *emerges from the miser's*
house, goes downstage and delivers the
prologue to the audience

LAR. Should any wonder who I am, I'll make it brief:
A household god am I [*indicating Euclio's house*]—and
   here from whence I came.
The family I have protected now for years.
I've dwelt here in this home and have safeguarded it
For both the grandpa and the father of its owner.
In secret long ago the grandad gave to me
[*Whispers confidentially*] A pot of gold, which he had buried
   in the hearth.
Imploring me to keep a watch on it for him.
And when at last he died, he was so miserly
He couldn't bring himself to tell his son about it.   10
And he preferred to leave the fellow penniless
Rather than inform him where the money was.
So all he left him was a tiny scrap of land
From which with toil he tilled a slender living.
Now when the man who first gave me the gold passed on,
I started to look closely at the son. To see
If he held me in greater honour than his sire.
But *he*—if anything, gave me still less respect.   20
I treated him in kind. And so he died as well.
He left behind a son, the one who lives here now,
And he's as bad as dad and grandad were before.
And yet his only daughter daily worships me.
She always brings me offerings of wine and incense
And garlands too. It's for this young girl's sake
I saw to it that Euclio unearthed the treasure.
To help him marry off his daughter, if he wished.
[*Confidentially*] An upper-class young man has ravished
   her.
The lad knows whom he's ravished, though she knows him
   not.

Nor does her father know that she's been ravishèd.
Today I'll see to it the codger from next door
Will ask to marry her. Now, here's my plan
To make it easier for him who ravished her
To get to marry her. Because as it turns out
Our neighbour is the uncle of the youth who wronged her
At the midnight revels of the Ceres festival.
But hark—old Euclio is bellowing again
He's kicking out his ancient maid so she won't know what's up.
I guess he wants to check and see his gold's still there.

> *The door flies open and Euclio the miser emerges*
> *angrily, swinging a club at his ancient female*
> *servant. He is filthy, wearing tattered garments*

EUCLIO [*enraged*]. Out out, I say get out, decamp, you
    snooperette—   40
Get out with those two sneaky-peeking eyes of yours!
STAPHYLA. Why beat a wretch like me?
EUCLIO.   To keep you wretched and
To cause you pain for being such a pain to me.
STAPHYLA. But why have you now expelled me from inside
    the house?
EUCLIO. Do *I* owe you a reason—bashed potato face?
Get even further from the door—right over there.
See how she dawdles—do you know how I'd fix you?
If I could only grab a club or pointed stick
I'd speed your tortoise-crawling in a snap, I would.
STAPHYLA [*melodramatically*]. Oh, how I wish the gods would
    string me up to death.   50
Death would be a better lot than slave to you.
EUCLIO [*aside*]. Just listen to that malefactrix mumbling maid.
    [*Aloud*] By Hercules, you bawd, I'll dig out both your
    eyes.
So you no longer spy on every move I make.
Go further back—no, even more—yes, stand right there!
By Hercules, you budge a single finger's breadth
A single finger *nail's*—or if you even steal a glance
Before I say you can, then, by Hercules, you'll get

A pretty lesson on the uses of the cross!
I've never seen a more pernicious hag than she   60
I'm in a fearful fright she'll trick me unawares
And sniff out where my lovely pot of gold's concealed.
That bitch has eyeballs in both front and back.
But now I'll check to see the gold's still where I hid it.
It's such a worry in a million wretched ways.

STAPHYLA. By Castor in my wildest dreams I can't imagine
What's happened to my master or what madness grips him.
Why, every single day he kicks me out ten times.   70
I don't know what affliction's taken hold of him.
He stays up all the night—then all day long he sits
Just like a crippled shoemaker inside the house.
[*Confidentially*] And how much longer can I hide his girl's
    disgrace?
[*Exploding*] The blessed birth's becoming bloody im-
    minent!*

*Suddenly old Euclio sprints back out and
addresses the audience*

EUCLIO. At last my mind's becalmed enough to let me leave.
I've just now seen that all is safe inside.   80
[*To maid*] Now you go back inside and stay on guard—
STAPHYLA.   What's that?
I stay 'on guard'? Are you afraid they'll steal the house?
We've nothing else at all to interest thieving folk.
The house is full of emptiness—and cobwebs.*

EUCLIO. It's amazing that—for your sake—mighty Jove
Did not make me a king like Philip or Darius.*
You snake, I want those cobwebs guarded—understand?
[*Moaning and groaning*] I'm poor, I'm *very* poor. I bear
    what heaven wills.
Now go inside and lock the door. I'll soon be back.
Take care not to allow a single stranger in.   90
Lest someone ask you for a light—put out our fire,
So that there won't be a chance that anyone will ask.
If I should find it burning, I'll extinguish *you*.
If anyone should ask for water—say that 'it's run off'.*
And knives or axes, mortar, pestle, all the stuff

That neighbours always come around and ask to use—
Tell them that thieves have come and robbed it all from us.
Indeed, while I'm away don't let a single soul
Come in. And let me even tell you this:
Should Lady Luck herself appear—don't let *her* in!   100
STAPHYLA. By Pollux, there's no fear of that I wouldn't think.
She's never come to us—or even been nearby!
EUCLIO. Shut up and go.
STAPHYLA.   I'll shut and go.
EUCLIO.   And close the house!
And double-bolt the door. I'll soon be back again.
[*To the audience*] Oh how I suffer when I have to leave my
    house.
Unwillingly I go, by Hercules, but go I must—
Because our councilman's announced a distribution*
And said he's giving out some coins to all of us.
If I should let this pass and not seek mine, why then
They'd all suspect that I had—you know—gold at home.   110
I mean it's not believable that someone poor
Would be so careless as to let a little coin go by.
But though I try to keep it hid, they seem to know
And all act friendlier than ever—greeting me,
Approaching, stopping, shaking hands and asking
If I'm well, how I'm doing—what I'm up to . . .
But now I'd better hurry where I'm heading. After that—
I'll then return back home as soon as possible.

> *The moment he dashes off-stage, his neighbour*
> MEGADORUS *and his sister* EUNOMIA *enter from*
> *the house next door*

EUNOMIA.

Brother please heed me, you need me I know,*   120
I'm showing concern that a sister should show.
Although I'm a woman and really don't matter,
(For men think that women just prattle and chatter)
I'll grant you, dear brother, it's possibly true
You probably think that I'm talkative too.*
Remember dear brother and do bear in mind

The ties of a brother and sister that bind.
We should both speak quite frankly and trust one another,
A woman should never hide things from her brother.
That's why I've invited you here out of doors   130
And don't fear to broach a small problem of yours.
Let's now talk of something important and grand.

MEGADORUS. O noblest of women do give me your hand.
EUNOMIA. What 'noblest' of women—who's perfect and quiet?
MEGADORUS. Why you—
EUNOMIA.   Me? You say so?
MEGADORUS.   Not if you deny it.
EUNOMIA. Be truthful dear brother, there's none to be had.
  No woman is noble—some just are less bad.   140
MEGADORUS. In that I agree, In that I agree,
  you'll never hear anything different from me.
EUNOMIA [returning to her previous topic]. Now listen dear
  brother—
MEGADORUS. I'm listening to you.
EUNOMIA. There's something important I want you to do.
MEGADORUS. Just tell me—I'll do it, your word's my com-
  mand.
EUNOMIA.
    It's something quite wonderful, something quite grand.
MEGADORUS. That's always your way.
EUNOMIA.   Oh, I hope so.
MEGADORUS.   Now speak.
EUNOMIA. You know dear that children bring pleasures
  unique.
  I want you to wed.
MEGADORUS. Oh no my dear sister you're killing me dead!
EUNOMIA.   Why these moans?   150
MEGADORUS. You're beating my brains out, your words are
  like stones.
EUNOMIA. Obey your dear sister, don't you want what's best?
MEGADORUS [shaking his head]. Before I would marry I'd be
  laid to rest.
        [For a moment they stop and stare at each other.
        Then MEGADORUS sighs in capitulation

MEGADORUS. All right, I'll marry, choose the girl—with one
    proviso—
    'Tomorrow we wed, the next day she's dead.'*
    If you'll agree to this—go on, prepare the party.
EUNOMIA. Don't worry, I'll get one with a gigantic dowry.
    But not too young—in fact one of a mellow age.
    So brother dear just say the word and she'll be yours.   160
MEGADORUS. Dear sister may I ask a question?
EUNOMIA.   Ask away.
MEGADORUS. What if a man of middle life should wed a girl
    that age
    And by some chance the old boy makes the lady pregnant.
    Do you have any doubt they'll name the baby Postumus?*
    But now, dear sister, I'll spare you all further troubles:
    Thank heaven and our ancestors, I'm rich enough.
    I can dispense with social climbing, pride, and cushy
        dowries,
    Their shouting and their bossiness, their carriages of ivory,
    And all their purple finery which can enslave a man.
EUNOMIA. Well tell me then, whom *will* you marry?
MEGADORUS.   Listen here, 170
    You know the poorish chap who lives next door to us?
EUNOMIA. He seems all right, By Castor.
MEGADORUS.   Well I want his daughter.
    And sister, don't object because the girl is poor.
    Say what you will—I like her kind of poverty.
EUNOMIA. I wish you luck.
MEGADORUS.   Me too.
EUNOMIA.   Is there anything more?*
MEGADORUS.   Just take care of yourself.
EUNOMIA. And you, dear brother.

                    [*She turns and goes back into their house*

MEGADORUS. Now I'll see if Euclio's at home.
    [*Glancing off-stage*] But there he is—returning from some
    place or another.

            Euclio enters and addresses the audience

EUCLIO. When I left I sensed the whole thing would fall
    through

And I was so loath to go—for no one from our district
Even came nor did the councilman distribute money.   180
So I hasten to make haste—my thoughts are home already.

MEGADORUS. Greetings Euclio—I hope you're well and
  flourishing.

EUCLIO [*suspiciously*]. God love you, Megadorus.

MEGADORUS.   Are things as you would like them?

EUCLIO [*to the audience*]. A trick—I sense a trick when rich
  men speak so lavishly to poor.

That fellow knows that I have gold, why else would he be
  so polite?

MEGADORUS. Do I take it that you're well?

EUCLIO.   Uh—not financially.

MEGADORUS. But they say that if you're feeling happy, that's
  money in the bank.

EUCLIO [*aside*]. Damn—that hag's showed him the gold it's
  clearly clear.

When I get home I'll cut her tongue out and I'll gouge her
  eyes!

MEGADORUS. Talking to yourself?

EUCLIO.   Uh yes, bemoaning poverty.   190

I don't have enough to give a dowry for my grown-up
  daughter.

So I can't contract her—

MEGADORUS.   Oh. Cheer up Euclio,

Marry she will—I'll help you. Tell me what you need.

EUCLIO [*aside*]. My own cash he's promising. He hungers for
  my gold,

Holding bread in one hand and a big rock in the other.

Never trust a rich man when he's civil to a pauper.

When he shakes your hand he really wants to shake you
  down!

He's just like an octopus—he's fastening his tentacles.

MEGADORUS. Pay attention Euclio, I'll tell you briefly what I
  want.

This is something good for both of us.

EUCLIO.   O wretched me!   200

Hooked and crooked my gold is—that's what this man's
  after.*

Now he wants to make a 'deal'—I have to check my house!

MEGADORUS. Where you going?

EUCLIO [*dashing towards his front door*]. I'll be back—I have
to check my home.

[*He goes in*

MEGADORUS [*puzzled, to the audience*]. All this started when
I mentioned marrying his daughter.

Seems to me he thinks I'm mocking him or something.

Never have I seen a fellow more tight-fisted in his poverty.

The miser emerges from his house once again

EUCLIO [*to the audience*]. Praise the gods the gold is safe—
safe if everything's all there.

What fear—before I got inside and looked I nearly died.

[*To his neighbour*] Megadorus, here I am—I'm at your
service.

MEGADORUS.   Thanks.
Would you be so kind as to reply to certain questions?   210

EUCLIO. Not at all—if they're not questions I don't want to
answer.

MEGADORUS. Tell me your opinion of my social standing.

EUCLIO.   Good.

MEGADORUS. Reputation?

EUCLIO.   Good.

MEGADORUS.   Behaviour?

EUCLIO.   Not too terrible.

MEGADORUS. How about my age?

EUCLIO.   It's growing every year
[*aside*] just like your money.

MEGADORUS. Certainly *I* always held *you* in esteem—a solid
citizen,

That is what I've always thought.

EUCLIO [*aside*].   The man has sniffed my gold!
[*To* MEGADORUS] What is it you want?

MEGADORUS.   Since we know one another well
Both of us will benefit—as well as your good daughter.

Your good daughter whom I wish to wed. Do pledge her
to me.

EUCLIO. Come on Megadorus, you're not dealing with me
decently.   220

[*Pained*] Making fun of someone without blame—and
without any money.

Really—I've done nothing to deserve this kind of treatment.

MEGADORUS. Pollux, I'm not making fun or mocking in the
very least,

Nor is that a decent thing to do.

EUCLIO.   But why *my* daughter?

MEGADORUS. Well, it will be beneficial to our families—both
yours and mine.

EUCLIO. Megadorus, it occurs to me that you're a man of
wealth—

Powerful politically—but I'm a pauper of impoverished
poverty.

Were I to do a deal with you about my daughter, it would
seem

You were an ox and I an ass. We wouldn't fit together.*

Never could we bear an equal load, I'd stumble in the mud. 230

You, the mighty ox, would scarcely know that I exist.

I'd be so badly treated—my own kind would hee-haw at
me.

Should we fall out, I'd be destabilized in every quarter.

All the asses would be biting me, the oxen goring me.

That's the risk when asses try to rise to oxish rank.

MEGADORUS. Nothing could be finer than if people who are
fine

Forge an alliance. Hear me and accept my honest offer.

Pledge your daughter—

EUCLIO.   But I've nothing for a dowry.*

MEGADORUS.   Never mind.

Virtue's the most important dowry—and she's rich in that.

EUCLIO. I'm saying that lest you should think I've found some 240
hidden treasure [*nervous laugh*].

MEGADORUS. Naturally, I understand. So you agree?

EUCLIO.   I do.

                    [*He is startled by a sudden noise in his house*
                                                         My god!

Am I dead?

MEGADORUS.   What's wrong?

EUCLIO.   Just now the sound of something iron.

                    [EUCLIO *speeds back into his house*

MEGADORUS [*shrugging*]. Just the workers digging in my
garden. [*Noticing*] Where's he gone?
Disappeared without an explanation. Now he snubs me
Just because I want to be his friend. How typical—
When a rich man tries befriending someone less well-off
The poor shrink back in fear and fearfully object,
But when the chance has passed them by too late they have
a change of heart.

EUCLIO *reappears*

EUCLIO [*calling back to* STAPHYLA]. Hercules, if I don't have
your tongue ripped out right at the roots
You have my permission to have me submitted for
castration!   250
MEGADORUS. Euclio, I see that you find me suitable
Despite my age—to make a fool of quite unfairly.
EUCLIO. Not at all by Pollux—and I couldn't if I wanted to.
MEGADORUS. Well now—does that mean I get your daughter?
EUCLIO.   On condition that
You stick by the agreement for the dowry that we—
MEGADORUS [*nodding assent*]. Deal?
EUCLIO.   A deal.
MEGADORUS. Bless us both.
EUCLIO. Agreed—but you won't forget what we've arranged.
I mean about the lack of dowry that my daughter brings
with her.
MEGADORUS. Right.
EUCLIO. I mean I know you rich folk can get muddled up.
Disagreeing with agreements you already have agreed.   260
MEGADORUS. I won't give you any problems. And would you
object
To a marriage ceremony—well—today?
EUCLIO.   That's fine.
MEGADORUS. Then I'll go make preparations. Is there some-
thing else?*
EUCLIO.   Just that—farewell.
MEGADORUS [*calling at his own doorway*]. Ho! Strobilus!
Look lively—we're off to the market-place!

[EUCLIO *watches carefully till he
is sure they are out of earshot*

EUCLIO. Gone! Oh, by the gods the power gold possesses!
  I think the fellow's overheard about my treasure.
  That's why he's panting so to join my family.

            [*He rushes to his own door and shouts*

  Where are you—tattle-taling terror of the neighbourhood?
  Claiming I would give a dowry for my daughter? Staphyla!
  Do you hear me? Hurry up and—polish all the crockery.
  My daughter's getting married—right away—to Megadorus. 270
STAPHYLA [*shocked*]. Heaven help us, no she can't—it's much
    too . . . premature!
EUCLIO. Shut up and be off. Have all prepared when I'm
  back from the forum.

  Shut the house up tight—I'll soon return.*

            [*He marches off towards the forum, leaving
            the old woman in a state of desperation*

STAPHYLA [*moaning*].   Now what to do?
  Mistress is in dire straits—and so am I.
  All of the disgrace will be exposed—the birth is very near.
  There's no way to cover what we've hidden up to now.
  Now I'll go inside and do what master ordered me to do.
  Castor, what a mega-mixture of such monstrous misery!

            [*She dashes off into the house. The
            stage is empty for a few moments**

Enter MEGADORUS' *slave* STROBILUS, *a motley
  procession of* COOKS (ANTHRAX *and* CONGRIO)*,
  FLUTE GIRLS (PHRYGIA *and* ELEUSIUM) *as well as
  various* SLAVES *bearing festive foods from the
  market. Traditionally, the cook wears a short
  tunic and carries a carving knife*

STROBILUS. When master shopped around the forum, hired
    the cooks,   280
  He then engaged the flute girls and he gave me orders
  To lead all back here and split them into halves.
ANTHRAX. By Hercules I'll tell you now you won't split *me*,
  But if you want me somewhere as a whole, I'll go.
CONGRIO. Yes, cutie-pie, you piece of public property,
  I'll bet if someone wanted you would do a split.*
STROBILUS. Now Anthrax, calm yourself, I didn't mean it
    that way.

Stop misconstruing. It's my master's wedding day.

ANTHRAX.   And who's he marrying?

STROBILUS. The daughter of old Euclio who lives next door. 290
That's why he'll get one half of all we've bought today.
Including half the cooks and half the music girls.

ANTHRAX. In other words we're going half and half with
Euclio.

STROBILUS. Yes—in those very words.

ANTHRAX.   What? Can't the man afford
To do the shopping for his own girl's wedding?

STROBILUS. You jest!

ANTHRAX.   What do you mean?

STROBILUS.   I mean he's mean!
That man's about as 'liquid' as a pumice stone!

ANTHRAX. You don't say.

CONGRIO [butting in].   Yes I do say.

STROBILUS.   Just see for yourself.
He calls on gods and men to witness that he's bankrupt,
totally wiped out,   300
If but a smoky wisp blows from his twiggy fire.
And at night he ties a bag around his mouth

ANTHRAX. Why?

STROBILUS. So he won't lose any breath while he's asleep.

ANTHRAX. Why doesn't he plug up his lower parts as well?
Then he won't even lose a fart when he's asleep.

STROBILUS. Believe me, you should trust what I am saying.

ANTHRAX. But honestly I do believe you.

STROBILUS.   And there's more.
He cries to heaven if we throw out water from a person's
bath.

ANTHRAX [facetiously]. In other words, he won't give us a
silver talent
To buy our freedom. Do you think there's not much
chance?   310

STROBILUS. The fellow wouldn't even let you have his *hunger*,
if you asked.
The other day when he had his nails cut by the barber
He scooped up all the bits and took them home with him.

ANTHRAX. By Pollux, what a miserable mingy miser!

STROBILUS. Indeed. Could anybody be more miserable or
   miserly?
   One day a kite pecked off a little grain of porridge.
   The fellow stormed down to the courthouse, all in tears,
   And uncontrollably he wailed and railed
   To have an order issued that the bird be jailed!
   Oh, if I had time I'd tell six hundred stories.   320
   But tell me which of you's the faster worker?

ANTHRAX. It's me. And I'm the better.

STROBILUS.   I mean cook not *crook.*

ANTHRAX. Well, *I'm* a cook.

STROBILUS.   And you?

CONGRIO.   Whatever I appear.

ANTHRAX [*mocking*]. No one ever hires you—except on
   market days
   When everybody's desperate.

CONGRIO.   *You're* a man of letters:
   C—R—O—O—K.

ANTHRAX.   And you're a man of *fetters.*

STROBILUS. All right, shut up now. And you take me the
   lamb that's fatter
   Right into our house.

ANTHRAX.   Righto.

STROBILUS.   Now you, Congrio,
   You take the lamb that's left and go to Euclio's.
   You follow him—and all you other lot to us.

CONGRIO.   But it's not fair!   330
   You misdivided, giving them the fatter lamb.

STROBILUS. So now you'll get the fatter flute girl—Phrygia,
   You go with him. And you, Eleusium,
   Come into our house.

CONGRIO.   Oh—you tricky one
   You're relegating me to that old cheapskate?
   If I ask for something there, I'll lose my voice.
   Before I get a thing.

STROBILUS.   Ungrateful idiot,
   What sense is doing right by you since any offer is a waste?*

CONGRIO. How come?

STROBILUS.   It's clear—at Euclio's

There won't be any crowds of people who will waste your
    time.   340
Whatever you might want to borrow—bring yourself from
    home.
On the other hand, *we're* stuffed with hordes of people—
Utensils, gold and silver, lots of clothing too.
If some should disappear—because I know that you can
    easily
Restrain your hands as long as there is nothing there to
    take—
They'd say the cooks have filched it—grab ahold of them.
And chain them, beat them, toss them in the pit.
Now this could never be at Euclio's. Because
There's nothing there to steal.

                        [Starting towards the miser's house

Now follow me!

CONGRIO.   I will.

STROBILUS [*knocking loudly*]. Hey Staphyla, come open up
    the door.

STAPHYLA [*from within*]. Who calls?   350

STROBILUS. It's Strobilus.

STAPHYLA.   What do you want?

STROBILUS.   I bring the cook,
    A flute girl and the food for the festivities.
    Megadorus told me to deliver them.

STAPHYLA. If it's to honour Ceres it's a *fast*ival.

STROBILUS. Why so?

STAPHYLA.   Because I don't see any wine at all.*

STROBILUS. Don't worry, it will be delivered right away once
    he gets back from the forum.

STAPHYLA. But we've no firewood to cook.

CONGRIO.   The house has beams?

STAPHYLA. By Pollux yes.

CONGRIO.   That's firewood—no need to get any.

STAPHYLA. You filthy pig! You're much too fond of Vulcan.*   360
    Just to cook one wretched dinner and collect your wretched
      pay
    You want to burn down our whole house?

CONGRIO. Why, not at all.

STAPHYLA [*indicating the others*]. Bring them all in.
STROBILUS.   All follow me!

The slave PYTHODICUS *enters* from* MEGADORUS' *house*
PYTHODICUS [*to those inside*]. Keep on working. Meanwhile
   I'll go see how all those cooks are doing.
  Pollux—what a task it is today just keeping watch on
   them.
  They would only be all right if they cooked dinner in the
   pit.
  Then we'd pull up all the food in little baskets;
  But then downstairs they'd all be gobbling everything they
   cooked.
  The devils down below would feast while the angels up on
   high are fasting.*
  But I shouldn't stand here jabbering as if there weren't
   things to do,
  And our house is absolutely plunderful and pillagey.   370

> *The stage is empty* for a moment. Then* EUCLIO
> *enters from stage right, carrying a small bag and*
> *a pathetic bouquet of half-dead flowers*

EUCLIO. I tried to screw my courage up today
  To have some fun—enjoy my daughter's wedding.
  I went to shop for fish—but it was overpriced.
  The lamb was overpriced, the beef was overpriced,
  The veal was overpriced, the pork and tuna too.
  And they were all the more expensive since I had no money.
  I stormed away, unable to buy anything!
  And that's how I outfoxed all of those cheating rogues.
  Then making my way home I started to consider:
  'If you should spend too much upon a festive bash   380
  You'll wake up the next morning and you'll have no cash!'
  Philosophizing thus with heart and stomach too
  These organs then persuaded all the rest of me
  To minimize the spending on my daughter's party.
  I've bought a pinch of incense and a bloom or two
  To place upon the altar of our Household God
  To make him see my daughter's married happily.

But look—my house—do I see an *open* door?
And now a noise within? Is someone robbing me?

> CONGRIO *appears at* EUCLIO's
> *door, calling to someone inside*

CONGRIO. A bigger pot—I need a bigger pot at once!   390
  This pot is much too small, go ask our neighbours.

> [*The very word hits* EUCLIO *like a thunderbolt*

EUCLIO. Oh no—I'm dead! My gold—he wants to steal my
  pot!
  I'm killed—unless I hurry hurriedly inside!
  [*To the heavens*] Apollo—I implore you—help me and assist
  me!
  Pierce with arrows all these treasure-taking thieves,
  Rescue me if you have ever helped a man in need before.
  But now I must run in before they ruin me totally!

> As EUCLIO *dashes into his own house,* ANTHRAX
> *appears in front of* MEGADORUS' *home*

ANTHRAX [*calling inside*]. Now Dromo, scale the fish and you
  Machaerio,
  You bone the eel and lamprey quick as possible.
  I'm going to ask Congrio to lend his bread-pan.   400
  Now if you're wise, you'll pluck that rooster really clean.
  I want it to be hairless as a fancy dancer.*
  [*Cocking his ear*] But what's this uproar coming from our
  neighbour's house?
  By Hercules the cooks must be at work for sure.
  I'd better rush back in or we'll have trouble too!

> [*He quickly retreats into*
> MEGADORUS' *house again*

> CONGRIO *and his helpers pile out of* EUCLIO's
> *house in panic*

CONGRIO. Help me everybody—citizens and foreigners and
  visitors alike!
  Clear the way for me to flee—open up the street for me!
  Never in my life have I prepared a meal for Bacchanalians.*
  How they pounded me and my assistants with their clubs!

Now I'm one big welt—I'll die for sure. The old man used
    me for his punching bag!   410
Nowhere in the world have they been freer with their use
    of wood.
How they loaded us with beatings and unloaded us outside!
Oh no, what now? I'm dead—the door's ajar. More orgiasts
    are coming.
Here he comes, he's after me. I know what's next, he's
    taught me well.

EUCLIO *comes out still swinging madly
        at the cooks*

EUCLIO. Stop thief! Stop thief!
CONGRIO.   What's all the shouting for you fool?
EUCLIO. Shouting for policemen to arrest you.
CONGRIO.   Why? What for?
EUCLIO. Carrying a knife.
CONGRIO [*waving the blade*]. To cook.
EUCLIO.   Don't threaten me!
CONGRIO. I was wrong—I should've stuck it right straight
    through you.
EUCLIO. Nowhere on this earth is there a bigger criminal
    than you!
No one that I'd beat to death with greater pleasure.   420
CONGRIO. Pollux—why the proof's already in your beating
All your pounding's made me softer than a dancer boy!
What gives you the right to hit me, filthy beggar?
EUCLIO.   Right?
Cheeky question—that means that you didn't get enough!
CONGRIO [*ducking the blow*]. Stop that! I'll make lots of
    trouble if I've any sense.
EUCLIO. I don't care. But I've sure knocked some sense into
    you now.
Why were you inside my house while I was gone?
Did I give an order? Answer me.
CONGRIO.   All right, shut up!
We just came to cook the wedding feast.
EUCLIO.   What's it to you

Whether I eat dinner cooked or raw—are you my guardian?   430

CONGRIO. For the last time—will you let us cook this dinner
    for you—yes or no?

EUCLIO. *You* tell me—will my belongings still be safe if I say
    yes?

CONGRIO. All I care about is whether *my* belongings will be
    safe.

  I don't want a thing of yours.

EUCLIO [*facetiously*].   Of course—and I believe you.

CONGRIO. Will you be so kind as to allow us to cook dinner?
  What exactly have we done or said to anger you?

EUCLIO. Criminal—you dare to ask—while snooping every-
    where,

Turning every private room of mine into a public place?

Had you only stayed where you belong—beside the oven

Then you wouldn't have the chopped-up head that you
    deserve.   440

[*Adopting a more solemn tone*] Now that you may know
    my policy, do listen here.

Should you now approach the door without my licence

You'll become the absolutest wretch that walks the earth.

Now you know my policy.

                [*He rushes back into his house*

CONGRIO.   Where are you going? Get back here at once.

By the goddess of all Thieves, will I take care of you.*

If you don't return my dishes, I'll start rioting right here.*

Now what should I do? Oh, what a nasty piece of luck.

Twice what I've received for cooking I'll be paying to a
    doctor now!

      EUCLIO *emerges again, this time carrying his*
           beloved pot of treasure

EUCLIO. Hercules, henceforth wherever I go she goes with me.

Nevermore will she be left exposed to such great dangers.   450

All right now you cooks and music girls, the lot of you

You can go inside with all your rented cronies.

Cook your food and serve it, hustle bustle as you please.

CONGRIO. Well at last, after you've drubbed and clubbed me
    till I'm full of holes.

EUCLIO. Go inside, don't make a speech, you were engaged
    to make a meal!

CONGRIO. Hey old man, I ought to bill you for my injuries,
    you know?

    When they hired me they said it was for making punch, not
    being punched.

EUCLIO. Go and sue me. Don't annoy me, go and cook your
    dinner now.

    Otherwise, you just can go to hell.

CONGRIO.   No—you go first, old man.
                  [*The cooks return inside*

EUCLIO. O ye immortal gods, he really flirts with danger   460

    If a poor man lets himself have dealings with a man who's
    rich.

    Look how Megadorus tricked a miserable man like me.

    Sending crooks—these so-called cooks—as if it was an
    honour

    When in truth he wanted to abscond [*points under his
    cloak*] with this thing here.

    Then just now, my hag's pet cocky cock nearly finished me
    completely.*

    Right where I had buried this, he started scratching busily.

    Then I lost my temper with the rooster caught red-handed—

    Snatching up my club I beat the rooster's brains out then
    and there.

    Pollux, I suspect the cooks had promised him a bribe to
    show

    Where I'd hidden this. But now I've snatched my pot—
    they've lost their chance.   470

    Never mind the rest, I simply knocked the cocky cock's
    own block off.

    Look—there's my future son-in-law now swaggering back
    from the forum.

    No way to avoid him now, I'll have to stop and chat a bit.

MEGADORUS [*to the audience*]. I've talked to many friends
    about my marriage plans—

    They spoke with admiration of my neighbour's daughter.

    And they said that I was acting admirably well.

    In fact I think if other rich men would do likewise

And marry girls of humble stock who don't have dowries 480
There also would be much more peace throughout the city.
And other folk would envy us far less than now.
Our wives would also show us more respect
And our expenses would be less extravagant.
I think this would be sound advice for most of us.
The argument would come from just the money-grubbing
    few—
Their greed's so great that no law can limit it
Or any shoemaker take its measure.*
Now you may ask—whom will the dowried ladies wed   490
If all men accept your preference for the poor?
Let them wed anyone—as long as they forsake their dowries
And bring along some virtues—in the place of cash in hand.
Believe me, they'd be better wives than they are now.
That way mules which nowadays are so expensive
Would then be cheaper than old Gallic nags.*

EUCLIO [aside]. By heaven, what joy it is to listen to the man.
    I loved his brilliant speech about frugality.

MEGADORUS. No more would wives complain 'You know
    the sum I brought you—
You never had more cash in your entire life.
And so—give me my due—in purple and in gold   500
In maids and mules and coachmen and in errand boys
Attendants, lackeys, and assorted carriages.'

EUCLIO [aside]. How well he knows the ways of all those
    matrons—
I wish they'd make him the commissioner of women.*

MEGADORUS. Why nowadays wherever you go in the city
You see more vehicles than you see on a country road.
But even this is lovelier if compared to when the creditors
    arrive:*
The cleaner, tailor, jeweller and embroiderer,
The woolifier, linen-maker, fringe-maker, tunic-maker,
Crimson-dyer, brown-dyer, violet-dyer,
The salesmen, craftsmen, tradesmen of every sort,   510
The bootmakers, sandal-maker, slipper-makers, girdle-
    makers.
Oh, look who's here· for money—it's the dry-cleaner, belt-
    maker.

Everybody's got his hand out standing all around you
And when at last you think you've paid off all these
   characters,
Why here's three hundred more collectors waiting for you.
The weavers, the tassel-makers, cabinet-makers just to start.
In they come, you pay them—and *then* you think you've
   seen the last   520
But in march the saffron-dyers—damn them all—
Assorted other pestilences, dunning you . . .

EUCLIO [*aside, with relish*]. I'd love to hail him, but I wouldn't
   interrupt.
What joy to hear all women well described.

MEGADORUS. When finally you've settled all these fripperies,
The soldier marches in demanding army tax.*
You go off to see your banker for a consultation,
The hungry soldier still believing that he'll get his cash,
But after you've discussed the matter with your banker,
You learn that you yourself owe *him* some cash as well!   530
The soldier's hopes are put off to another day.
These tribulations and unbearable expenses
Are just a few of all the ills that come with dowries.
But she who brings no cash does bring obedience,
While rich girls kill their husbands with their mischief and
   extravagance.
[*Noticing the miser*] My future relative—how are you
   Euclio?

EUCLIO. I found your observations to be tasty morsels.

MEGADORUS. So then you heard?

EUCLIO.   From the beginning to the end.

MEGADORUS [*eyeing the old man's appearance*]. Uhh—by the
   way, if you could be a trifle neater—
I mean—it is your daughter's wedding after all.   540

EUCLIO. A man can only dress to suit his rank—and income.
One always has to keep his origins in mind.
By Pollux, neither I nor any other pauper
Has got—you know—a pot of money stashed at home.

MEGADORUS. Indeed you have enough. And with good luck,
   the gods in heaven will bless what you have got already.

EUCLIO [*warily*]. 'Got already'? I don't like the sound of that.
That means he *knows* I've got—the hag betrayed me!

MEGADORUS. Just what are you debating with yourself inside
    your head?

EUCLIO [*aggressively*]. I'm wondering how I can charge you.

MEGADORUS.   Charge me—why? 550

EUCLIO [*outraged*]. You even ask—after you've filled my
    household to the brim

With crooks in all the nooks pretending to be cooks

And sending me five hundred of these so-called chefs

And each with half a dozen hands like Geryon.*

And even eye-filled Argus couldn't guard them all*

As once he did to Io for the sake of Juno.

And that's not even mentioning the music girl

Who by herself could quaff the fountain of Pirene,*

The one at Corinth—that is if it ran with wine.

And as for groceries—

MEGADORUS.   Enough to feed a legion. 560

And I even sent a lamb.

EUCLIO.   Oh yes, about the lamb.

It makes me angry and I want to pick a bone.

MEGADORUS. And what exactly is the bone you want to pick?

EUCLIO. The lamb itself—it is *only* bone—no meat at all!*

The animal's so skinny you can see the light

Exactly as you can with all those lamps from Carthage.*

MEGADORUS. I brought it to be slaughtered.

EUCLIO.   But you were mistaken.

You should have had it buried, it's already dead.

        [*But* MEGADORUS *persists in his good humour*

MEGADORUS. Today dear Euclio, I want to drink with you.

EUCLIO. I shall not drink, by Hercules.

MEGADORUS.   But I'll command 570

A cask of my best vintage wine to be brought over.

EUCLIO. I won't by Hercules, I've sworn myself to water.

MEGADORUS. I'll get you good and 'splashed' today, I swear
    I will,

However 'sworn to water'—

EUCLIO [*to the audience*].   Now I know what's up.

He wants to get me 'splashed' with wine in hopes

That what belongs to me will somehow emigrate to him.

But I'll be on my guard and spirit this from here.

I'll see to it he wastes his time and even wastes his wine.
MEGADORUS. If you'll excuse me, I'll go bathe and sacrifice.

[*He bows courteously and goes into his house*

EUCLIO [*addressing his treasure*]. By Pollux, you have loads
    of enemies, dear pot,   580
As well as all the gold you're holding there inside.
The best thing I can do, dear pot, is carry you
And then entrust you safely to the shrine of Trust.*
You know me don't you, trusty Trust, and I know you.
Don't you dare change your name if I entrust this to you.
I'm banking on your famed trustworthiness.

[*He dashes off-stage*

Enter a slave of LYCONIDES
[STROBILUS?] *soliloquizing*

STROBILUS. Here's the way a slave who's worth his salt should
    act: the way I do.
Quickly and obediently, follow orders cheerfully.
For if a slave sincerely seeks to serve his master skilfully
He ought to do his master's business first, and then his
    own.   590
Even if he's sleeping he must serve his master in his dreams.
If his master is in love—which is the current situation—
He must keep the master from succumbing to his passion
    totally.
Hold him back for his own good, not push him into
    anything.
Look at little boys who learn to swim and use a wicker
    raft,
Making it less tiring and easier to float and move their
    arms.
That's what a slave should be, a raft to hold his lovesick
    master up.
Keep his head above the water and not sink just like a
    piece of lead.
He should learn to read his master's face and know his
    every wish.
Faster than a speeding chariot a good slave hastens to his
    duties.   600

And whoever's conscientious won't be feeling any leather,
Nor will he be forced to polish any iron round his ankles.
[*Explaining to the audience*] You see, Lyconides is crazy
  for the daughter of poor Euclio.
When he heard his sweetheart would be wed to Megadorus
  here,
He then sent me to find out exactly what was happening.
Now, avoiding notice, I'll just sit here by the holy altar
And from here I'll check both sides—and see what they're
  all doing.

    As he hides, EUCLIO *emerges from the temple*

EUCLIO [*calling in*]. Trust, I'm trusting you not to tell anyone
  about my gold.
  [*To himself*] Nothing to be scared of, Euclio, it's too well
    hid.
  Quite a bit of booty—if a man should come across my
    trove.   610
  What a pot all stuffed with gold. [*Aloud*] But please protect
    it, Holy Trust.
  Now I'll bathe, make sacrifice—and not delay my son-in-
    law
  So he can wed my daughter just as soon as he arrives to
    claim her.
  Now mind you, Trust, please, please make sure I get my
    pot back safe and sound.
  After all, I chose your shrine because you are so—trust-
    worthy.

      [*He bustles into his house. After a moment*
      STROBILUS *comes out of hiding and exclaims*

STROBILUS. By the gods—what deed is this that I've just heard
  the miser mention?
Has he really stashed a loaded pot of gold here in the
  temple?
Please, Trust, don't be faithfuller to Euclio than to me.*
And if I'm not mistaken he is the father of my master's
  sweetheart.
In I go to search the shrine in every little tiny nook   620
While the miser's busy. If I find the gold, believe me Trust,
I'll pour a gallon jug of honied wine to you—

And then I'll drain my trusty jug myself.*

> [*He rushes into the temple*
>
> *A moment later* EUCLIO *bustles out again from his house and addresses the audience*

EUCLIO. Not for nothing did a raven just now squawk on my left side in there.

And he kept on scraping at the ground while he was squawking too.

All at once my heart began to somersault inside in my chest,

Nearly flying out of me—but now's the time to run like mad!

> [*He charges into the temple and a moment later re-emerges, dragging* STROBILUS

EUCLIO. Out, out you worm, what hole have you just crawled from?

How did you suddenly appear? Now that you have you'll disappear.

Mangy malefactor! I'll destroy you in a thousand wretched ways!   630

> [*He begins throwing wild punches*

STROBILUS. What the hell is eating you, old man? What do you want with me?

[*Ducking with every swing*] Why are you attacking me? Why snatching me? Why beating me?

EUCLIO. Absolutely beatable is what you are—you triple thief!

STROBILUS. What did I steal from you?

EUCLIO.   Give it back.

STOBILUS.   Give what back?

EUCLIO.   You ask?

STROBILUS. Nothing have I stolen from you—

EUCLIO.   Then return what you have stolen from yourself.
                                                                            Come now.

STROBILUS. Come where?

EUCLIO.   You won't get away with this.

STROBILUS.   What do you want?

EUCLIO. Get it up.

STROBILUS.   You're not my type. I just can't get it up for you.*

EUCLIO. Up with it—and off with all your jokes. The matter's
   serious.

STROBILUS. Up with what? Just call a spade a spade—and
   tell me up with what?

  Hercules, I haven't touched a single thing.

EUCLIO.   Show me your hands. 640

STROBILUS. Look, I'll show you both of them.

EUCLIO.   I see—now what about the third?

STROBILUS [*to the audience*]. Furies and a monumental madness make the man insane.

  Tell the truth—you've done me an injustice—

EUCLIO.   By not hanging you!

  But hang you will quite soon if you will not confess.

STROBILUS.   To *what*?

EUCLIO. Whatever you've just filched.

STROBILUS.   By all the gods I haven't filched a thing.
   [*Aside*] As I would have liked to.

EUCLIO.   Come on now and shake your mantle out!

STROBILUS. As you wish.

EUCLIO.   You're hiding something in your tunic?

STROBILUS [*with a leer*].   Grope me anywhere.

EUCLIO. Sweet talk from a criminal, to make me think you
   didn't steal it.

  All your trickery is clear. Come show me your right hand
   again.

STROBILUS. Here.

EUCLIO.   Let's see the left again.

STROBILUS.   Examine both for all I care. 650

EUCLIO. Never mind the searching. Give it back.

STROBILUS.   Give *what*?

EUCLIO.   Don't mess about!
  Yes you do have it.

STROBILUS.   Have? Have what?

EUCLIO.   Aha! I'll bet you'd like to know.
  Just give back the thing of mine you took.

STROBILUS.   You're absolutely crazy.

  Having felt me everywhere, you haven't found a thing of
   yours.

                [*Suddenly* EUCLIO *perceives noises from
             the shrine. Once again he grows frantic*

EUCLIO. Wait a minute—who's in there? Who else was with
  you there inside?

  Hercules, I'm dead—there's someone making a noise in
  there as well.

  [*Then, remembering* STROBILUS] If I let him go, he'll bolt.
  But I've searched him. All right, off!

  Go—you're free.

STROBILUS.   Jupiter and all the gods destroy you!

EUCLIO [*sarcastically*].   Oh, what gratitude.

  Back into the temple now and break the neck of his
  accomplice.

  [*To* STROBILUS *again*]. Off with you! Will you be gone or not?

STROBILUS. I'm gone.

EUCLIO.   And don't come back!   660

STROBILUS. I'd rather die a wretched rotten deadly death

  Than let that codger go without a punishment.

  For now, I'm sure, he won't dare hide his gold in here.

  He'll move, change his address and take it all with him.

  But hush—the door's just creaked. Look, look—he's dragging
  out the gold.

  I'll hide here by the doorway for a little while.

EUCLIO. I realize my mistake in trusting Trust too much.

  But now she almost made a mockery of me.

  And if the raven hadn't rescued me—I would be finished.

  By Hercules I wish that bird would now come back, the
  one that tipped me off.

  I'd treat him to a lavish heap—   670

  Of thanks. It would be such a waste to give him food.

  Now I must hit upon a lonely spot to transfer this.

  Silvanus' grove stands far beyond the city walls

  All overrun with willows and weeds—that's the place.

  That's it—I'll trust Silvanus rather than keep trusting
  Trust.

STROBILUS. What joy—the gods have brought a salvo of
  salvation!

  I'll sprint ahead and be there waiting up a tree.

  I'll watch the miser and see where he hides the gold.

  So what if master ordered me to keep watch here?   680

  A box on the ear is worth a pot of you know what!

  Enter young LYCONIDES *with* EUNOMIA

LYCONIDES. Now mother, you know everything as well as I
   About how I behaved with the old miser's daughter
   And now I beg and rebeg Mother, as I've begged before
   Do take this matter up with uncle, mother dear.

EUNOMIA. You know I want for you whatever you might
      want.
   I'm certain I'll successfully convince my brother.
   What's more, it is the proper thing—if as you say
   You ... forced the blameless girl when you had drunk too
      much.

LYCONIDES. I'd never lie to you. You know that, mother
   dear.   690

         [*From inside the house come the anguished
               moans of* EUCLIO's *daughter* PHAEDRIA

PHAEDRIA [*from off-stage*]. Oh help me nurse, I beg you
   please, my belly hurts!
   Juno, childbirth goddess, help!

LYCONIDES.   You hear that, mother?
   What need for further words—the girl is giving birth.

EUNOMIA. Come in with me, my boy, into my brother's house,
   I'll try to talk him into doing what you want.

LYCONIDES. Go on, I'll follow you. [*Looking round*] I wonder
   where Strobilus is.
   I told him to wait here. But since he's helping me
   It would be wrong to be upset or lose control.
   I'll go and hear the session that decides my fate.   700

STROBILUS. I'm rich—not all the fabled birds from realms of
      gold
   Can match my wealth and never mind those paltry little
      kings
   Whose names I hardly care to mention—merely shreds and
      patches!
   I am now that fabled Philip, king of gold. Oh, what a day.*
   I left here just in time. I got there well before the miser
   And hid myself far up a tree and watched.
   Then I observed him when he came to hide the treasure.
   The minute he was gone, I slid down from the tree,
   I quickly disinterred the pot of gold—and skipped!
   I saw the miser coming home—he saw me not,   710

For cleverly I hugged the roadside just a little bit.

[STROBILUS *scampers into* MEGADORUS' *house.*

A second later EUCLIO *arrives on-stage—*
in a state of utter desperation

EUCLIO. I'm killed and I'm dead and I'm finished for ever. To
run or to not run—to grab him—but grab whom?
I don't know—I can't see where I'm going. I'm blind. Oh,
where am I? Who am I? I'm totally lost.
I can't think straight. [*To the audience*] Please help me, I
beseech on my knees.
Please, I beg and I implore you—just show me who stole
it.
[*To a spectator in the front row*] And what are you saying?
I'll believe you for sure. Your bearing's so honest, your
expression so pure.
But what is it—why laugh you? I know that you're all
crooks here!
So you're dressed in white togas and have the best seats,
There are crooks 'mongst the mighty—and swindlers and
cheats.
What—none of you has it? Oh no, then I'm dead.   720
You mean you can't tell me?
[*With incredulous despair*] Then tell me *who's* got it. I'm
losing my head!
[*Working himself up into a frenzy*] Oh alas and alack
from the pain I will crack—if I don't get it back I'll just
die.
The most wretched of days has in such painful ways
Brought me total starvation and great ruination.
I'm the wretch of the earth and I rue my own birth.
[*He sobs*] Without gold what can I hold?
For I lost what I've guarded so close day and night,
Depriving myself of all joy and delight.
Now I've starved my own soul and the blackguards who
stole—
Have now caused me an injury none can console.   730

Young LYCONIDES *enters from* MEGADORUS' *house*

LYCONIDES. Who's this fellow bellowing and howling pitifully
    outside our gates?

No—it looks like Euclio. I'm finished utterly. My secret's
    out!

Now he knows already that his daughter's given birth—I'm
    lost.

Should I go or stay, advance or flee? By Pollux, I have no
    idea.

EUCLIO. Who's that who's talking?

LYCONIDES.   Wretched me!

EUCLIO.   No, *I'm* the wretched of the wretched,
    Stricken with titanic tribulations.

LYCONIDES.   Oh do cheer up, sir.

EUCLIO. How for pity's sake?

LYCONIDES. Because the dirty deed that you're bemoaning—
    I confess—I did it.

EUCLIO [*stunned*].   What is this I hear from you?

LYCONIDES. Nothing but the truth.

EUCLIO.   Whatever have I done to you young man?

Why did you misbehave so, bringing such misfortune on us
    all?

LYCONIDES. Passion—ruthless God—compelled me irresistibly.

EUCLIO.   But how?

LYCONIDES. I confess it, I was wrong. The whole affair was
    all my fault.

That's why I've come here to see you, to implore forgiveness.

EUCLIO. How'd you ever dare to lay a finger on what wasn't
    yours?   740

LYCONIDES. Nothing can be changed, the deed is done—and
    cannot be undone.

Heaven willed it, I suppose. How could it happen otherwise?

EUCLIO. Heaven also willed it that I thong you up and murder
    you?*

LYCONIDES. Don't say that.

EUCLIO.   Then why without permission
    did you lay your hands on my sweet thing?

LYCONIDES [*contritely*]. Love impelled me. Also too much
    wine.

EUCLIO.   Colossal arrogance!

How could you dare invent a fiction so implausible?
By your reasoning we all could be allowed to go and rob
Matrons in their finery right in the open on the street.
We could then excuse ourselves by saying that we're 'drunk
  on love'.
Love and wine are very cheap these days, I see.   750
Drunken sots and lovers can do anything they damn well
  please.

LYCONIDES. Just remember sir, I came to you to pardon my
  sheer folly.

EUCLIO. I don't care for men who misbehave and then
  apologize.
You were well aware you had no right to—and you
  shouldn't touch!

LYCONIDES. Granted that I touched what I should not.
But since I dared to touch her, I don't mind to have her
  now,
Keeping her for ever.

EUCLIO.   Keeping her? You mean against my will?

LYCONIDES. Not against your will—but then it's fitting that
  she should be mine.
Soon you'll find out, Euclio, the reasons why this is appropriate.

EUCLIO. I already have a reason to take you straight into
  court.
That's unless you give back—

LYCONIDES.   Give what back?

EUCLIO.   What you've just robbed from me.   760

LYCONIDES [stunned]. What on earth are you discussing? I've
  not robbed a thing from you.

EUCLIO. Jupiter—the man pretends he doesn't know!

LYCONIDES.   Unless you tell me.

EUCLIO [histrionically]. Pot of gold! That's what you stole
  from me and just confessed you did.

LYCONIDES. Never have I said such things or done such things.

EUCLIO.   You dare deny it?

LYCONIDES. Absolutely. I deny and redeny it. Never saw your
  potted gold.
Never knew you had it.

EUCLIO.   From the grove you filched it—give it back!
Come now, hand it over.

[*Desperate offer*] I might even let you keep a half.

Even though you robbed me, I won't make a fuss. Now
hand it over.

LYCONIDES. Euclio, have you gone crazy, calling me a common
thief?

I confessed about a different matter—private and discreet. 770

It's important. I should talk with you at length . . . if you
have time.

EUCLIO. Then you truly didn't steal my gold?

LYCONIDES.   I didn't—truly, truly.

EUCLIO. Do you *know* who stole it?

LYCONIDES.   Truly not.

EUCLIO.   But if you hear who did

Then will you come and tell me?

LYCONIDES.   Yes of course.

EUCLIO.   And if the thief

Offers you a share of loot or asks you to conceal him?

LYCONIDES.   I'll say no!

EUCLIO. If you don't keep your word? What then?

LYCONIDES.   Then let great Jupiter thunderbolt me.

EUCLIO. Good, I'm satisfied. Now speak your mind.*

LYCONIDES.   I'll introduce myself

Here's my birth: my uncle's Megadorus and my father was
Antimachus. I'm called Lyconides, My mother is Eunomia. 780

EUCLIO. I know the family. What do you want, young man?
That's what I would like to know.

LYCONIDES. You have a daughter.

EUCLIO.   That's correct—at least at home I do.

LYCONIDES. Pledged to marry Uncle Megadorus—

EUCLIO.   That is quite correct.

LYCONIDES. Uncle's told me to announce that he's renouncing
her today.

EUCLIO. What—when all's prepared, the ceremony set—the
man's renouncing?

All the immortal gods and goddesses should curse him
utterly.

He's the wretched reason that I've lost my pot of gold today.

LYCONIDES. Do cheer up and hold your curses. Rather ask
for blessings now

    For yourself and for your daughter—say with me 'so please
the Gods'.

EUCLIO [*nodding*]. Please the gods.

LYCONIDES. And may I ask for blessings for myself as well.
Now listen here:

    No man on this earth's so base he's not ashamed by some
misdeed he's done,   790

    Wanting to unsmirch his name. Now I appeal to you,

    If unwittingly I've wronged you—or your daughter—please

    Pardon me and let me marry her—as, by the way, the laws
demand.

    Freely I confess that I have wronged your daughter
dreadfully,

    Driven by the wine and wildness at the festival of Ceres.

EUCLIO. By the gods—what horror are you now revealing?

LYCONIDES.   Please don't yell.

    Look, I'm making you a grandad on your daughter's
wedding day.

    Count the months—it works out perfectly. She's had the
child.*

    That explains why uncle has revoked his promise—for my
sake.

    Go inside, you'll see it's all as I described.

EUCLIO.   I'm truly lost! 800

    Countless catastrophic cataclysms now confound my life.

    Let's go in and see what truth there may be in this.

LYCONIDES.   In a moment.

    All the storms are now subsiding, we're near port, it seems
to me.

    Only where the devil is my slave Strobilus?

    I should wait outside for a while, then follow Euclio
inside.

    At the moment he needs time to come to grips with all the
news.

    Doubtless at the moment the old woman is recounting
everything.

    Suddenly STROBILUS *bursts euphorically on-stage*

STROBILUS. Triumph. Joy and jubilation are showered on me
    from the gods.

Now I own a four-pound pot of gold. What man on earth
    is richer?

No one in the whole of Athens has been blessed by heaven
    more.*   810

LYCONIDES. Surely if I'm not mistaken I heard someone speak
    just then.

STROBILUS. Do I not see my master?

LYCONIDES.   Is it not my slave that I behold?

STROBILUS. There he is.

LYCONIDES.   It's him all right.

STROBILUS.   I'll greet him.

LYCONIDES.   I'll go meet him now.

I assume he's followed orders to inform my darling's nurse.

STROBILUS [aside]. Now I wonder, should I tell him of the
    booty I've discovered?

Not so fast. I ought to ask him first to free me. Here I go.

Master—I have found—

LYCONIDES.   Found what?

STROBILUS.   Not just what children find in beans,*
    Shouting 'eureka'.

LYCONIDES.   Are you mocking me again?

STROBILUS. Master, please, I want to tell you.

LYCONIDES.   Tell me.

STROBILUS.   I have found today 820
    Riches beyond measure.

LYCONIDES.   Where?

STROBILUS.   Four pounds of it—a pot of gold.

LYCONIDES. What is this I hear from you?

STROBILUS.   I sneaked it from old Euclio.

LYCONIDES. Where's the gold?

STROBILUS.   I've got it in a chest at home.
                               Now please, sir, set me free!

LYCONIDES. You're asking me to set you free—you filthy fount
    of felony?

STROBILUS [backing down]. Stop it, sir, I know just what
    you're up to.

It was all a joke. And you were readying to beat me.

Only tell me what you *would* have done if I had really found it?

LYCONIDES. Sorry, but you haven't fooled me. *Give me back the gold.*

STROBILUS. What gold?

LYCONIDES [*nodding*]. The gold that's Euclio's.

STROBILUS. Where is it?

LYCONIDES. You just said it's in a chest.

STROBILUS [*bluffing*]. Oh, I do babble nonsense, don't I? 830

LYCONIDES. Do you know how I'll—

STROBILUS. By Hercules, you'll have to kill me or you'll never get it.

TRANSLATOR'S NOTE. *The manuscript breaks off here, but we can infer what transpired from the argument (see Introduction). There are a few fragmentary verses, one of which provides a clue to the play's ending. We must assume that* EUCLIO *finally relents and gives the pot of gold to the newly-wed parents:*

I never had a moment's peace—not day or night. Now I can rest.

EXPLANATORY NOTES

THE BRAGGART SOLDIER

3 *parasite*: parasites' character-names suggest their functions: here Artotrogus, 'bread muncher'; in *The Brothers Menaechmus*, Peniculus, 'the sponge'; in *Stichus*, Gelasimus, 'funny boy'.

4 *your accounts*: the Latin *recte rationem tenes* suggests 'accurate book-keeping'. The mercenary soldier ironically reveals his preoccupation with money. As we shall see, Palaestrio will play upon this avarice to trick him later (cf. line 952).

5 *King Seleucus*: it is not known which of the Syrian kings of this name is intended. The comic point here is that the soldier is boasting of his regal connections by mentioning a *king* (which he does once again in line 77).

6 *follow!*: the soldier himself acts regally by referring to his followers as *satellites*, the term used for members of a royal retinue.

full of crap: the Latin is *stercoreus*, meaning 'full of excrement'. Such explicit scatology is extremely rare in Plautus, who is quite unlike Aristophanes in this respect.

good old Athens: it was typical of Roman comedy to stress its Athenian origins. Cf. Introduction, p. xix.

8 *skylight*: the *impluvium* was an opening in the roof of Roman houses through which the sun could shine and the rain fall (the latter would be collected for household use).

bones . . . dice: the metaphor sounds extremely modern, but it is not only in Plautus' Latin (*talus* can mean an ankle-bone *or* a die), but may even have been in his Greek original (*astragalos* has the very same double meaning).

9 *on the cross*: Plautus' comedy abounds in grim threats of torture and crucifixion for misbehaving slaves. Note Sceledrus' terror in line 310, and Palaestrio's playing upon it in 359–360.

10 *'Seasoned' women*: both the metaphor and the tone are typically Plautine. All Plautus' comedies express a cynical distrust, even dislike at times, of female behaviour. Cf. Palaestrio's remark in line 786, and Periplectomenus' 'what mangy merchandise a woman is' in line

894. This attitude may in part be derived from Euripides, who often expresses his cynical mistrust of women's wiles.

11 *foreign poet*: this may be Plautus' theatrical colleague Naevius, who, as the legend goes, was chained up in prison for slandering the Metelli, an influential Roman family, in one of his plays. Since this comedy supposedly takes place in Greece, the Roman poet—whoever he may be—is ironically referred to as 'foreign', *barbarus*.

slavewise and theatrically: Plautus frequently alludes to theatrical matters, as part of his tongue-in-cheek irony. Thus one of his characters assures the audience near the conclusion of *Pseudolus* that he will not ambush his tricky slave as is the typical practice 'in other comedies' (line 1240). Tranio in *The Haunted House* is extremely well versed in the comic tradition (cf. lines 1149 ff.). See Introduction, p. xxxi.

slip to sleep: in lines 214–32, I follow the assignment of speakers proposed by Eduard Fraenkel: see *Museum Helveticum*, 25 (1968), 231 ff. Two important features characterize Palaestrio's lines here. First the plenitude of (alliterative) military metaphors, and second, the slave's highly theatrical dialogue with himself. See N. Slater, *Plautus in Performance* (Princeton, 1985), *passim*.

12 *clever as a stone*: the soldier's intellect is again likened to a rock in line 1024.

13 *my equipment*: the Latin refers specifically to Roman siege machines.

15 *storehouse stall*: the Latin *stabulum* can mean either stable or whorehouse.

16 *carrots*: the Latin states, in a roundabout way, that Sceledrus has been eating food (*lolium*, darnel) which is bad for his eyes.

17 *stupi-vision*: Plautus has coined the adjective *stultividus*.

18 *not even that*: Sceledrus claims that Palaestrio has been with their household for three years, yet Palaestrio himself stated that he had only been there a very short while (line 95, 'nam ego hau diu apud hunc servitutem servio'). Plautus has been criticized for this kind of inconsistency, but it is doubtful whether his audience noticed it.

20 *forefathers—and five-fathers*: a special Roman joke, for legally speaking, slaves were *nullo patre*, that is, considered as having no father at all. Hence when Plautus lets Sceledrus speak of numerous ancestors, he compounds the impossibility and increases the fun.

22 *Diana of Ephesus*: the temple of Diana at Ephesus was one of the seven wonders of the world. When Shakespeare translates *The Brothers Menaechmus* into *The Comedy of Errors*, he transfers the locale

of the play from Epidamnus to Ephesus, where Emilia, long-lost
mother of the twins, is the abbess at the priory which is descended
from Diana's temple.

22 *who am I?*: there is an abrupt change from iambic to trochaic verse
here.

23 *decent . . . indecent*: Plautus puns on the Greek words *dikaia* and
adikos, 'right' and 'wrong'. To have the pun sound right in English,
pronounce Dicea to rhyme with 'Lisa'.

24 *back involved in this*: i.e., for a whipping.

Go and sue me!: though it sounds like modern slang, the phrase
literally translates Plautus' *lege agito*.

30 *Do you want something else?*: a literal rendering of the Latin, which
was a Roman way of saying 'Goodbye'. It is not meant to be taken
literally as it is by Periplectomenus here.

our little senate: it is characteristic of Plautus' slave heroes that they
see themselves as leading Roman senators. Cf. Tranio in *The Haunted
House* 688. Note that they might vote without an elder statesman,
for Palaestrio is the leader!

31 *produce yourselves!*: Palaestrio is extremely long-winded here, even
by Plautine standards. Moreover, his verbosity is of dubious comic
value.

33 *Animulian*: most critics suggest that the inhabitants of Animulia, a
small town in Apulia, south-eastern Italy, had a bad reputation for
one reason or another. Or perhaps Plautus is punning on the word
animal, the old man arguing that he is not a beast, but very civilized.
Cf. the enigmatic joke on the town of Sarsina in *The Haunted House*
770.

fruity fairies: the Latin words are *cinaedus*, which refers to boy
ballet-dancers of dubious sexuality, and *malacus*, meaning 'delicate'.
Interestingly enough, as Mason Hammond, Arthur M. Mack, and
Walter Moskalew note in their edition (*Plautus, Miles Gloriosus*
(Cambridge, Mass., 1970), p. 133), both these Latin words are taken
directly from the Greek. This was a typical practice of the Romans
when they wished to describe 'people or practices which they regarded as characteristic of degenerate Greeks, but not of themselves'.

34 *profit*: line 675 omitted.

my house: cf. *The Brothers Menaechmus* 713-18, on wifely 'bitchiness'.

35 *to his good name*: this discussion of children has a faintly Roman
touch. But Periplectomenus' rejoinder that he doesn't want offspring
of his own (line 705) is a most un-Roman sentiment. Think of what
Aeneas suffers, all for the sake of his son's future!

38 *for a trimming*: 'trimming' sounds modern, but Plautus' *admutiletur* has precisely that tonsorial tone. Much of Plautus' vocabulary for trickery sounds very up to date.

were the truth: the old man means that many unhappily married husbands would be glad to have the soldier relieve them of their onerous connubial responsibilities. Plautus is replete with anti-wife jokes, roundabout and direct.

39 *ribbons and the rest*: you could tell by her hairstyle if a Roman woman was married or single.

in fine condition: the text is uncertain here. The translator has given the general sense of it.

40 *all my troops*: Palaestrio speaks of *manuplares*, specifically Roman troop-divisions. Cf. note on *The Haunted House* 312. In performance, this is an ideal spot for the intermission.

41 *He's busy now*: the translator is hard pressed to explain the purpose of the Lurcio–Palaestrio repartee (lines 816–69). The plot is not advanced, and Lurcio never appears again. At least Artotrogus in the opening scene serves as a so-called 'protatic' character, whose *raison d'être* is to aid exposition. Here he also serves as a foil to the soldier. Cf. G. E. Duckworth, *The Nature of Roman Comedy* (Princeton, 1952; revised edn. Bristol, 1994), 108 ff.

Perhaps one of Plautus' actors needed some extra time to change costume. This explanation has been offered for several moments in his comedies which seem otherwise to be needless padding. It is also possible that a member of the troupe which performed this play was popular for doing a drunken 'turn'—and Plautus simply had to accommodate a comedian, as Shakespeare did many a time. If we accept this explanation, we then may imagine that the actor who plays Lurcio here was so successful that Plautus wrote him another inebriated part—Callidamates in *The Haunted House*. See p. 145 ff.

42 *danced wildly*: here and in line 857 below we find a topical allusion to bacchanalian behaviour, that is, the orgiastic dancing involved in the worship of the wine-god Bacchus. This wild worship was newly introduced to Italy in Plautus' day, and was outlawed by a decree of the senate in 186 BC. (There is another allusion in *The Pot of Gold* 408.) *Bacchor*, the verb for 'dance wildly', appears here, I believe, for the very first time in Latin literature. Virgil uses this verb at significant moments in the *Aeneid*, with very great dramatic effect, e.g. at 4. 301: 'Saevit inops animi, totamque incensa per urbem bacchatur' ('[Dido] rages, out of her mind, reeling in flames, in a dance through the city'). Cf. also *Aeneid* 6. 78 and 7. 385.

46 *Promising new venture's*: the Latin is 'condicio nova et luculenta',

which might also be rendered as 'a new and profitable business'. Note how Palaestrio employs commercial terms to get the greedy soldier interested in love-affairs. Cf. line 957, 'the first deposit on a love account', in which a very technical term, *arrabo* (down payment), is used.

49 *she becomes my bride*: strange words from Palaestrio! Neither before this nor at any time later does he speak of his own love-affairs. It may just be a tossed-off line, simply to get the soldier to concentrate on Milphidippa's mistress. Yet in Resaissance comedies master and man wooing mistress and maid became a staple plot item, influenced by the 'zany' of the *commedia dell'arte*, the servant who apes his master. This may be yet another instance of Plautus mocking theatrical convention.

50 *heaven grant me this*: we must imagine some brief musical introduction to this one and only 'sing scene' in the play.

51 *storming our Troy here?*: the metaphor of assaulting a city, meaning to outwit someone, appears frequently in Plautus. Cf. *Epidicus* 163; *Bacchides* 829; *Pseudolus* 585 ff., 761 ff. It is most significant that it is always a *slave* who plans the attack on the citadel.

54 *born of the earth*: in the Latin *Ops*, the mother figure analogous to the Greek Rhea.

56 *male and female!*: homosexual jokes or allusions are very rare in Plautus. We do find others in *The Haunted House* 890, and *The Pot of Gold* 285–6.

58 *with all our tricks*: see note on line 1025.

in your dowry: the Roman legal process of *divortium* (referred to in line 1167) stipulated the return of the wife's dowry upon separation.

61 *for bad girls to be worse girls*: cf. the notorious cinematic *femme fatale* Mae West: 'When I'm good I'm very good, but when I'm bad I'm better.'

63 *Isle of Lesbos*: Sappho, the famous poet, lived on the Isle of Lesbos in the late seventh and early sixth century BC. The legend alluded to here concerns her wild infatuation for a ferryman named Phaon. When he rejected her advances, she committed suicide.

64 *my grandmother was . . . Venus*: is Plautus mocking the Aeneas legend, then newly introduced in Rome? Aeneas was, of course, the son of Venus. Lucretius warmly hails this very Roman goddess in the first words of his *De Rerum Natura* as *Aeneadum genetrix*, the originator of the race of Aeneas.

65 *Achilles*: here the misogynistic playwright reduces the cause for the wrath of Achilles to *propter amorem*, 'all for love'. Needless to say, this is not Homer's view. We are reminded of Shakespeare's cynical reduction of the Trojan War as expressed by Thersites in *Troilus and Cressida* (II. iii. 67 ff.): 'All the argument is a whore and a cuckold— a good quarrel to draw emulous factions and bleed to death on.'

66 *dev*-otion: 'Ocean-devotion'—not a very good pun in the Latin either. Plautus is punning on *mare*, 'sea' (line 1308), and *amare*, 'to love' (line 1309). Most editors, in fact, believe the word-play too feeble to be Plautine, and read *amoris*, 'love', in line 1308.

71 *Venus and Mars: the* Roman gods. Cf. lines 11-12, where the soldier is said to surpass the fighting talents of the god of war. Surely Pyrgopolynices is some sort of Roman caricature. Cf John Arthur Hanson, 'The Glorious Military', in T. A. Dorey and Donald R. Dudley (eds.), *Roman Drama* (New York, 1965), 51-85.

72 *this lecher's vital parts*: in the Latin, Cario threatens to slice the soldier's *abdomen*. But since the punishment for adultery was castration, both the Braggart—and the audience—knew very well what was in jeopardy.

73 *a hundred drachmae*: this is an enormous sum of money. Greek workmen were paid a single drachma a day.

THE BROTHERS MENAECHMUS

77 *In every play*: Plautus criticizes other Roman playwrights for boasting of their 'authenticity', their fidelity to the Greek models, a practice which evidently had some snob appeal (to judge from Terence's prologues, in a later age). Plautus, as he here ironically proves, preferred mob appeal. See Introduction, pp. xiv-xv.

78 *the very same*: this 'explanation' is also calculated to add something to the comic confusion about which Menaechmus twin is which.

he owes a debt: the text is uncertain. This is the translator's guess.

Metre by metre: the Latin *pedibus* could mean human feet or feet of verse. A pun.

was all he had: there was a pun in the Greek original which Plautus has not succeeded in rendering in Latin. The same Greek word, *tokos*, means both children and money.

he died: this blithe attitude toward death, and lack of sympathy for the adoptive father, is echoed verbatim by Plautus in line 77 of *Poenulus*.

79 *and on and on*: Plautus' prologue is incomplete, lacking at least one verse. The translator has added this line, which at least has the virtue of giving the prologue-actor something to say as he strolls off-stage.

80 *festivals*: the Latin refers specifically to the festival of Ceres, a holiday in April, when public banquets were held in Rome.

ungrateful too: this is the first 'lyric' in the play. There will be four more (lines 351 ff., 571 ff., 753 ff., 966 ff.).

83 *the city prophets*: the text is fragmentary. Peniculus seems to be referring to the College of Augurs, official prophets of Rome.

odours quite unwashable: never a praiser of women, Plautus none the less stoops very, very rarely to jokes this unsavoury.

rub-a-dub-dubbing: the Latin is 'furtum scortum prandium'. This triad has never been rendered into English with all its assonantal splendour. Harry Levin has offered 'pinching, wenching, and lunching'. Still another attractive suggestion is 'purloin, sirloin, her loin', although the reference to the steak seems anachronistic. Perhaps the reader can concoct a thrilling threesome.

84 *outtop*: Erotium's sexual innuendo that Menaechmus will always be *superior* as far as she is concerned, recalls Martial's wry epigram advising that a wife should always be *inferior* (8. 12. 3–4): 'Inferior matrona suo sit, Prisce, marito | non aliter fiunt femina virque pares'. ('Priscus, a woman should always be beneath her husband, | Otherwise they won't be equal in relationship').

85 *duties with such diligence*: Menaechmus calls his mistress *morigera*, a dutiful epithet usually reserved for Roman wives. Cf. *The Haunted House* 189.

along those lines: all foods 'along those lines' were forbidden to Romans by various censorship rulings, especially the puritanical food prohibitions put forth by the Elder Cato. See Introduction, p. xxviii.

86 *tell me please*: one of the all-time obvious cue lines.

exotic Greece: Greece beyond the mainland; most specifically, Magna Graecia, the Greek settlements in southern Italy. The precise area is hard to define. According to some, 'exotic Greece' might extend as far north as Naples.

87 *no kin . . . bro-kin*: this pun renders Plautus' play on *geminum*, 'twin brother' and *gemes*, 'you'll groan'.

'undamaged': Plautus puns on the name of the town, Epidamnus, and *damnum*, which means 'financial ruin'.

88 *my back is dead*: non-clever slaves in comedy (especially Plautine comedy) are always worried about whiplashes on their backs—the

reward for misbehaviour. Cf. *The Braggart Soldier* 447; *The Haunted House* 991.

88 *for sacred pigs*: as the context suggests, pigs were used as expiatory animals, offered up to cure diseases, especially mental ones.

90 *the party's parts*: Cylindrus talks grandiloquently, as comic cooks were wont to. The Latin says, in stately fashion, that he is about to bring delicacies to Vulcan, the fire-god—a fancy way of saying 'stove'.

94 *King Phintia*: there is enough historical accuracy here to suggest that Plautus *might* have found these names in his Greek model. On the other hand, the names would be well known to the Romans who had fought in Sicily during the Punic Wars.

100 *given me today*: in a modern production, this would seem an ideal moment for the intermission.

this tradition: Menaechmus talks a great deal about 'tradition', *mos* in the Latin, leading many scholars to believe that this is a 'Roman song', for the benefit of the *patroni* and *clientes* in the house (i.e. almost everybody). This is likely, for the word *mos* was a very important one. The Romans, as anyone who has read Cicero will know, constantly harped upon *mos maiorum*, their forefathers' tradition.

101 *step into court*: to make all this litigation intelligible to the modern reader, the translator has merely given the gist of Menaechmus' legal manœuvring, which involves a procedure *per sponsionem*, a type of out-of-court arbitration. For a full explanation, see the edition of Moseley and Hammond, pp. 90–1. The important points are that (*a*) Menaechmus was forced to defend a client, (*b*) the client was clearly guilty, and (*c*) notwithstanding his guilt, the client was an idiot, who spoiled all of Menaechmus' efforts on his behalf.

104 *pretending*: line 639a omitted.

105 *I didn't give it to her*: the emphatic *non dedisse* in the Latin has much the same *double entendre* as the English phrase. We recall Ovid's plea to his mistress, urging her to reject her husband's amorous advances (*Amores* 1. 4. 69–70): 'Sed quaecumque tamen noctem fortuna sequetur | cras mihi constanti voce dedisse nega!' ('And yet, whatever chances to happen this night, tomorrow— | In unshaking tones, deny you gave him anything').

107 *universally kicked out*: perhaps not an adequate rendering of *exclusissumus*, a Plautine coinage based on the adjective *exclusus*, 'kicked out'. Most literally, I suppose, we could say 'kickedest-out', but the word does not play very well.

109 *father-in-law of Hercules*: Plautus, showing off his erudition, refers

to Porthaon, grandfather of Deianira, wife of Hercules. The aim, of
course, is mytho-hyperbolic: 'I don't know you from Adam', or some
such.

109 *friend of Agamemnon*: Plautus uses Calchas, prophet of the Greek
army at Troy. The translator has substituted Calchas' employer,
King Agamemnon.

110 *big-dowry wives*: Plautus abounds in jokes about the pains which
accompany dowried wives. Here even the woman's own father complains of the convention. Cf. *The Braggart Soldier* 766; *The Haunted
House* 281; *The Pot of Gold* 165–9 (and note).

111 *what his business is*: the old man advises her to be *morigera*, as the
ideal Roman wife should be.

113 *with perjury*: it may seem odd to the modern reader that, after
calling your antagonist a smelly goat, you then call him (merely) a
perjurer. But we must remember how the Romans praised plain-
dealing and honesty; by their standards, how you reek was less
important than how you speak.

114 *compared to him*: reading *Tithonus* for Lindsay's *Titanus*. Tithonus
was Aurora's lover, immortal but not immutable. With time he became
a mere wrinkle.

115 *horses' hoofbeats*: in '*see* the sound of horses' hoofbeats', Menaechmus
anticipates the nonsensical outburst of Shakespeare's Pyramus: 'I see
a voice!' (*Midsummer Night's Dream*, v. i. 194).

hauls me from the car?: needless to say, Menaechmus II is making
all this up as he goes along. But Moseley and Hammond, in their
note to this line, point out that Menaechmus has improvised this
'staying hand', to keep him from attacking an old man. The Romans
revered their elders; any assault on an old person, even on the comic
stage, was unthinkable.

Enter OLD MAN: the old man does get back with the doctor rather
quickly. And he complains of having had to wait, at that. Perhaps
there was a musical interlude. Or perhaps, counter to the comic
spirit, we are being too literal in noticing.

116 *or is he frantic?*: 'depressed' and 'frantic' in the Latin are *larvatus*,
literally, 'haunted by ghosts', and *cerritus*, 'out of his head'.

his royal patron: the Latin is *rex*, 'king', the title by which a parasite
would refer to his benefactor.

118 *like a Nestor now*: Nestor, elder statesman of the Greeks at Troy.
Homeric legends were just becoming fashionable at Rome, which
may explain Plautus' frequent references to them.

119 *All's well*: Plautus too is tampering with a proverb.

120 *for me, that's best*: a few lines of dubious authenticity have been omitted here.

for something nice: the meaning of this line is unsure. I have made a conjecture.

126 *and help me as well*: the absurdly logical process that Messenio now undertakes has puzzled many. Why are they so hesitant? Isn't it clear that the brothers have found each other? Why this detailed investigation? In his French edition of the play, Alfred Ernout suggests that we here see the 'cautious attitude characteristic of the Romans'. This may well be the case. And yet there is an even simpler explanation: Plautus never stops until he gets the nth laugh out of his audience. And he does wring quite a few more jokes out of this protracted recognition dialogue.

THE HAUNTED HOUSE

133 *Greek-it up*: the Latin verb *pergraecari*, also used in lines 64 and 960. See Introduction, p. xix (Horace uses the verb *graecari* in *Satires* 2. 2. 11).

135 *the Piraeus*: principal port of Athens. Plautus is wont to make a gallimaufry of Greek and Roman geography. The exit across the stage from the (Athenian) Pireaus leads towards the (Roman) forum.

a doleful lament: I have rendered Philolaches' famous 'Man is a House' song rather freely, keeping the sense and making a mishmash of the metre. This is the first 'lyric' in the play. There will be four more: at 313 ff., 690 ff., 783 ff., 858 ff.

138 *perform her toilette*: because the conventional city-street set made it impossible for Roman comic playwrights to show interiors, the authors had to bring the 'inside' outside.

harvest stored away: a puzzling allusion. Is it some sort of proverb? Or is it a Plautine reference to the Roman harvest, the occasion at which the play may have been presented? The latter seems more likely. Call it an 'in' joke, whose precise connotations are lost to us.

139 *To be so dutiful*: the Latin is *morem gerere*, which connotes the devotion of an ideal (Roman) wife.

140 *monogamous*: what I have rendered 'monogamous' is *obsequens*, 'compliant', in the Latin. *Obsequentia* was a particularly Roman wifely virtue, frequently lauded on memorial inscriptions.

141 *a wifely hairdo*: you could tell by her coiffure if a Roman lady was married. Cf. *The Braggart Soldier* 791 ff.

rather sell him: to be sold into slavery was, for a Roman, a fate worse than death. Roman fathers, who had the power to execute their sons, could *not* sell them into bondage. Moreover, the Roman reverence for their elders cannot be overemphasized. Hence, to behold Philolaches' impious desire to sell his father, not to mention his wishing the old man dead (line 233), would be especially shocking (and gratifying?) for the Roman audience.

142 *box of jewellery*: the metre changes from iambic to trochaic.

a glass to cling to: in Scapha's speech here, and in the conversation that follows, there is a crescendo of sexual puns, with special emphasis on the similarity between *speculum*, 'mirror', and *peculium*, which can mean penis. We know that at times the *s* in *speculum* was not strongly pronounced. Surely the bawdy Scapha would be carefree with her *s*'s, accentuating the positive, as it were. Once the low tone of innuendo is established, almost every word can assume sexual overtones. *Speculum* is not unlike the word *specus*, which can refer to a woman's genital area. Thus, by the time the conversation reaches line 271 and we encounter a phrase like '... in mentem venit de speculo', we can no longer naïvely think that Plautus means: 'it came into her mind about the mirror'. No, into our minds come the words *mentula* and *specus*, male and female sex organs. The result is that when Philematium calls for a little table, *mensula* (line 308), the word is denuded of its orginal innocence. We can be quite sure that the Roman audience felt the courtesan was calling for her boyfriend's *mentula*.

thing to—Philematium: this kind of joke is called a *para prosdokian* (Greek for 'counter to expectation'), what we would call a 'twist'. We expected him to be offering the gift to Scapha, but no—everything for his sweetheart. As for the nature of his potential gift, see the previous note.

143 *smell of silver now*: we must infer that the mirror is made of silver. Scapha is being extra-ironic about Philematium's fidelity.

144 *people in this theatre know*: Plautus frequently has his characters address the audience directly, although this practice was no innovation even when Aristophanes did it. Yet the allusion here is especially Roman: then (as now) greed often inspired marriages of convenience, which ultimately proved inconvenient; cf. Simo's song, lines 690 ff. For similar Plautine jokes on the pains which accompany dowried wives, see *The Brothers Menaechmus* 766; *The Braggart Soldier* 680–1; *The Pot of Gold* 165–9.

144 *twenty minae*: 60 minae make a talent. Simo's house is worth more
than 6 talents (see line 913); thus, a mina is worth 1/360 of the price
of a house on Main Street.

145 *Soldiers are assembling*: the soldiers referred to are Roman
manuplares, companies of 120 men, thirty of which composed a
legion. No doubt this pleased the military men in Plautus' audience.
And, since everybody was a soldier, it pleased everybody. Cf. *The
Braggart Soldier* 815.

tititit-tipsy to you: 'Tititit-tipsy' seemed a justifiable rendering of
mamma-madere. *Madere* means 'to be drunk', and *mamma* means
'breast'.

147 *next to nothing*: this is probably a reference from the Greek original,
composed at a time (late fourth–early third century BC) when mercenaries were replacing Greek citizen armies.

149 *kill your father*: another parricidal utterance, no less shocking to the
Romans than Philolaches' unspeakable thoughts in lines 229 and
233. See note on *The Brothers Menaechmus* 870.

150 *dutiful to you*: the girls offer to be *morigerae*, i.e. loyal as wives. Cf.
line 189.

locked up tight: in all that follows, the verb *occludere*, 'to lock up
tight', is used over and over, almost giving a characterization to the
house itself.

151 *games he'll get when dead*: the Latin word *ludus* means not only a
game or theatrical performance but a 'deception' as well. What will
be a deception for Theopropides will be a show for everyone else.
Tranio also alludes to the practice of holding funeral games for
distinguished persons (Terence's *Adelphoe* was presented on one such
occasion). But in so doing he is wishing his master dead. Yet another
parricidal utterance!

fill him full of it: this may sound anachronistic, but the Latin is
sarcinam imponere, 'to load him up'. See note on *The Braggart
Soldier* 768.

154 *across the sea*: the name Tranio has invented is Diapontius, which is
straightforward Greek, meaning 'from across the sea'. The actor's
hesitation before coming out with his place of birth as 'across the
sea' would show the audience that Tranio was improvising on the
spot—and stalling for time.

156 *the 'haunted' house*: when this play is being acted, this would seem
the ideal spot for an intermission.

157 *as foxes eat a pear*: perhaps an allusion to a then-current proverb,
now lost to us.

157 *Tranini*: the moneylender calls Tranio *Tranius*, which may be a diminutive, or a pet name of some sort.

160 *His father's son he is*: the Latin verb is *patrissare*, from a similar
Greek coinage, literally meaning 'fatherizing'.

165 *shady things are shady*: Plautus is playing on the word *umbra*,
'shadow', and the town of Sarsina in Umbria, which most scholars
believe was his birthplace. This translator believes that Plautus never
could resist a pun, so why not *umbra* and *umbria*? Cf. his pun on
Animula, a town in Apulia, in *The Braggart Soldier* 648.

166 *Alexander and Agathocles*: Alexander is, of course, the Great, a
conqueror whose exploits were much admired by the Romans.
Agathocles of Syracuse (361–289 BC) fought some brilliant campaigns against the Carthaginians. In 304 BC, he crowned himself
King of Syracuse, and was at this time the only ruler among the
Western Greeks to own this title. It was most likely Plautus who
linked Alexander and Agathocles. The soldierly Romans would know
both the names well. The clever slave comparing himself to a heroic
general is a distinctive feature of Plautine comedy.

167 *sensitive of you, my boy*: Theopropides thinks Tranio is being
humanus. This is the only time Plautus employs the adjective to
connote anything like 'humane', in the manner of Terence's famous
utterance: 'homo sum: humani nil a me alienum puto' ('I am a man:
I consider nothing human alien to me') (*Heauton Timorumenos* 77).

168 *pasta-eating foreign workmen*: there is a double (and doubly ironic)
Roman reference here. What I have rendered as *pasta*, is in the Latin,
puls, a kind of bland porridge which was the Romans' staple food.
'Foreign' translates Plautus' *barbarus*, 'barbarian', which is how the
Greeks were wont to refer to the Romans, to the latter's displeasure.
This sort of self-mockery, then, has Plautus saying—to Romans—'no
lousy Roman workman made this!' Cf. note on *The Braggart Soldier*
211.

169 *can't hurt you*: the translator does not know whether it was a stuffed
dog, a painted dog, a real dog, or an imaginary one. Perhaps the last
guess is best (and least troublesome for the producer).

170 *nest egg*: in Latin, *peculium*, the private funds which slaves were
urged to amass to buy their freedom. The better the slave, the larger
his *peculium*; no need to say how bad a fellow with a *peculium* of
trouble is. For another meaning of *peculium*, see the note on line
250.

171 *share the master's bed*: a homosexual joke.

counterfeit groins: Pierre Grimal suggests that this odd line was a pun in the Greek original, whose innuendo is made clear in the lines that follow. Also note *The Pot of Gold* 285–6.

173 *tell my son I'm back*: of course no one ever told Theopropides his son was in the country—at least not in the text as we have it. Nobody in the audience would notice the inconsistency.

174 *a new official*: there is no exact English equivalent for the Roman *praefectus*, a kind of city administrator.

176 *thirty minae, sir*: Phaniscus' reply to the old man contains an exclamation to Apollo in Greek. I thought it best to drop it entirely rather than confuse the issue by using French—which is the standard practice of translators who render the occasional Greek phrases which pop up in Plautus. His audience had at least a smattering of (Sicilian) Greek.

full-time festive frolicking: my fanfare of *f*'s suggests Plautus' fantastic fit of alliteration, all with the letter *p*, e.g. 'Et postquam eius hinc pater | Sit profectus peregre, perpotasse . . .' etc. (976–7). All of this has an ironic echo in line 983: *perdidit patrem*, 'father's fully finished'.

177 *bankrupt Hercules*: The Latin refers to *quaestus Herculis*, 'the profits of Hercules'. The mythical strong man was also a god of gain, as he would be offered a tithe of any great money that might come a Roman's way. Thus, to bankrupt Hercules would be to ruin the richest person in the universe.

freedom to protect your back: as already noted, all the non-clever slaves in Plautine comedy (i.e. those unlike Tranio and Palaestrio) are terribly worried about their backs being whipped because they have disobeyed their masters (e.g. Sceledrus in *The Braggart Soldier*, Messenio in *The Brothers Menaechmus*). The dichotomy between this class and the insouciant slave-schemers is well drawn in the opening *agon* of this comedy, in the differing attitudes toward punishment of Grumio and Tranio.

I saw a funeral: Simo's 'what's new' quip is rather grim. It may be merely a kind of sick joke (uncharacteristic of Plautus), or else an oblique way of an old man saying: 'There's not much time left . . . for either of us.' Since the play celebrates celebration, i.e. living-it-up, this latter suggestion seems more likely.

178 *I'm invited out*: evidently it was a custom (in Greece? Rome?) to invite a newly arrived friend to dinner. Cf. line 1129, where Callidamates does indeed offer old Theopropides a welcome-back meal.

179 *That's why . . . a different story*: the bracketed lines are the translator's conjecture of an extremely fragmentary text.

180 *siege conditions into safety*: we note once again the clever slave's predilection for military language. Cf. the note on line 775.

with lots of line: Theopropides compares himself to a fisherman, Tranio to a fish. This has led at least one noted scholar to suggest the origin of Tranio's name in the Greek *thranis* or swordfish.

181 *hunk of stone*: for another 'stupid as a stone' allusion, cf. *The Braggart Soldier* 1024.

hicks . . . sticks: 'Veniunt ruri rustici'; most likely a familiar expression, with a few extra connotations now lost to us.

what a nice arrival: it is Theopropides who is being ironic here. He is happy over the arrival of Tranio, his potential victim, not of his son, as he expects Tranio to understand.

trial by torture: getting at the truth by torturing a man's slaves was, alas, an actual practice.

182 *leaps onto altar*: fleeing to an altar for sanctuary was a familiar practice of slaves in Greek comedy as well—not to mention Euripidean heroines (Creusa in Euripides' *Ion* is a fine example). The holy altar meant immunity for the person who sat upon it. Whether there was always an altar on the Roman stage, from the religious ceremony which would precede the play, has been a subject of much discussion. Most evidence suggests that there was indeed a permanent altar as part of the *mise-en-scène*.

184 *that's so stupid*: Callidamates argues that Tranio's very flight to the altar is a blatant confession of guilt. This line has been given entirely to Callidamates. Cf. Sonnenschein ad loc.

noble families do otherwise?: this could very well be an allusion to aristocratic youths in Plautus' Rome.

185 *Diphilus or Philemon*: see Introduction, p. xxxi.

THE POT OF GOLD

188 SLAVE OF LYCONIDES: the Latin text causes difficulty here, by identifying both Megadorus' bondsman and Lyconides' slave as 'Strobilus'. Most critics agree that the young man's slave is a different character (the Oxford text lists him as merely 'Lyconides' slave'). W. Ludwig ('Aululariaprobleme', *Philologus*, 105 (1961), 255 ff.) suggests that in the Greek original the two characters' names were somewhat similar—ultimately causing a scribal corruption. In any event, the path of greatest convenience would be to combine the roles, at least for performance.

191 *bloody imminent*: lines 76-8 contain an indecipherable joke and have been omitted here. Literally translated, it reads: 'Nor, as I think, is there anything better for me [to do], than to tie a noose around my neck and turn myself into a long letter [I].'

full of emptiness—and cobwebs: clearly a proverbial expression for financial embarrassment. Cf. Catullus 13. 8: 'plenus sacculus est aranearum' ('my purse is full of cobwebs'). (See also, among others, Propertius 2. 6. 35.)

Philip or Darius: both Philip II and Darius were proverbially rich. Not coincidentally, they were also names of (Greek) coins.

If anyone should ask for water: the symbol for banishment in Rome was the *aquae et ignis interdictio*, the prohibition of the lending of water and fire. Fixated on his private treasure, Euclio has in effect estranged his society from himself. (See D. Konstan, *Roman Comedy* Ithaca, NY, 1983), 36 n. 5.

192 *our councilman's announced*: the Latin *magister curiae* may be a Roman rendering of the Greek *demarchos* in the original. In either case, it is a neighbourhood official. The Greek functionary collected funds; we are not sure what Roman practice, if any, is alluded to.

Brother please heed me: the following and other 'lyric' passages are rendered more freely than the rest of the play. Sacrifice in precision—and the occasional line—is made for the sake of atmosphere. At least one critic believes that lines 120-76 were so musical that brother and sister actually *danced*. See Victor Castellani, 'Plautus versus *Komoidia*: Popular Farce at Rome', in J. Redmond (ed.), *Themes in Drama* (Cambridge, 1988) x. 76 n. 20.

I'm talkative too: of course she is doing exactly what she complains of.

194 *the next day she's dead*: surprisingly cruel coming from Megadorus, yet one of the oldest 'jokes' on record. Perhaps best known is the epigram of Hipponax (sixth century BC): 'A woman gives you two good days: the day you marry her—and when you bury her.'

Postumus: an inevitable consequence of the father's advanced age.

Is there anything more?: less a real question than the common Roman formula for taking leave. Plautus often plays with his characters, having them take it literally and make some kind of quip. Cf. note on *The Braggart Soldier* 575.

195 *hooked*: the Latin for 'hooked' is *harpagatum*, from *harpago*, a kind of hook or harpoon. It is not only a Plautine coinage, but a possible inspiration for the name of Molière's miser, Harpagon. Thomas

(*T. Macci Plauti Aulularia* (Oxford, 1913)) suggests that the French playwright was more directly inspired by Luigi Groto's comedy *La Emilia*, whose dramatis personae includes a skinflint called Arpago.

197 *You were an ox and I an ass*: this extended metaphor is an example of what Eduard Fraenkel deemed quintessentially Plautine style. It should be noted that the Roman playwright goes a bit wild and grossly overworks the conceit of the image. *Plautinisches im Plautus* (Berlin, 1922); revised edition translated by Franco Munari as *Elementi Plautini in Plauto* (Florence, 1960).

nothing for a dowry: Euclio's pathological resistance to giving a dowry became in Molière's version the famous *sans dot*, echoed and re-echoed in theatrical history.

198 *something else?*: again the departure formula (see above, on line 175).

199 *Shut the house up tight*: a traditional obsession with misers. Cf. Shylock's insistence that his house be closed securely. Cf. *Merchant of Venice*, II. v. 28 ff: 'Hear you me, Jessica, | Lock up my doors . . . stop my house's ears'.

empty for a few moments: perhaps there was a brief musical interlude on the flute.

ANTHRAX *and* CONGRIO: Thomas notes (p. 91) that this is the longest cook scene in all of Roman comedy (cf. *The Brothers Menaechmus* 219 ff.). This figure has an important function in Menander's *Dyskolos*.

a split: homoerotic innuendo—the verb *dividere* hinting at penetration. J. N. Adams discusses this passage in *The Latin Sexual Vocabulary* (London, 1982), 151.

201 *a waste?*: text obscure; the general sense is given. Castellani, *Themes in Drama*, x. 58.

202 *I don't see any wine*: the drunken housekeeper is another New Comedy stereotype. We should have expected this remark from Staphyla, whose name in Greek means 'bunch of grapes'.

pig . . . Vulcan: the original contains a pun on *inpurate* a term of abuse, and *pur*, the Greek word for fire.

203 PYTHODICUS *enters*: a puzzling little scene which serves no apparent purpose; and Pythodicus has no other role in the play. It is doubtless a later addition—but why?

down below . . . on high: the Latin puns on *inferi* and *superi*, referring to subterranean and celestial gods respectively. (Obviously omit in performance.)

203 *The stage is empty*: perhaps another musical interlude by the flute-player.

204 *hairless as a fancy dancer*: Roman dancers shaved their body hair. They are synonymous with effeminacy.

Bacchanalians: a reference to the Bacchic orgies notorious for their wildness. (See Introduction, p. xl.)

206 *goddess of all Thieves*: Laverna, a Roman divinity (perhaps of Etruscan origin). She had a grove on the Via Salaria where her worshippers prayed—silently—for success in their malefactions.

I'll start rioting: an allusion to the practice of the injured party making loud noises outside the house of his wrongdoer.

207 *cocky cock*: the Latin puns on the word *gallus*, rooster.

208 *shoemaker take its measure*: a joke whose meaning is not altogether clear.

old Gallic nags: another obscure allusion in some way intended to illustrate the fruits of frugality.

commissioner of women: a reference to the Greek office of *gynaikonomos*. Megadorus' entire speech is thought to be a Plautine elaboration. Some have detected in it a topical reference to the *Lex Oppia* of 215 BC (repealed in 195), a puritanical Roman attempt to combat female extravagance.

creditors: it is impossible to know exactly what sort of tradesmen are alluded to in some names in the list which follows. Many of these words appear here for the only time in Latin and include specialists like the *murobatharius*, which the *Oxford Latin Dictionary* simply—and unhelpfully—glosses as 'a probably corrupt word in Plautus *Aulularia*'. The translator has merely guessed.

209 *army tax*: perhaps alluding to the *tributum*, a war tax. It has also been suggested that the soldier, long retired, is demanding a kind of pension from well-to-do citizens.

210 *Geryon*: a three-headed, three-bodied giant of Greek mythology.

Argus: a herdsman sent by Juno to guard her rival (for Zeus' affections) Io. He is often described in Greek as *panoptes*, 'all eyes'. After Hermes killed him, these orbs went into the peacock's tail.

fountain of Pirene: a fabled spring where Bellerophon caught and harnessed the winged horse Pegasus.

all bone: a Latin pun on the words *curio* which is a Roman ward official, and *cura*, 'worry', 'care'.

lamps from Carthage: Carthaginian lamps were said to be translucent.

211 *Trust*: the goddess Fides, Good Faith or Trust, is one of the most ancient Roman divinities.

212 *faithfuller to Euclio*: the language evokes the *fides* that was the basis of the patron–client relationship, implying a bond between Strobilus and the god which should not be violated. It is the kind of slave sophistry so typical of Plautus.

213 *trusty jug*: the Latin *fidelia* equals a large pot or bucket—a pun on *fides*.

   get it up: another homosexual joke. The Latin *id datare* suggests erotic provocation.

216 *Philip, king of gold*: as mentioned above (see note on line 86), King Philip was a legendarily wealthy monarch—and also the name of a coin. This sort of allusion is typical of Plautine style.

218 *thong you up*: the Latin *in nervo* does of course mean in custody, but it can also mean penis and, in the plural, sexual powers or virility. These meanings are attested for the first time only in Horace and Ovid and yet it would not be impossible that Plautus might be making a racy pun.

220 *Good, I'm satisfied*: this is hardly subtle dramaturgy. After being in a mortal panic about his stolen gold, Euclio suddenly shifts mood completely and is cordial to Lyconides. That this is a comedy is only partial excuse. We should note that Molière adapts only the 'quiproquo' half of this scene—i.e. the misunderstanding between Euclio and Lyconides in which the miser assumes that the young man is confessing to the theft.

221 *Count the months*: the Latin states explicitly that she is in her tenth month—but then the reckoning is lunar.

222 *No one in the whole of Athens*: this tongue-in-cheek emphasis that the action is taking place in Athens was a familiar ploy to evoke Roman smiles.

   what children find in beans: there are many explanations of this allusion. An attractive one is offered by Thomas, who notes that what boys find in beans is often a worm known as *midas*—a golden suggestion, even if far-fetched.